PRACTICING MUSIC BY DESIGN

Practicing Music by Design: Historic Virtuosi on Peak Performance explores pedagogical practices for achieving expert skill in performance. It is an account of the relationship between historic practices and modern research, examining the defining characteristics and applications of eight common components of practice from the perspectives of performing artists, master teachers, and scientists. The author presents research past and present designed to help musicians understand the abstract principles behind the concepts. After studying *Practicing Music by Design*, students and performers will be able to identify areas in their practice that prevent them from developing.

The tenets articulated here are universal, not instrument-specific, borne of modern research and the methods of legendary virtuosi and teachers. Those figures discussed include:

- Luminaries Franz Liszt and Frederic Chopin
- Renowned performers Anton Rubinstein, Mark Hambourg, Ignace Paderewski, and Sergei Rachmaninoff
- Extraordinary teachers Theodor Leschetizky, Rafael Joseffy, Leopold Auer, Carl Flesch, and Ivan Galamian
- Lesser-known musicians who wrote perceptively on the subject, such as violinists Frank Thistleton, Rowsby Woof, Achille Rivarde, and Sydney Robjohns

Practicing Music by Design forges old with new connections between research and practice, outlining the *practice* practices of some of the most virtuosic concert performers in history while ultimately addressing the question: How does all this work to make for better musicians and artists?

Christopher Berg is a Carolina Distinguished Professor at the University of South Carolina School of Music, where he runs the classical guitar program.

PRACTICING MUSIC BY DESIGN

Historic Virtuosi on Peak Performance

Christopher Berg

University of South Carolina

Routledge
Taylor & Francis Group

NEW YORK AND LONDON

First published 2019
by Routledge
52 Vanderbilt Avenue, New York, NY 10017

and by Routledge
2 Park Square, Milton Park, Abingdon, Oxon, OX14 4RN

Routledge is an imprint of the Taylor & Francis Group, an informa business

Library of Congress Cataloging-in-Publication Data
A catalog record for this book has been requested

ISBN: 978-0-367-19006-4 (hbk)
ISBN: 978-0-367-19007-1 (pbk)
ISBN: 978-0-429-19979-0 (ebk)

Typeset in Bembo
by Apex CoVantage, LLC

What should they know of England who only England know?
—RUDYARD KIPLING

CONTENTS

EXAMPLES AND TABLE

Examples

Table

PREFACE

In the Spring of 2016, after I had finished reading the last of a half-dozen recent books on the development of expert skill, fleeting thoughts that had cropped up in my reading coalesced into a steady chorus. These short-lived thoughts were things like "Mark Hambourg wrote something similar in 1922," or "I wonder if the author is familiar with Theodor Leschetizky's teaching?" and "This is different from what's recommended in some guitar methods." The idea behind *Practicing Music by Design: Historic Virtuosi on Peak Performance* began with the recognition that there was a relationship between the recent neurological, psychological, and physiological research that informed these modern books and the practices of legendary performers and teachers of the past.

Practice occurs behind closed doors, and usually only its product can be observed by others. Who can infer the complexities and subtleties of a process by witnessing only its product? To put it crudely, who can infer the existence of a pig from seeing only a sausage?

Practice purports to lead to an artistic and creative performance of a piece of music, and although the quality of performance depends on the quality of practice, *performance as an act* has little in common with the innumerable acts of practice that make a performance possible. This doesn't mean that practice and performance are not inextricably bound together, but what drives the creation of the most potent connections between the two?

This book is about the formation of the most artistic and technically rewarding of these bonds: the *drivers* of good practice. Why do *this* instead of *that*? And why do it one way as opposed to another? What does one need to know, or be able to do, before taking on advanced works? Why break a piece up into smaller sections instead of playing through the entire work repeatedly? Can mental work enhance physical skill? How does that work? Why practice slowly, other than because your teacher says to do so? How does one bring artistic interpretations into being? What personal traits interfere with or enhance practice? What is the relationship between the study of technical exercises and the repertoire we wish to play? How do we recognize and work on problem areas in a piece? Why do some live performances on stage not feel as secure and brilliant as the previous day's run-through in the practice room? How does all this work to make us better musicians and artists?

Some method books and advice about practice are simply accounts of what the author thinks is effective or beneficial. These writings often consist of prescriptive or proscriptive advice such as "Do this for thirty minutes, and this for another twenty minutes, but don't practice any more than four hours a day," and so on. The *how* and *why* behind the *what* of practice are seldom explored. There is rarely reference to other books in the field or research that corroborates an author's statements. Instead, these works exist as atomized monologues, or as Rowsby Woof (1883–1943) put it in his *Technique and Interpretation in Violin-Playing* from 1920: "It is perhaps natural to most people to rate their own experiences too highly, and to imagine that their own classifications of old doctrines are new—not merely as regards classification, but also as to the doctrines themselves."[1]

The great cellist Pablo Casals (1876–1973) gave a succinct summary of the defects of such works in the preface to Diran Alexanian's (1881–1954) *Traité Théorique et Pratique du Violoncelle* in 1922: "[A] great number of [methods] have passed through my hands, strengthening each time my conviction that only routine and empiricism contributed to the production of such works."[2] It will likely be a surprise for readers to learn that an older but now obsolete meaning of the word "empiricism" given in the Oxford English Dictionary is "a reliance on previous experience, unsystematic observation, or trial and error, rather than formal learning or an understanding of underlying principles." The OED gives an example of the word used this way as recently as 1969, and this is undoubtedly the meaning Casals intended in 1922.

Written advice about music practice most often occurs in books that are instrument-specific. Although there are certainly instrument-specific attributes that might call for variation in the application of the tenets I explore in this book, the ideas behind these tenets are universal, as borne out by modern research. If you're looking for a simple "how-to" book with lists of practice routines or possible quick fixes, this is not it. *Practicing Music by Design* is more of a "why-do" book. If serious musicians and teachers are to change or refine their practices, it is necessary that they understand why. Without understanding, one is left vulnerable to boredom and frustration and is liable to waste time trying to solve symptoms of problems rather than actual problems.

I hope to show the relationship between documented practices of legendary artists from the past and recent neurological, psychological, and physiological research on the development of high-level skill. Although the artists I discuss had unique artistic voices, there is a consistency in the way they developed these voices. Herbert Whone put it nicely in *The Simplicity of Playing the Violin* from 1972: "What is intended is that a basic and universal logic should be understood in order later that individual characteristics may flourish."[3]

There is more than the universal logic of one's instrumental discipline that needs to be considered, however. High-level practice and performance include the development and mastery of many separate skills and sensitivities. We'll hear from legendary musicians, but we'll also hear from those with expertise in neurology, psychology, physiology, and creativity. Along the way, perhaps we'll notice that Theodor Leschetizky's teaching may have anticipated the work of Nobel Laureate Charles Sherrington or Frederick Matthias Alexander; that Frederic Chopin and guitarist Fernando Sor may have anticipated the way that today's psychologists understand the difference between "rule learners" and "example learners"; that Ivan Galamian's practices were identical to concepts later developed by psychologist Robert Bjork; and that violinist Achille Rivarde's ideas about the dangers of approaching a work with preconceived notions is echoed in later research by Mihaly Csikszentmihalyi on creativity and problem-*finding*. And that almost all great performers understood the technical and artistic benefits of incorporating variety in their practice. Once these links are understood, readers will have a point of reference to help them recognize practices that might dull their ears, imaginations, and artistic perceptions.

The books on developing exceptional skill that I read in 2016 explore how modern research can improve athletic and academic performance. These books are invaluable to us because it's unlikely a performing musician will be familiar with journals such as *Psychological Science*; *Trends in Neurosciences, Neuropsychologia, Behavioral, and Brain Sciences*; *Cognitive Brain Research*; *Journal of Verbal Learning and Verbal Behavior*; or the *Journal of General Psychology*, to name a handful of the sources modern authors use to develop and support their arguments.

This neurological, physiological, and psychological research confirms the efficacy of the way many legendary artists of the past studied and practiced as they acquired high-levels of virtuoso technique and musical artistry. Their writings—or writings about them—allow us to see practices in action that would be substantiated by research that would occur decades later. Among these artists are Franz Liszt and Frederic Chopin; legendary performers such as Anton Rubinstein, Mark Hambourg, Ignace Paderewski, Josef Hofmann, Alfred Cortot, Josef Lhévinne, Sergei Rachmaninoff, and Walter Gieseking; the extraordinary teachers Theodor Leschetizky, Rafael Joseffy, Leopold Auer, Carl Flesch, and Ivan Galamian; and lesser-known musicians who wrote perceptively about developing high-levels of artistic skill on their instrument, such as violinists Frank Thistleton, Rowsby Woof, Achille Rivarde, and Sydney Robjohns.

Through a series of books, interviews in anthologies such as James Francis Cooke's *Great Pianists on Piano-Playing* (1913); Harriette Moore Brower's two volumes of *Piano Mastery* (1915 and 1917);[4] and articles in popular music magazines such as *The Etude, The Musical Times,* or *The Musical Courier, practice* practices are presented that have been empirically tested by outstanding artists and confirm the results of later research. This confirmation takes the form of brilliant concert careers, historical recordings, written accounts of performances, and pedagogical successes. Musicians able to see the agreement between these approaches to practice and modern research will be able to design extraordinarily dynamic and rewarding practice sessions.

Eight components, or tenets, of practice turn up consistently in the writings of legendary artists and teachers (not all did write—much like today): building a foundation of knowledge and skill, chunking, mental work, slow practice, variety in repetition, continuity, phrase-storming (my term), and an openness to feedback and self-criticism. These eight components parallel concepts presented in recent literature that explore how brain and body learn best. Familiarity with these ideas can improve one's mental understanding and perceptions, physical skills, ability to generate and effect artistic ideas, and enhance the relationship among the three.

The first chapter of *Practicing Music by Design* lays the groundwork for why a detailed exploration of these ideas is important. The succeeding eight chapters examine the defining characteristics and applications of each from the perspectives of performing artists, master teachers, neurologists, physiologists, and psychologists.

Notes

1. Rowsby Woof, *Technique and Interpretation in Violin-Playing* (New York and London: Longmans, Green and E. Arnold, 1920), iii.
2. Diran Alexanian and Frederick Fairbanks, *Traité Théorique et Pratique du Violoncelle; Theoretical and Practical Treatise of the Violoncello* (Paris: A. Z. Mathot, 1922), 3.
3. Herbert Whone, *The Simplicity of Playing the Violin* (London: Victor Gollancz Ltd, 1989), 16.
4. To distinguish between these two volumes, after the initial reference I will always include the year, and I will always include the words "Second Series" in the short form of the title for the second book. (The first volume was not called "First Series.")

Sources

Alexanian, Diran, and Frederick Fairbanks. *Traité Théorique et Pratique du Violoncelle; Theoretical and Practical Treatise of the Violoncello.* Paris: A. Z. Mathot, 1922.
Whone, Herbert. *The Simplicity of Playing the Violin.* London: Victor Gollancz ltd, 1989.
Woof, Rowsby. *Technique and Interpretation in Violin-Playing.* New York and London: Longmans, Green and E. Arnold, 1920.

ACKNOWLEDGMENTS

This work was originally intended to serve as a guide for my students to help them understand the reasons behind the practice advice I give them, especially when that advice seemed counter-intuitive or was contrary to cherished popular mythologies connected to an admired artist. I had no thought of publication until pianist Marina Lomazov, my colleague at the University of South Carolina School of Music and who now teaches at the Eastman School of Music, read an early draft of the book and asked if it was available publicly. I offer my thanks to Marina for helping me see that perhaps this book could find an audience beyond those who study with me.

I am especially grateful to Constance Ditzel, Senior Editor at Routledge, for skillfully guiding me through the steps leading to the final submission of my manuscript. Thanks are also due to Marie Louise Roberts, who managed the project, and the excellent copyeditors who made my prose easier to read.

Pianist, singer, and historian Susan Parker Shimp, my friend and sometime duo partner, read early drafts of the manuscript and provided numerous insightful comments.

Cellist Robert Jesselson, friend and colleague at the University of South Carolina, also read an early draft of the manuscript and offered many suggestions. His comments, along with numerous conversations throughout our four-decade friendship, have been particularly helpful.

I am also grateful for two serendipitous but well-timed email exchanges that were initially unrelated to the book. Phillip Ulanowsky, my best friend and roommate from high school, began to send me material about his father, pianist Paul Ulanowsky, a member of the well-known Bach Aria Group. Phillip sent me an unpublished address his father had given in 1962. Within this address was material that was tailor-made for the opening of chapter 6.

Pianist Sara Davis Buechner and I had corresponded about how our paths had crossed while I was a student at Peabody Conservatory. She sent me an address she had given in honor of her teacher, Reynaldo Reyes, on the occasion of his retirement from 50 years of teaching at Towson University. Within this touching and wonderful talk, I found the perfect way to end chapter 5.

Each of you has my gratitude, and the book is better because of you. The responsibility for errors or confusing writing lies solely with me.

Finally, my family has been preternaturally patient with me, especially as I became increasingly distracted in my everyday life as I tried to give form and expression to the inchoate mass of material swirling around in my head.

1

INTRODUCTION

It hardly needs stating that the ways in which people experience music have changed throughout the centuries. Some ways of hearing live music have been at court, a concert hall, salon, or buying a score and playing it yourself at home. Exposure to recorded music has been through listening to the radio, 78s, 45s, LPs, cassettes, CDs, MP3s, and ubiquitous distribution channels on the internet.

Courts, cassettes, and crackly 78s are gone, but there are still concert halls, recitals, and people making music at home, although the latter is surely rarer than it once was. Despite the ease of creating music with samples and virtual instruments, classical musicians make music with real instruments in performance settings. It takes years of study and practice to do this with fluency and artistry. Those involved in working to master an instrumental discipline, studying, interpreting, and performing concert literature at the highest level do most of this work behind the closed door of the practice and teaching studio.

The level of technique required to master an instrumental discipline may have expanded over time, often in response to compositional innovations, an increased awareness of how to use ourselves better, or in response to changes in the instrument itself, but what goes on behind the studio doors of master musicians—the tenets of high-level practice that I explore in this book—has scarcely changed. Great artists of the past were aware that there were ways of working that could help them assimilate material quickly; attend to technical and artistic refinements; recognize and solve problems; and prevent their ears, aesthetic senses, and imaginations from growing dull. These artists—like many today—may not have known why these practices worked, but their writings, or writings about them, reveal ways of working that anticipated later neurological, psychological, and physiological research.

These legendary musicians also pointed out practices they saw as hindering students' technical and artistic development. These faulty practices usually centered around a reliance on imitation and mindless repetition at the expense of solid foundational work and learning to recognize and reduce problems to their basic level.

The essential problem of teaching and practice is that good teachers try to have their students fulfill as many of the criteria of the advanced, fast, or complicated version of something as they acquire the skill and knowledge of the elementary, slow, or simple version of the thing. This isn't possible all the time, but skilled teachers are attuned to this and are adept at recognizing when it is possible. Students of these skilled teachers don't need to know these advanced criteria, but they have been prepared to meet these criteria in the future. Those teaching themselves won't have an awareness of these advanced criteria, only their product, which isn't the same thing.

Although I want the ideas explored in this book to be of immediate and practical value to students and teachers as they design, or redesign, their practice, it may not be possible for an inexperienced student to make use of this material right away without expert guidance. I explore tenets of practice in terms of their *practical* value, but I also explore the *concepts* that corroborate these tenets, which can lead one to more polished and refined ways of working in the future. The application of concepts to particular situations is "know-how"; first-hand knowledge of the concepts themselves requires cultivated thought.

Cultivated thought about practice can help students understand the differences between the limits of a skill that's undeveloped because not enough time has been spent on it, the limits of a skill that's undeveloped because of the way in which one has been working, or the limits of a skill that is undeveloped because of the constraints of the central nervous system. To the inexperienced ear and eye, these limits appear the same, but learning how to work better can help one override certain constraints of the central nervous system and is a distinctive feature of exceptional skill. When these differences are not understood, progress can become stalled and practice increasingly futile. When practice is viewed simply as know-how, it can become a confining checklist that reveals nothing of its origin, its value, or its purpose. By drawing parallels between the practices of legendary performers of the past and modern research, I hope to remove the opacity of how one develops the skill to create compelling artistic interpretations.

An approach such as this is cultivated *and* practical: cultivated because it opens a path to spacious thinking about practice; practical because practices are validated by their *efficacy*, as demonstrated by the outstanding careers and pedagogical successes of those from whom I draw. Too often, though, students confuse *efficacy* for *expediency*. In music study, the expedient should be linked to the highest levels of artistry. It takes years to grasp the boundlessness of artistic possibilities, and it's easy for one's concept of expediency to be shaped only by the short-term. Unless one is well-schooled in the existing knowledge, techniques, and artistic accomplishments within one's field, one's sense of expediency runs the risk of being shaped by vision that is unimaginative and derivative.

Method books and treatises usually attest to authors' predilections for rehashing approaches that already exist or, as may be more common, reveal authors working under the illusion that they have discovered certain "intuitive" insights about practice but which gainsay documented research. In many ways, these authors are like the group of blind men who try to describe an elephant by experiencing only one of its parts (trunk, tusks, tail, side) without understanding the whole, and their preoccupation with immediate experience defends them against an outbreak of second thoughts. Although the transmutation of one's own learning experience into directives for others often passes for pedagogy, it has served to give both practice and pedagogy a bad name. The best drivers of good practice design are counterintuitive, especially to the self-taught and beginners.

Daniel Coyle's 2009 book, *The Talent Code*, went a long way toward explaining why some things work well and others do not. His explanations and discussions of the role of *myelin* in building skill are especially useful. Coyle draws most of his examples from the world of sports, but one can easily infer how they might be applied to high-level music study.[1] I recommend Coyle's book to those who want to refine their work, find out why their current efforts aren't producing the results they desire, and to those who wish to understand how they can better teach their students.

Although I draw upon Coyle's work in this book, as well as that of Geoffrey Colvin, author of *Talent Is Overrated* (2008); Matthew Syed, author of *Bounce: Mozart, Federer, Picasso, Beckham, and the Science of Success* (2010); Peter Brown et al., authors of *Make It Stick: The Science of Successful Learning* (2014), and Zach Schonbrun, author of *The Performance Cortex: How Neuroscience Is Redefining Athletic Genius* (2018), *Practicing Music by Design* is not a reiteration of their work and related work by others. It turns out that the above authors were unaware of a body of literature that anticipates and confirms the research they draw upon by more than seven or eight decades. Even many of today's musicians are unfamiliar with the historical literature at which I'll be looking.

Coyle, Colvin, Syed, and Schonbrun focus primarily on sports, although there is an occasional mention of the work musicians do. Brown and his coauthors focus more on academic work and how best to study. These authors all refer to psychologist K. Anders Ericsson and his work on deliberate practice. Ericsson, who has spent much of his career probing questions related to the acquisition of exceptional skill, introduced the term "deliberate practice" in 1993. Athletes, however, are latecomers to the world of deliberate practice. The first modern Olympics occurred in 1896, a time when many of the artists I'll discuss were working toward or had achieved an exceptional level of performance. The early modern Olympics were nothing like today's Olympics: There were no sports psychologists, physicians specializing in sports medicine, or studies that explored how mental work can enhance physical performance.

There is a lot that musicians and athletes have in common, although comparisons break down when it comes to the nature of their skills. Coyle has a section in his book called "Why Teaching Soccer is Different from Teaching Violin." The differences are whether an activity requires "flexible-circuit skills" or "consistent-circuit skills":

> Skills like soccer, writing, and comedy are flexible-circuit skills, meaning that they require us to grow vast ivy-vine circuits that we can flick through to navigate an ever-changing set of obstacles. Playing violin, golf, gymnastics, and figure skating, on the other hand, are consistent-circuit skills, depending utterly on a solid foundation of technique that enables us to reliably re-create the fundamentals of an ideal performance. (This is why self-taught violinists, skaters, and gymnasts rarely reach world-class level and why self-taught novelists, comedians, and soccer players do all the time.) The universal rule remains the same: *good coaching supports the desired circuit.*[2]

Much of Coyle's research involved visiting what he called "talent hotbeds," places throughout the world that consistently turn out top athletes. Had he been able to go back in time to the turn of the twentieth century and visit the Moscow Imperial Conservatory, or the studios and master classes of teachers like Theodor Leschetizky (1830–1915), he would have recognized these as talent hotbeds as well.

"The Making of an Expert" by K. Anders Ericsson, Michael J. Prietula, and Edward T. Cokel, which was the cover story of the July 2007 issue of the *Harvard Business Review*, included two comments by violinists Leopold Auer (1845–1930) and Ivan Galamian (1903–1981) within its seven pages to illustrate the authors' points. Perhaps because the article was in a business journal, it wasn't obvious that these famous teachers were examples of an untapped wealth of literature by prototypical exponents of deliberate practice.[3]

The terminology of prototypical deliberate practicers and teachers of deliberate practice from the past may differ from ours, written clarity varies from source to source, and some writings hold a student's talent—or lack of it—to account for whether students reach a high level of artistry, but to perceptive musicians the parallels between these historical texts and more recent ones are unmistakable. An unusually large number of musicians from the past have acknowledged that it's the way in which one works that leads to success.

I'm a concert guitarist, and I know the technical, procedural, and artistic problems of the guitar best. I occasionally use examples of these problems as proxies for the problems all high-level musicians face. Perhaps other instrumentalists will recognize similar types of problems in the practices of their disciplines. With the exception of this introductory chapter, my voice as a teacher is largely absent from this book. *Practicing Music by Design* is not about my ideas, methods, or how I apply what I explore here to my own work or to my students' development. I will start, though, by relaying several experiences I've had that stimulated me to search for a deeper understanding of problems I've encountered that seemed to stem from faulty assumptions about how best to work. These encounters serve as a springboard to the larger and extended discussions of the tenets of exceptional practice in subsequent chapters.

Ian

Sometime in the mid-1980s, a French horn teacher at another university received a grant to study with me during the summer. Ian (not his real name) was an amateur guitarist, and the idea was that after some summer training with me he would be better qualified to teach guitar students at his school. Ian was self-taught and could make his way through a few pieces, but his technique was undeveloped and rough, which left his musicianship on the instrument lacking nuance and refinement.

I had a difficult time with Ian. He was in thrall to all the *Inner Game of . . .* books that appeared in the 1970s and 1980s. *The Inner Game of Music* explained the fundamental problem of development as a conflict between Self 1 and Self 2. Self 1 was our interference; Self 2 was a reservoir of potential within us all. There's no doubt that students can get in the way of their own development, but Ian viewed his problems as simply having the wrong mindset. This prevented him from looking at his study in any sort of analytical or intellectual way.

Ian thought that if he could just think of the right thing or was given the right attitudinal directive and let go of Self 1, music and technique would flow, and he wouldn't have to think about how to develop them. Technical problems would disappear, and his artistic potential would be realized. It seemed to me that the approach so appealing to Ian was influenced by the human potential movement of the mid-to-late twentieth century. This movement may have brought individuals into a more meaningful connection with their inner lives, but as a method of *training*, it was lazy, feckless, and narcissistic. Social critic Christopher Lasch (1932–1994) saw that this therapeutic sensibility created an "antagonism to education itself—an inability to take an interest in anything beyond immediate experience."[4]

Barry Green and Timothy Gallwey don't discuss Ideo-Kinetics in *The Inner Game of Music*, but Luigi Bonpensiere's *New Pathways to Piano Technique* from 1953 espouses an Ideo-Kinetic process in which physical preparation and execution are never considered, or, as Bonpensiere put it, one need only "Imagine the act as if already performed—and lo! it is done."[5] Proper technique, according to this approach, is created by thinking only of the musical result. George Kochevitsky, who has surveyed the history of various schools of thought about piano playing, believed that Bonpensiere's Ideo-Kinetics carried this idea to the point of absurdity and that it called for "a spiritual attitude taught by Zen Buddhism, a doctrine with which Bonpensiere was evidently rather superficially acquainted."[6]

The chief tenet of Zen Buddhism is that we are already enlightened but have forgotten, which is why we seek enlightenment; hence, all the stories of Zen masters saying inscrutable things and having initiates meditate on koans to help them see the flaws in logical reasoning to jolt them into enlightenment. When this tenet governs the process of becoming a guitarist, pianist, or master of any highly skilled activity, it necessarily rests upon the assumption that we are already skilled but have forgotten. We just need to think of the right things— or not think about the wrong things. But Zen focuses on the mundane— chop wood, carry water—or, as Harold McCarthy wrote in his 1955 review of Eugen Herrigel's *Zen in the Art of Archery*, "when Zen is divorced from the usual activities of daily life, it ceases to be Zen altogether and becomes a cult for those who are preoccupied with mysticism rather than with the living of life."[7] McCarthy adds that there is nothing mundane about archery: "[I]t is a special skill, art, and discipline which is added to without growing out of the matrix of daily life."[8] The same is true of developing skill on an instrument; it is cultivated outside the matrix of daily life. It is not something we knew at birth but forgot after being indoctrinated into a system of logical reasoning.

Surely, this attitude would serve to denigrate the efforts of those who have dedicated their lives to developing their skill and artistry on an instrument; at least it would be were the *Zen of . . .* and *Inner Game of . . .* approaches not destined to be so unsuccessful when used as substitutes for actual training. But a lack of success is more likely to be attributed to a lack of talent than it is to a lack of direction or solid mentorship.

We will explore in chapter 4 how the right type of mental work in expert practice can help one achieve remarkable results, but mental work cannot make one a fine pianist or guitarist without the commensurate work of building skill.

I failed with Ian, and he left before his six weeks of study were up. Although I tried to articulate reasoned arguments, I couldn't persuade him to engage in practices that would benefit him. I also couldn't give him a koan to meditate on in the hopes he would be jolted into a state of logical reasoning. I learned too late, as Jonathan Swift notes, "It is useless to attempt to reason a man out of a thing he was never reasoned into."[9]

The Governor's School

One summer in the early 1990s, I was asked to teach at the South Carolina Governor's School for the Arts. I drove from Columbia to Greenville twice a week to teach two high school guitar students. As with my university students, I wanted them to have the best start toward becoming well-trained musicians and to become independent learners.

I spent a lot of time with them—several lessons a week as well as extra time—and we started with basics. There was to be a student recital at the end of the six-week session, and the head of the school pressed me to have the guitarists play. "We want them to have a real conservatory-type experience, so they can see what it's like to be a professional musician," she said. "If you really want them to have a conservatory experience," I told her, "they've been having it. *If* they manage to get admitted to a conservatory, and *if* their teachers are any good, they'll be taken through a period of rigorous technical training. They'll probably play open strings for several weeks or more, study how their left hands work, followed by intensive scale and arpeggio work before they're even given an etude or repertoire piece. I've been doing what they'd do at a conservatory, so maybe now they'll be a little ahead. That's the reality they're facing."

Here I encountered the assumption that creating the conditions for successful performance inheres in the act of performing. But *learning goals* are not the same as *performance goals*. The two are entirely different, as the work of psychologist Carol Dweck has shown: When you're focused on performance goals, you're invested in validating your ability; when you're focused on learning goals, your concern is acquiring and developing new knowledge and skills.[10] A premature focus on performance goals can limit a student's potential.[11] When students are practicing well, they can develop technique, build mental structures, and fix mistakes because practice is designed to look to the future. When they're focused on performance, there's an immediacy to their attention and a preoccupation with appearing accomplished. Unless a student's performance grows out of corresponding learning goals, or are continually balanced by learning goals, students can become stuck in a cycle of not being able to prepare for anything other than the immediate future. *But training is the process of preparing for the long-term future.*

I would have done these two students a disservice had I designed their work solely with performance goals in mind, which I would have had to do if performing in the recital at the session's end had been the primary focus. Learning goals are governed by a separate set of mental processes than performance goals. It can be excellent pedagogy to create *learning goals for performance* once students have reached a certain level—as we'll see in chapter 7—but it was my assessment that these students wouldn't benefit from performance goals without vital preparatory work, which would have required more than the six weeks we had available given their level when the session began.

As it turned out, these two students went on to have successful careers. One became an Honors College student at the University of South Carolina and majored in guitar performance. He later earned a Ph.D. in composition from Duke University and is now a professor at a state university where he is an active performer and composer. The other student attended the North Carolina School of the Arts where he majored in guitar performance. He then came to the University of South Carolina where he received his master's degree in guitar performance. He has since developed the largest private music school in South Carolina.

My experience at the South Carolina Governor's School for the Arts illustrates two contrasting ideas about beginning serious training and how this training can interfere with or enhance the acquisition of expert skill.

Skill Acquisition

In 1993, K. Anders Ericsson and his colleagues wrote that "research on skill acquisition indicates that performance in the initial phases of practice is determined by characteristics quite different from those that determine performance during later phases."[12] Ericsson uses the word "performance" in terms of executing a high-level skill, not necessarily music performance on stage, but his findings are relevant to the early training of musicians: Practice during the development stage leads to "far greater changes in basic perceptual and motor abilities than previously thought."[13] This is especially true for activities that are comprised of numerous interdependent and interlocking high-level skills, such as found in virtuoso violin, guitar, or piano technique.

Early training should focus on securing more and better organized knowledge of one's area of study, which includes understanding and mastering the separate components that make up a larger skill. Changes in "basic perceptual and motor abilities," along with the acquisition of better organized knowledge, create optimal conditions for successful advanced study. As students become more advanced, they can focus on acquiring and applying the mental skills needed to transcend the limits of short-term memory and to combine the separate components of a movement so they can be performed as a fluent whole and transcend the limits of what Ericsson calls "serial reaction time."[14]

According to neurophysiologist Nikolai Bernstein, an important figure in the field of motor learning and motor control, "Actions are not simply movements. Most of them are whole sequences of movements that together solve a motor problem."[15] Virtuoso musicians and artist-teachers design practice for themselves and their students that integrates individual movements into sequences that create high-level technical and artistic actions. We'll explore how these movements are integrated with each other to solve technical and artistic problems in chapter 3.

Understanding the difference between movements that are processed by the brain serially, that is, one after another, and the *consolidation* of movements so they can be executed as part of a fluent whole is an example of how one can benefit by having been prepared to meet the requirements of advanced criteria early in one's training.

Many of the refined movements skilled musicians make are initiated and executed within a period of time that is less than what is known as "response latency" by those who study motor control. Response latency is the interval of time between when a stimulus is perceived and a response to the stimulus begins.[16] This latency is brief, up to 200 milliseconds, but in high-level music performance, transcending latency for difficult movements, or studying a series

of movements so they coalesce into an effortless whole, is necessary for technical and artistic success. The ability to transcend what I call "initiation latency"
in virtuoso playing contributes to the illusion that advanced performers have
all the time they need. Creating the conditions for this work should be one of
the goals of exceptional early training. We'll return to this often-unrecognized
aspect of skill acquisition and how early training can either facilitate it or render
it inaccessible in chapter 3. (High-level musicians should think of Ericsson's
phrase as transcending the limits of "serial *initiation* time.")

The most successful early training creates the conditions for high-level mastery. One can't teach students who need training the same way one would teach
more advanced students. My role with my Governor's School students was to
develop the characteristics essential for the initial phases of their practice; the
characteristics necessary for advanced study would grow out of this inceptive
work.

More Than Just the Next Repetition

In one of my posts on *The Guitar Whisperer Blog*, I wrote about the widespread
practice of guitarists and teachers shirking foundational technical work in favor
of what I call the "technique-from-pieces fallacy," a bewilderingly widespread
practice. We'll look at this more in the next chapter, but the problem is that
without extracting and understanding the underlying principles involved,
which is unlikely if there is no storehouse or foundation of prior knowledge
and skill, students rely on what researchers call "massed practice," which is
mindlessly repeating something over and over. With this approach, one necessarily relies on short-term memory. One may even experience what appears to
be rapid improvement, but as Peter Brown writes, "you haven't done much to
strengthen the underlying representation of those skills. Your performance in
the moment is not an indication of durable learning."[17]

After initial rapid improvement, one ends up stranded on a plateau, and it's
not the plateau that George Leonard, the author of *Mastery*, writes about and
that masters experience where all kinds of good things are happening below the
surface in preparation for a sudden jump to a new level.[18] But the jump never is
sudden; it's been painstakingly prepared for. The plateau reached through shallow practice is less of a plateau than an impenetrable barrier.

When one focuses primarily on the quantity of practice and the desired result
(performance goals), or one's practice is either poorly designed or not designed at
all, one may experience initial improvement and success. But Lauren Tashman,
a professor of sports psychology, writes that those engaged in the work of mastering a discipline may reach a plateau where they can perform successfully at that
level, *but they will not be able to develop their skills to an expert level.*[19] This plateau
may even be high enough to enable a music student to complete an undergraduate performance degree without realizing that something is wrong, but further
advancement is impossible without a drastic change of direction.

Focusing on the amount of practice and the substitution of a goal for how to reach it are too facile, inherently unmusical, uncreative, and do a disservice to the music *and* the student. Some legendary artists and artist-teachers agree. The great violin teacher Carl Flesch (1873–1944) thought that the musical meaning of a piece (or passage) subject to this way of working would be "entirely lost in the course of time," and one would "no longer be able to feel and express it with . . . immediacy and freshness."[20] Flesch decried reducing the piece to the "rank of a practice piece,"[21] and felt that "musical meaning will be lost along the way of excessive repetition."[22]

Robert Bjork, chair of the psychology department at UCLA, explains why massed practice doesn't work as well as other forms of practice:

> We tend to think of our memory as a tape recorder, but that's wrong. It's a living structure, a scaffold of nearly infinite size. The more we generate impulses, encountering and overcoming difficulties, the more scaffolding we build. The more scaffolding we build, the faster we learn.[23]

Building scaffolding implies a process that is stepwise and designed. Some difficulties are desirable, if approached in the right way and in the right order, because they force us to focus and reconstruct a skill, which speeds our movement toward mastery.

Desirable Difficulties

Some of these "desirable difficulties,"[24] a term introduced by Robert and Elizabeth Bjork, are created in music study by adding variety to repetition, something great musicians of the past have written about at least since the time of Franz Liszt (1811–1886). In volume one of *Contemporary Violin Technique* from 1966, Ivan Galamian presented what could be seen as a prescient definition of Bjork's term:

> Since technical mastery depends more upon control of mind over muscle than upon mere agility of fingers, the direct way to such mastery lies through working procedures which present a constant challenge to the student's thinking processes. For this reason *new problems must always be faced and solved*.[25]

Galamian's book contains an extraordinary number of rhythmic and bowing patterns that are to be applied to scales, arpeggios, intervals, and other musical material. Galamian's "working procedures" are an example of how a musician can build scaffolding.

This way of working has not been emphasized as much in guitar study as it has been in the historical pedagogical literature for the piano and violin. This literature documents how great musicians applied many variations to exercises and to sections of a piece. Chapter 6 explores why variety in repetition is beneficial. Chapter 8 illustrates how creating variations in practice will liberate one's ear, facilitate experimentation, and increase one's sensitivity to artistic nuance.

Fallacies Explored and Too Much Energy

Guitarists commenting on my blog post, however, were staunch defenders of their practices, but they instead served as providers of textbook examples of fallacious approaches to study:

> One thing that I feel most of the teachers, writers and so on out there seem to forget is exactly what we/they are here to do. Apart from getting people from A to Z on the fretboard, it is to release the student's mind of inhibition, to enable as near perfect as possible muscle control, to guide them as they make new discoveries. For some people, using repertoire to learn technique is great; for others it is a crappy method. Personally, I like to see a practical application in action. If that means using half-a-dozen bars of "Recuerdos [de la Alhambra]" to improve a student's tremolo, I will.[26]

No one can argue with the intention of helping students learn the fingerboard, liberating them from restrictive inhibitions, developing their muscle control, and guiding them in new discoveries. However, this writer is mistaking one of the components of initial study—developing technique—as a discrete entity that simply needs to be worked out in context. Technique is a series of distinct micro skills that need to be mastered separately before they can be successfully combined. When and how this combination takes place is a distinctive feature of superior practice.

By what means is one to determine that using repertoire to learn technique is practical for some but not for others? The author of the above comment at first claims that this decision is based upon the student but follows it with *his* preference: "I like to see a practical application in action." What's seen as practical is often the seemingly expedient decoupled from the artistic.

The above quotation is not atypical and embodies a faux-practicality and faux-artistic expediency, which happens to gainsay the practices of some of the most extraordinary musicians of the past as well as recent neurological, physiological, and psychological research about how expert skill is developed.

How exactly does one help students to release their mental inhibitions? It turns out there are some well-documented ways to do this, but they'll only work once the necessary foundation of knowledge and skill has been established and a level of technical quality has been reached. The better question is "How does one develop the conditions for students to achieve freedom and spontaneity in performance?" The answers lie in having developed a solid foundation and well-designed physical and mental practice.

How do you ensure students are developing "perfect as possible muscle control?" George Kochevitsky writes, "The elimination of too much muscle action is the real basis for developing technical agility."[27] Once one has developed technical agility appropriate to the level of literature being studied, the development of physical and mental skills is best accomplished by mastering small chunks and then stitching them together. Trying to assimilate too many things at once ensures students will increase their level of physical and mental tension.

If a guitar student is learning Francisco Tárrega's *Recuerdos de la Alhambra* as a means of learning tremolo technique (a technique that gives the illusion of long, sustained notes), the student faces the challenge of trying to master too many things simultaneously—the notes, left-hand movements, tremolo technique, and how to interpret the piece or passage—and may end up mastering nothing. In the best cases, learning and assimilation will be slow; in the worst of cases, students will develop habits of frustration and uncoordinated movement, which will require time later to develop better habits with which to replace them. Recent research has shown that the better one knows individual skills before combining them, the stronger one's learning of the whole will be.[28] This speaks directly to the importance of what is known as "hierarchical chunking" and is a necessary condition for transcending latency in virtuoso playing, both of which we'll explore in chapter 3. Someone who gradually assimilates skills needs decreasing amounts of energy to execute a task. When more mental energy is needed simply to get the notes, less energy is available to attend to artistic concerns.

Guiding students in new discoveries is best accomplished by ensuring students have developed a rich body of knowledge and experience so that sparks of ideas or inspiration will have something with which to interact.

The technique-from-pieces approach is an inherently unmusical practice disguised as an artistic one. The interpretive aspects of the piece will be the thing not receiving attention if one's foundation of prior knowledge and skill doesn't include what's needed to play the piece or passage, which it won't *if the stated purpose of studying the piece is to acquire that knowledge and skill*. One's ear will likely become habituated to a struggling, exercise-like rendition of the score, and the possibility of spontaneity and freedom in the future will decrease over time. Pianist Ferruccio Busoni (1866–1924) warned of how easy it is to forget about musical meaning while engaged in the technical practice of a piece.[29] If Busoni was concerned about this, then so should novice music students. (This fallacy will get more attention in the next chapter, but I mention it here to show that this approach requires more mental energy, which ends up compromising basic musicianship as well as technical fluency.)

One of the overarching goals of study and practice is to create the conditions for spontaneity and freedom in the future. As a corollary, anything that would impede spontaneity in performance (poor technique, faulty memory, lack of focus) must be transcended. Vladimir Horowitz (1903–1989), a towering figure in twentieth-century pianism, thought that performance should be more than just another repetition:

> [Pianists] practice and practice, and repeat passages and parts a hundred times over. Then they go on the stage, and repeat them for the hundred-and-first time. . . . But, on stage, you have to take chances to make the music really live.[30]

In 1921, the great violinist and teacher Leopold Auer (1845–1930) described the phenomenon of a struggling, exercise-like approach to a piece crowding out the ability to attend to artistic details. He attributed a student's deficiencies in expressing nuance to the student being *"too much absorbed in the actual playing of the notes."*[31] The student wasn't ready for the piece to be interpreted because the student's energy and brain power were appropriated by the mechanics of getting the piece played.

This observation has since been shown to be exactly what happens. Functional Magnetic Resonance Imaging (fMRI) shows the presence of increased brain activity while one is learning a new skill. As one assimilates and acquires a skill, brain activity decreases, leaving energy for approaching higher levels of skill or adding more skills.[32] Psychologist and Nobel Laureate Daniel Kahneman encapsulates the results of this neurological research: "As you become skilled in a task, its demand for energy diminishes. Studies of the brain have shown that the pattern of activity associated with an action changes as skill increases, with fewer brain regions involved."[33]

Auer knew this empirically before neurologists could prove it or would even be interested in formulating the question. Auer's student *was* devoting all his brainpower to trying to play the notes, and there was nothing left over for interpretation, despite poetic exhortations coming from his teacher. Taking a piece or passage from a piece to learn a new technique is stultifying in three ways: A fluent rendering of the notes suffers, which will dull the ear; one's technique suffers because there's limited mental energy to devote to it; and one's ability to create high-level structures of knowledge and skill is compromised. Although one would be playing a piece of music, this practice is inherently unmusical and imposes a sentence of drudgery and self-doubt upon one's future self.

There is another way one can expend too much energy, to the detriment of attending to the artistic and interpretive aspects of a piece: tension. The recognition of excessive tension and knowing how to eliminate it is a vexatious problem in pedagogy and is not understood by all. Relaxation in instrumental technique is the release of one set of muscles while opposing muscles are active. The ability to modulate and regulate the timing of these exchanges contributes to a high level of technique and artistry. Harmful tension results when opposing muscle groups contract at the same time. An often-overlooked result of harmful tension is that it can compromise one's mental acuity. An illustration of the effects of what is obviously too much tension and effort comes from Konstantin Stanislavsky (1863–1938), founder of the Moscow Art Theater and developer of the influential "Stanislavsky Method" of acting. He had his students lift and hold a corner of a piano while asked to recite multiplication tables. They couldn't do it until they set the piano down.

George Kochevitsky, who relates this story in *The Art of Piano Playing*, states that "muscular overstrain produces a disturbance of the whole mental activity."[34] Overstrain can begin to feel normal to poorly trained students and be mistaken for Robert Bjork's desirable difficulties. How are students to know the differences between mental activity that is compromised because they haven't studied and practiced well, mental energy that is strained because they're trying to assimilate too many things simultaneously, or mental energy that is strained because they're playing with too much tension? It's more difficult than narrowing it down to one thing because it's usually a stew of all three.

The Trial-and-Error Fallacy

Kochevitsky sees trial and error as an ineffective way to acquire skill and develop as an artist.[35] Yet, it is often promoted by the self-taught:

> I discovered the right and wrong ways to do most of the things I do by trial and error and by the most unbelievably close examination of my own technique. . . . I drove myself nearly insane with the demands I made on myself . . . and I tell you here and now, that if I'd had to sit and play scales for hours on end, I'd have . . . gone for the alternative career I had in mind—motor racing.[36]

In one respect, high-level study always involves experimenting, evaluating the results, and moving on from there, and we will discuss these steps and the necessity of uncontaminated feedback and self-criticism in chapter 9. But why go through trial and error—or have students go through trial and error—for something that someone else has figured out? Those teaching themselves cannot know the advanced criteria for the skill they're trying to learn. If they don't know these advanced criteria and how to meet them, they can't provide themselves with accurate feedback and won't know whether the "trial" resulted in error or success relative to their long-term development. They are likely to be misled by short-term results.

Howard Austin, who received his Ph.D. from the Department of Electrical Engineering and Computer Science at the Massachusetts Institute of Technology in 1976, devoted his dissertation to an analysis of juggling. Austin's study was meant to be read by artificial intelligence researchers and cognitive psychologists, although he also thought it would be helpful to anyone interested in motor control. His study was "the first attempt to discuss a complex (as opposed to a simple) motor skill in computational terms."[37]

Austin designed his study so that some of the novice jugglers were given instruction and others were given none. He found that self-taught jugglers spend most of their time acquiring information that those with teachers are given early on.[38] The self-taught sometimes develop "aberrant models or stumble across the correct model by accident."[39] Austin's data show that even if the self-taught "have enough problem-solving experience to avoid frustration and eventually succeed, it takes the uninstructed juggler 2–4 times as long as the instructed juggler to reach a given level of progress."[40] Half of the self-taught juggling students failed completely.[41]

Even outstanding artists who initially transcend the limits of being self-taught—which relies on trial and error—do not always remain exempt from adverse effects manifesting themselves decades later. Concert guitarist Julian Bream (b. 1933), who exerted a powerful artistic influence upon guitarists studying in the last third of the twentieth century, provides an example of the difficulty connecting cause with effect and the length of time it takes for faulty practices to reveal themselves as harmful.

Guitarists born in the first half of the twentieth century had no avenues for formal study and little choice other than to try to teach themselves. Bream describes with candor "a sort of paralysis" he suffered in his left hand several times during his career:

> I went to a number of specialists, and I found out that I had been playing the guitar in a wrong and faulty way for thirty years. This, I'm afraid, is one of the real problems of being self-taught. Nobody shows you how exactly to put your fingers on the instrument, therefore you just pick it up "naturally." This works, to a certain extent, but you can develop some muscles at the expense of others, and this is exactly that happened to me.[42]

Bream changed his left-hand technique when he was thirty-nine years old through what he called an "irksome routine" of exercises that he did every morning. He never promoted his self-taught approach as pedagogical advice for others, but his commentary illustrates the problem of discerning what works in the interests of one's long-term development versus one's short-term development. And there is the pesky problem of what limits inhere in the phrase "to a certain extent": The self-taught can never know.

Fernando Sor (1778–1839), composer, performer, and the most thoughtful nineteenth-century guitar pedagogue, writes about the importance of specificity in his *Method for the Spanish Guitar*:

> Rules, not given from authority merely, but with the reasons for which they were established, make a better impression received by persuasion

> than by memory; for, certainly, to say, "I do such a thing, because I have
> been told to do so," has not the same force as to say, "I do such a thing,
> because in being advised to do so, I have been shown the reasons for it,
> and I perceive its intention and utility."[43]

In the best case, the self-taught only have second-hand access to "rules given
from authority" but not the "reasons for which they were established."

Teaching is a skilled profession and the famous quotation about a defendant
representing himself in court—"A man who is his own lawyer has a fool for a
client"—[44]surely applies to those who try to be their own teachers of a high-
level skill. One need not go "nearly insane" in order to achieve a high level of
artistic ability.

The assumption that instead of using repertoire for technical study one must
sit and play scales for hours is reductive and doesn't consider the way great artists used scale practice to develop touch, articulation, and dynamic control and
to recognize and solve the minutest of technical and musical problems. We'll
look at how this is done in chapter 6.

The It-Works-for-Me Fallacy

There's another fallacy of study that doesn't acknowledge that there might be a
difference between what we think we know and what we could know:

> I just think that it's a nonsense to try and teach everyone the same way.
> We're all different and we teach and learn differently to one another. I
> don't recommend my own style of learning to anyone—it is quite hon-
> estly too tough for most students to handle—but it worked for me. To
> learn from repertoire or not . . . well it depends who you are and how
> you learn best.[45]

Although no counter statement or observation can be presented to show that
this statement is false, it doesn't follow that the statement is correct. It is not fal-
sifiable, which means were it false, there would be a way to show that it's false
through experiment or analysis, but the invocation of this remark shuts down
any critical discussion. It is subjective and unanalyzed experience masquerading
as valid information. Could something else have worked better? What other
factors might have affected one's work? How is the efficacy of one's work measured? This fallacy is especially pernicious because what works could simply be
short-term skill acquisition. The measure of something working is whether or
not one's functioning improves with subsequent work.[46] Unfortunately, when
problems start showing up and one's progress comes to a standstill, it's usually
years after study with a teacher has ceased, and it's almost impossible to connect
cause with effect. Historian Daniel Boorstin (1914–2004) points out that illusions of knowledge are obstacles to discovery.[47]

Developing expert skill is not as individualized as one might think, although the manifestations of skill are unique among individuals. The most efficient ways of practicing and studying are not intuitive and are likely to remain undiscovered by those without a guide. Unless the "me" who is figuring out "what works" knows these strategies, the chances are that "It works for me" should be, "It seems to work for me, but maybe it could work better." Expert teachers can target the development of specific skills that are prerequisites for mastery. The uninitiated often mistake pedagogical specificity for pedagogical autocracy and chafe beneath it.

The "it-works-for-me" gambit as a justification for a particular pedagogical approach usually masks a specious argument: the assumption that the possession of expertise in one area, in this case performance, means one also has expertise in another domain, such as teaching. They are separate skills, although existing within the same field.

Michael Oakeshott (1901–1990), English philosopher and political theorist, offers some insight why this might be: "There is an important difference between learning which is concerned with the degree of understanding necessary to practice a skill, and learning which is expressly focused upon an enterprise of understanding and explaining."[48] David Foster Wallace has a more damning explanation: "[T]hose who receive and act out the gift of athletic genius must, perforce, be blind and dumb about it—and not because blindness and dumbness are the price of the gift, but because they are its essence."[49]

I disagree with Wallace about blindness and dumbness being the essence of the gift, but Wallace's statement illustrates that pedagogical blindness and dumbness are a commonplace among those who have a high-level of skill. He suggests that it's naïve to think otherwise: If we "expect geniuses-in-motion to be also geniuses-in-reflection," he writes, "then their failure to be that shouldn't really seem any crueler or more disillusioning than Kant's glass jaw [a boxer's inability to take a punch] or [T. S.] Eliot's inability to hit the curve."[50]

If one's advice to others is to be useful, one had best develop expertise as a teacher. One does not automatically come by this skill by acquiring skill as a performer. Carl Flesch wrote in Book Two of *The Art of Violin Playing*:

> An abyss yawns between the *learning* and the *teaching* of an art. The one who learns has only the experience of his own case, the one who teaches must understand the immeasurable multiplicity of all that occurs, and must learn how to handle it. The recognition of the manifold nature of pedagogic science is a study in itself.[51]

Bridging the Yawning Abyss

One outstanding pianist who undertook this study was Claudio Arrau (1903–1991). Arrau was a child prodigy who was sent to study at the Stern Conservatory in Berlin with a grant from the Chilean government when he was eight years old. He studied with Martin Krause (1853–1918), one of Liszt's last students. After Krause's death in 1918, Arrau began the process of turning that which had been subconscious into that which was conscious:

> It all became conscious long after Krause died. At first, I played without thinking about technique, because I had this natural gift. Much later, I decided it was better to be conscious of how I played. I put a mirror next to my piano—it must have been when I was eighteen or nineteen. Then I began to notice the rotation, the vibration, the use of arm weight, and so on.[52]

Arrau was unusually self-aware and described this process in an article in *The Piano Quarterly* in 1973:

> A few years later when I started teaching, I started watching myself when I did something the right way. I put up a huge mirror in my studio in Berlin. The mirror was standing on the floor and I would ask myself, 'What am I doing and how do I do it?' I brought it up to consciousness, so to speak. And so gradually I began to know exactly whence every movement came. Where came the impetus.[53]

One of the goals of this book is to bridge the yawning abyss between the teaching and the learning of an art and to remove the vagueness of "it depends who you are and how you learn best."[54] This statement is a room-temperature nod to individuality, but the woolliness of it causes one to teach "everyone all the same way" because of its failure to focus on real problems. How students learn best is by having developed—or by having it developed for them—well-designed practice. Well-designed means understanding the best that neurologists, physiologists, psychologists, and great artists have discovered and applied. There is a remarkable consilience between the documented study and teaching approaches used by legendary pianists and violinists and recent discoveries on learning and the acquisition of high-level skill.

Transformation, Not Mindless Repetition

The great pianists and violinists who wrote about using a passage from a piece as an exercise always wrote about *transforming* the passage by studying it with different rhythms, dynamics, accents, articulations, bowings for violinists, and transposition and voicings for pianists. Neurological, physiological, and psychological research has confirmed that working this way confers significant artistic and technical benefits. None of the great musicians of the past wrote about learning technique as it occurs in etudes and repertoire, or the mindless repetition of scales, except to condemn these practices. Using repertoire as a means of staying in shape once one has developed to a certain point is a different thing, but, even then, pianists like Ignace Paderewski (1860–1941) claimed always to practice scales and exercises—but he said that "one must know which exercises to choose and how to practise them."[55] Both Ferruccio Busoni and Arthur Rubinstein (1887–1982) withdrew from performing for a time to overhaul their technique. They didn't overhaul their technique by playing pieces; they had already been doing that for years.

The Rote to Ruin

There's another fallacy—perhaps it's more of a paradox—that confuses the mindful repetition one must do in practice with the "thinking too much" that can sabotage a performance. They are not the same thing.

Repetition is necessary for practice, but one must learn to practice *mindful* repetition. Ellen J. Langer, the author of *The Power of Mindful Learning*, asks: Does it make sense

> to freeze our understanding of the skill before trying it out in different contexts and, at various stages, adjust it to our own strengths and experiences? Does it make sense to stick to what we first learned when that learning occurred when we were most naive?[56]

What she is pointing to is the danger of learning a skill without the recognition that one might need to meet different criteria in order to develop the higher-level version of the skill. She adds that

> [W]hen people overlearn a task so that they can perform it by rote, the individual steps that make up the skill come together in larger and larger units. As a consequence, the smaller components of the activity are essentially lost, yet it is by adjusting and varying these pieces that we can improve our performance.[57]

The desirable difficulties caused by applying continual variety in repetition decrease rote learning and improve mindfulness. Rote learners will have difficulty varying the small components of a skill, a process that enhances artistic and technical fluency.

Langer's small components that get lost through rote learning can be physical or mental. An example of a lost physical component for guitarists or players of bowed strings might be how one shifts in scales: If one has not practiced shifting mindfully, it will be absorbed into the larger activity of playing a scale. But, if it's the shift that is slowing the scale down, it will be difficult to isolate to improve it. (These small components are not at all like the chunks we'll discuss in chapter 3 because they are not based on existing high-level structures.)

There is another example of how mindless repetition can lock minute details away into the larger whole and make them irretrievable. Suppose a student has a problem in measure seventeen of a piece and is asked to play that measure to work on the problem. Students who have learned by rote can't start playing from anywhere and must go back to the beginning of the piece, section, or phrase. When they get to measure seventeen, the purpose of their practice is forgotten, and they have engaged in another mindless repetition. Measure seventeen has become absorbed into a mindless whole and is irretrievable. Any problem in measure seventeen, a bad fingering or a wrong note, will be difficult to change.

Here's the paradox: We need to be able to think carefully and specifically about the small components that make up a larger skill as we're learning something. This initial mindfulness leads to acquiring the ability to adjust these small components later if we need to throw off the shackles of a bad habit and change something. As we gain a higher level of sensitivity and musical understanding, we can continually refine our habits.

If we've learned material through mindless repetition and try to become mindful after the fact, we'll create a paralyzing conflict between the reflexive central nervous system and the slower decision making process of the prefrontal cortex. This paralysis can lead to an unsettling preoccupation with technique and memory during a performance, and things can fall apart.

The key is to understand the nature of mindlessness.

Mindlessness. Mindfulness. Return to Mindlessness

There are two types of mindlessness, the confusion of which causes the artistic growth of many musicians to become stunted. One of the goals of well-designed practice is to help make the transition from the first type of mindlessness to the second type.

Henry Skrimshander, the protagonist of Chad Harbach's novel *The Art of Fielding*, carries with him a book by legendary (fictional) shortstop Aparicio Rodriguez, which contains enlightenment-provoking statements about baseball (or life): "There are three stages: Thoughtless being. Thought. Return to thoughtless being. Do not confuse the first and third stages. Thoughtless being is attained by everyone, the return to thoughtless being by a very few."[58]

Pianist Max Pauer (1866–1945) expressed it this way in 1913: "The whole idea of technic then is to achieve a position *through* conscious effort, where one may *dispense* with conscious effort. Not until this can be accomplished can we hope for real self-expression in playing."[59] Not quite a decade later, violinist Frank Thistleton wrote about the importance of applying one's knowledge in practice. Then follows a description of the result of mindful practice: "[A]fter a time, it is not necessary to think how we do things, but *it is essential that we know how we obtain certain results whilst we are practising.*"[60]

We can never reach the third stage without passing through the second. The mindlessness of the first stage is the mindless work—in the sense of not being fully engaged or not knowing the implications of what one is doing—of the untrained. This is the sense in which Langer uses the term. She suggests that this mindlessness "is characterized by an entrapment in old categories; by automatic behavior that precludes attending to new signals; and by action that operates from a single perspective."[61] Each of these three characteristics can prevent one's artistry from developing beyond a rudimentary level. In contrast, the mindlessness of the third stage is the mindlessness of one who has integrated skills so well with their purpose that there is no thought, only artistic action, as recognized by Pauer.

When one tries to perform thinking he or she has achieved the mindlessness of a master, but the mindlessness has not been informed by mindful work— which is what Ian thought he could do—there will be present a layer of self-conscious monitoring, which is unartistic, distracting, and a barrier to freedom. Even if one has developed skills mindfully, thinking in the wrong way at the wrong time can hamper performance. In *The Performance Cortex*, a book that explores the workings of the brain's motor control system in high-level athletes, Zach Schonbrun writes, "[T]hinking about the plan will often disrupt the plan. A tennis player does not consciously consider which muscles to activate in order to return a backhand."[62]

This was something well understood by Theodor Leschetizky, one of the great piano teachers of the late nineteenth and early twentieth centuries. He thought that if one's initial study of a work was not mindful, that is, characterized by the kind of mental work we'll look at in chapter 4, pianists who rely solely on muscle and aural memory and who play well when alone become "absolutely stranded before an audience. The presence of other people compels them to concentrate their attention on what they are doing, and they find they do not actually know what that is."[63] In a 1902 letter to Malwine Brée, Leschetizky declared, "I am from principle, no friend of theoretical Piano-Methods,"[64] but later qualified this, as reported by Annette Hullah: "There is but one part of my teaching that may be called a 'Method,' if you like; and that is the way in which I teach my pupils to learn a piece of music."[65]

Mindful work will liberate us from a preoccupation with technique, memory, or fear during a performance and contribute to the conditions for us to be able to do that which we should be doing: spontaneously sculpting sound in each moment. We'll look at this again when we discuss explicit and implicit skill in chapter 3.

Leschetizky's approach to new literature, whether for himself or his pupils, was rigorous and required concentrated thought and intellectual engagement with the material. He thought that no amount of mechanical repetition can help one obtain anything of permanence. "[T]he player who repeats the same passage, wearily expectant that he will accomplish it in process of time, is a lost soul on a hopeless quest."[66]

Approaches to study similar to Leschetizky's might be viewed as overly intellectual by some. There has long been a part of American society that is anti-intellectual and has an antipathy to the past. In 1835, Alexis de Tocqueville wrote in *Democracy in America*: "Those who went before are soon forgotten; of those who will come after, no one has any idea: the interest of man is confined to those in close propinquity to himself."[67] Richard Hofstadter, following the blaze left by de Tocqueville, writes in *Anti-Intellectualism in American Life* from 1963 that in the United States "the play of the mind is perhaps the only form of play that is not looked upon with the most tender indulgence."[68]

This anti-intellectual strain and antipathy to the past is suspicious of an intellectual approach to the arts, but this is a superficial criticism and falls into the thought-cliché that whatever emanates from the untrained possesses a Rousseau-like "authenticity" that the expert can't possibly hold.[69] This authenticity (not to be confused with the way the word "authenticity" was once used in relation to historical performance) is synonymous with something being unprocessed and sees the feelings of the inner self, whether or not they are informed by fact, history, or critical thought, as the ultimate guide to rightness. But having a strong feeling about something says nothing about a thing's rightness unless it clarifies one's inner life and one's emotional relationship to the world. Problems arise when the culture of authenticity transmutes feelings to opinions and opinions to facts. As Daniel Patrick Moynihan famously said, "You are entitled to your own opinion, but you are not entitled to your own facts."[70]

The aesthetics or tenets of the early music movement are now a part of mainstream musical thought and high-level instruction. Performance treatises have been examined, recordings once considered anachronistic are now historical and have been fodder for the scholar and artist alike, and we are the richer for it. But is anyone investigating the pedagogical works of legendary teachers and performers that document their teaching and practice methods to see if they can enrich our understanding of how one acquires exceptional skill? Is there a usefulness in the study of "historical pedagogy," or is the modern artist to assume that *any* modern approach to study necessarily usurps *any* practices advanced by great artists and teachers from the past? De Tocqueville also wrote, "Since the past no longer clarifies the future, the mind moves in shadows."[71]

The techniques and methods of the best of these legendary artists were modern before there was modernity, effective, and transcend both maestro inerrancy, which would alchemically transform a contemporary master's performing ability into teaching ability, and the infallibility of the uninformed self, which needs no alchemy because it is already assumed to be gold.

Hobgoblins of Little Minds

The approaches of Ian, the head of the SC Governor's School for the Arts, and the common use of a solipsistic, faux-practical approach to study are consistent in their lack of pedagogical precision. Teachers only need to do the easy thing and go right to the end: There's a problem with his technique, assign him a piece that uses that technique; she says she's a visual learner? Good, watch me demonstrate. It's too easy and deceives students into thinking they're on the road to mastery when they're only on the road to familiarity.

To many, though, these "practical" approaches seem intuitively correct and pragmatic. If the student flounders, he or she isn't talented and doesn't have what it takes. This is correct: They don't have what it takes, but it's not what you think. *What it takes is for them to have a teacher who can help them design their study to make use of the best that is known about how exceptional skill develops.*

Peter Brown and his coauthors open their book, *Make it Stick: The Science of Successful Learning*, by stating that "the most effective learning strategies are not intuitive"[72] and that "learning is an acquired skill."[73] Matthew Syed, author of *Bounce: Mozart, Federer, Picasso, Beckham, and the Science of Success*, calls talent a disempowering myth, which causes many to quit something if they don't make rapid initial progress.[74] What Syed calls the "talent myth" has long allowed teachers to abrogate their responsibilities by attributing a student's lack of progress to a lack of talent.

A Little Island in an Infinite Sea

What these consistent approaches to practice have in common is that they confuse the means with the ends. Philosopher and psychologist John Dewey (1859–1952) reminds us that "The 'end' is merely a series of acts viewed at a remote stage; and a means is merely the series viewed at an earlier one."[75] Dewey's statement becomes less cryptic when one realizes that he's referring to what Francis Matthias Alexander (1869–1955), who developed the influential Alexander Technique,[76] called the "means whereby" one more effectively reaches an "end." The means whereby are embedded in the end and are visible to those who are well trained, have developed skill consciously, and have not worked directly for an imagined end. One can't accurately view the end without having passed through a well-designed series of means, and one won't know the optimal design of these means except in retrospect, unless one has a skilled guide.

Dewey knew what he was talking about when it came to understanding the differences between ends and means. In 1916, he wrote about the error of taking "an effect for the cause of the effect,"[77] which is what happens when one mistakes performance goals for learning goals. Dewey met F. M. Alexander in 1916 and took lessons in the Alexander Technique for the next thirty-five years. Dewey wrote the preface for three of Alexander's books, including *Constructive Conscious Control of the Individual*, published in 1923. In this book, Alexander put his finger precisely on the problems explored in the above anecdotes: that of pursuing the ends above the means and the difficulty of replacing a bad habit with a better one. We will look at this in greater detail in chapter 5.

Dewey says that ends that are foreseen are "a little island in an infinite sea"[78] and called them "the refuge of the timid."[79] From this we can extrapolate that approaches based on imitation or an assumption that one knows a fixed end are approaches favored by the timorous. By mastering the means, one can work in a way that favors the venturesome. Unforeseen ends are endless in their refinements.

Foolish Consistencies

Approaches to study that promote the ends at the expense of the means may be fixed and consistent, but they are foolish, and as Emerson wrote in *Self-Reliance*, "A foolish consistency is the hobgoblin of little minds, adored by little statesmen and philosophers and divines."[80] The tenets of good practice I examine in this book—building a foundation of knowledge and skill, chunking, mental work, slow practice, variety in repetition, continuity, phrase-storming, and feedback and self-criticism—I regard as *unfoolish* consistencies. Implementation of these unfoolish consistencies will help musicians design their practice and develop the means to pass continuously through a series of endless ends.

Notes

1. Coyle does use the work of musicians for some of his examples, but his primary focus is on athletes.
2. Daniel Coyle, *The Talent Code: Greatness Isn't Born: It's Grown: Here's How* (New York: Bantam, 2009), 194–195. [Italics added.]
3. Coyle mentions Galamian's founding of Meadowmount, which Coyle visited. Colvin repeats the Auer comment.
4. Christopher Lasch, *The Culture of Narcissism: American Life in an Age of Diminishing Expectations* (New York: Norton, 1979), 149.
5. Quoted in George Kochevitsky, *The Art of Piano Playing: A Scientific Approach* (Princeton, NJ: Summy-Birchard Music, 1967), 17.
6. Ibid.
7. Harold E. McCarthy, "Review of Zen in the Art of Archery by Eugen Herrigel; R. F. C. Hull," *Philosophy East and West* Vol. 5, No. 3 (1955): 263–264.
8. Ibid. There is much more that could be said about Herrigel's book. Yamada Shōji, writing in 2001, claims that Herrigel's teacher, Kenzô Awa (1880–1939), may never have practiced Zen and it is difficult to detect Zen elements in his teachings. (Yamada Shōji, "The Myth of Zen in the Art of Archery," *Japanese Journal of Religious Studies* Vol. 28, No. 1/2 (2001): 1–30). This is relevant to musicians because Herrigel's book is occasionally referenced in writings about technique and practice.
9. This remark has been attributed to Swift but is more likely a paraphrase of an observation that appears in Swift's "A Letter to a Young Gentleman, Lately Entered into Holy Orders" from 1720: "Reasoning will never make a man correct an ill opinion, which by reasoning he never acquired."
10. Heidi Grant and Carol S. Dweck, "Clarifying Achievement Goals and Their Impact," *Journal of Personality and Social Psychology* Vol. 85, No. 3 (2003): 541–553.
11. Peter C. Brown, Henry L. Roediger, III, and Mark A. McDaniel, *Make It Stick: The Science of Successful Learning* (Cambridge, MA: Belknap Press, 2014), 180.

12. K. A. Ericsson, R. Th. Krampe, and C. Tesch-Römer, "The Role of Deliberate Practice in the Acquisition of Expert Performance," *Psychological Review* Vol. 100, No. 3 (1993): 397.
13. Ibid.
14. Ibid.
15. Zach Schonbrun, *The Performance Cortex: How Neuroscience is Redefining Athletic Genius* (New York: Dutton, 2018), 204.
16. Howard Austin, "A Computational Theory of Physical Skill" (PhD diss., Cambridge, MA: Massachusetts Institute of Technology, 1976), 103–104.
17. Brown, *Make It Stick*, 74.
18. George Leonard, *Mastery: The Keys to Success and Long-Term Fulfillment* (New York, NY: Plume, 1992), 7–17.
19. Lauren S. Tashman, "The Development of Expertise in Performance: The Role of Memory, Knowledge, Learning, and Practice," *Journal of Multidisciplinary Research* Vol. 5, No. 3 (2013): 42.
20. Carl Flesch, *The Art of Violin Playing, Book One* (New York: Carl Fischer, Inc., 1924; Revised Edition, 1939), 107.
21. Ibid.
22. Ibid., 166.
23. Quoted in Coyle, *The Talent Code*, 19. Motor researchers also use the word "scaffolding" for the early step-by-step phase of skill acquisition.
24. See: Brown, *Make It Stick*, 68–69.
25. Ivan Galamian and Frederick Neumann, *Contemporary Violin Technique*, Vol. 1 (Boston, MA: Galaxy Music Corporation, 1966), ii. [Italics added.]
26. Anonymous Internet comment. The three internet comments used in this chapter are difficult to document. They are all in response to a blog post of mine, "Reducing Music to Technique: Intelligent Bunglers and Brainless Acrobats." I don't host comments on my blog, but the post—and others in my practice series—have been shared on Facebook, which is where the comments appeared. Readers might be able to find the comment threads by searching for the post title *within* Facebook. Some commenters were especially agitated, but their arguments exemplified the fallacies I try to dispel: the technique-from-pieces fallacy, the trial-and-error fallacy, and the it-works-for-me fallacy. The blog is at http://blog.christopherberg.com.
27. Kochevitsky, *The Art of Piano Playing*, 13.
28. Lynne M. Reder et al., "Building Knowledge Requires Bricks, Not Sand: The Critical Role of Familiar Constituents in Learning," *Psychonomic Bulletin & Review* (2015): 1–7.
29. Kochevitsky, *The Art of Piano Playing*, 50.
30. Quoted in David Dubal, *The World of the Concert Pianist* (London: Victor Gollancz, 1985), 205.
31. Leopold Auer, *Violin Playing as I Teach It* (New York: Frederick A. Stokes Company, 1921), 148. [Italics added.]
32. See: Nicole M. Hill and Walter Schneider, "Brain Changes in the Development of Expertise: Neuroanatomical and Neurophysiological Evidence about Skill-Based Adaptations," in *The Cambridge Handbook of Expertise and Expert Performance*, ed. K. Anders Ericsson, Neil Charness, Paul J. Feltovich, and Robert R. Hoffman (New York: Cambridge, 2006), 653–682.
33. Daniel Kahneman, *Thinking, Fast and Slow* (New York: Farrar, Straus and Giroux, 2013), 35.
34. Kochevitsky, *The Art of Piano Playing*, 39.
35. Ibid., 18.
36. Anonymous Internet comment.

37. Austin, "A Computational Theory," 9.
38. Ibid., 175.
39. Ibid.
40. Ibid., 176.
41. Ibid., 352.
42. "Julian Bream discuss about [sic] playing the guitar in a wrong way." www.you tube.com/watch?v=0XGySXMG2GY. This is a video clip that has been excerpted from what appears to be a television program made in the 1980s. There is no indication what the original video was or when it was made.
43. Fernando Sor, *Method for the Spanish Guitar*, trans. A. Merrick (London: R. Cocks & Co., n.d.; New York: Da Capo Press, 1971), 24. Citations refer to the Da Capo edition.
44. Although many have said this, the first utterance of this may be by English clergyman and academic Henry Kitt (1761–1825) in *The Flowers of Wit* from 1814.
45. Anonymous Internet comment.
46. Christopher Berg, *Mastering Guitar Technique* (Pacific, MO: Mel Bay Publications, 1997), 21.
47. Daniel J. Boorstin, *The Discoverers, A History of Man's Search to Know His World and Himself* (New York: Random House, 1985), xv.
48. Michael Oakeshott, *What Is History? And Other Essays* (Charlottesville, VA: Imprint Academic, 2004).
49. David Foster Wallace, "How Tracy Austin Broke My Heart," in *Consider the Lobster and Other Essays* (New York: Back Bay Books and Little, Brown, 2007), 155.
50. Ibid., 153.
51. Carl Flesch, *The Art of Violin Playing, Book Two* (New York: Carl Fischer, Inc., 1930), 129.
52. Quoted in Victoria A. von Arx, *Piano Lessons with Claudio Arrau: A Guide to His Philosophy and Techniques* (New York: Oxford University Press, 2014), 18. Arrau's story is remarkable. Most prodigies would avoid thinking about how they do something lest they fall into the trap of turning an implicit skill into an explicit skill.
53. Quoted in ibid., 19.
54. Peter Brown and his coauthors present convincing evidence that being taught in one's preferred "learning style" confers no special benefit and even harms learning. See chapter 6 of Brown, *Make It Stick*.
55. T. P. Currier, "Some Characteristics of Paderewski the Pianist," *Modern Music and Musicians* (1918): 25.
56. Ellen J. Langer, *The Power of Mindful Learning* (Reading, MA: Addison-Wesley Publishing Company, Inc., 1997), 13.
57. Ibid., 17–18.
58. Chad Harbach, *The Art of Fielding* (New York: Little, Brown and Company, 2011), 16.
59. James Francis Cooke, *Great Pianists on Piano Playing* (Philadelphia: Theodore Presser Co., 1913), 199.
60. Frank Thistleton, *The Art of Violin Playing for Players and Teachers* (London: The Strad, 1924), 15. [Italics added.]
61. Langer, *The Power of Mindful Learning*, 4.
62. Schonbrun, *The Performance Cortex*, 112–113.
63. Annette Hullah, *Theodor Leschetizky* (London and New York: J. Lane Company, 1906), 45.
64. Malwine Brée and Theodor Baker, *The Groundwork of the Leschetizky Method* (New York: G. Schirmer, 1902), iii.
65. Hullah, *Theodor Leschetizky*, 42.
66. Ibid., 49.
67. Alexis de Tocqueville, *Democracy in America* (New York: Knopf, 1951), 2:99.

68. Richard Hofstadter, *Anti-Intellectualism in American Life* (New York: Alfred A. Knopf, 1963), 3.
69. Pianist Olga Samaroff touched upon this in 1913. See chapter 4.
70. There's more about the origin of this quote. It could be traced back to Bernard Baruch, but it's Moynihan with whom it and its variants are most often associated.
71. Alexis de Tocqueville, *Democracy in America: Historical-Critical Edition of De la démocratie en Amérique*, ed. Eduardo Nolla, trans. from the French by James T. Schleifer, Vol. 4 (Indianapolis: Liberty Fund, 2010), 1279. De Tocqueveille's words have also been translated as "When the past no longer illuminates the future, the spirit walks in darkness."
72. Brown, *Make It Stick*, ix.
73. Ibid., 3.
74. Matthew Syed, *Bounce: Mozart, Federer, Picasso, Beckham, and the Science of Success* (New York: Harper Perennial, 2011), 51.
75. John Dewey, *Human Nature and Conduct; an Introduction to Social Psychology* (New York: Holt, 1922), 35.
76. The Alexander Technique is routinely studied by musicians, actors, and other performing artists.
77. John Dewey, *Democracy and Education: An Introduction to the Philosophy of Education* (New York: The Macmillan Company, 1916), 41.
78. Dewey, *Human Nature and Conduct*, 262.
79. Ibid., 237.
80. Ralph Waldo Emerson, *The Essay on Self-Reliance* (East Aurora, NY: The Roycrofters, 1908), 23.

Sources

Arx, Victoria A. von. *Piano Lessons with Claudio Arrau: A Guide to His Philosophy and Techniques*. New York: Oxford University Press, 2014.

Auer, Leopold. *Violin Playing as I Teach It*. New York: Frederick A. Stokes Company, 1921.

Austin, Howard. "A Computational Theory of Physical Skill." PhD diss. Massachusetts Institute of Technology, Cambridge, MA, 1976.

Berg, Christopher. *Mastering Guitar Technique: Process & Essence*. Pacific, MO: Mel Bay Publications, 1997.

Bonpensiere, Luigi. *New Pathways to Piano Technique: A Study of the Relations between Mind and Body with Special Reference to Piano Playing*. New York: Philosophical Library, 1953.

Boorstin, Daniel J. *The Discoverers, a History of Man's Search to Know His World and Himself*. New York: Random House, 1985.

Brée, Malwine, and Theodor Baker. *The Groundwork of the Leschetizky Method*. New York: G. Schirmer, 1902.

Brown, Peter C., Henry L. Roediger, III, and Mark A. McDaniel. *Make It Stick: The Science of Successful Learning*. Cambridge, MA: Belknap Press, 2014.

Cooke, James Francis. *Great Pianists on Piano Playing*. Philadelphia: Theodore Presser Co., 1913.

Coyle, Daniel. *The Talent Code: Greatness Isn't Born: It's Grown: Here's How*. New York: Bantam, 2009.

Currier, T. P. "Some Characteristics of Paderewski the Pianist." *Modern Music and Musicians. Vol. 1: The Pianist's Guide*, 24–25. New York: The University Society, 1918.

Dewey, John. *Democracy and Education: An Introduction to the Philosophy of Education*. New York: The Macmillan Company, 1916.

Dewey, John. *Human Nature and Conduct: An Introduction to Social Psychology*. New York: Holt, 1922.

Dubal, David. *The World of the Concert Pianist*. London: Victor Gollancz, 1985.

Emerson, Ralph Waldo. *The Essay on Self-Reliance*. East Aurora, NY: The Roycrofters, 1908.

Ericsson, K. A., R. T. Krampe, and C. Tesch-Römer. "The Role of Deliberate Practice in the Acquisition of Expert Performance." *Psychological Review* (1993): 363–406.

Flesch, Carl. *The Art of Violin Playing, Book One*. New York: Carl Fischer, Inc., 1924.

Flesch, Carl. *The Art of Violin Playing, Book Two*. New York: Carl Fischer, Inc., 1930.

Galamian, Ivan, and Frederick Neumann. *Contemporary Violin Technique*. Vol. 1. Boston, MA: Galaxy Music Corporation, 1966.

Grant, Heidi, and Carol S. Dweck. "Clarifying Achievement Goals and Their Impact." *Journal of Personality and Social Psychology* Vol. 85, No. 3 (2003): 541–553.

Green, Barry, and W. Timothy Gallwey. *The Inner Game of Music*. Garden City, NY: Anchor Press and Doubleday, 1986.

Harbach, Chad. *The Art of Fielding*. New York: Little, Brown and Company, 2011.

Hill, Nicole M., and Walter Schneider. "Brain Changes in the Development of Expertise: Neuroanatomical and Neurophysiological Evidence about Skill-Based Adaptations." In *The Cambridge Handbook of Expertise and Expert Performance*, edited by K. A. Ericsson, N. Charness, P. J. Feltovich, and R. R. Hoffman, 653–682. New York: Cambridge University Press, 2006.

Hofstadter, Richard. *Anti-Intellectualism in American Life*. New York: Alfred A. Knopf, 1963.

Hullah, Annette. *Theodor Leschetizky*. London and New York: J. Lane Company, 1906.

Kahneman, Daniel. *Thinking, Fast and Slow*. New York: Farrar, Straus and Giroux, 2013.

Kochevitsky, George. *The Art of Piano Playing: A Scientific Approach*. Princeton, NJ: Summy-Birchard, 1967.

Langer, Ellen J. *The Power of Mindful Learning*. Reading, MA: Addison-Wesley Publishing Company, Inc., 1998.

Lasch, Christopher. *Culture of Narcissism: American Life in an Age of Diminishing Expectations*. New York: W. W. Norton & Company, 1991.

Leonard, George. *Mastery: The Keys to Success and Long-Term Fulfillment*. New York: Plume, 1992.

McCarthy, Harold E. "Review of Zen in the Art of Archery by Eugen Herrigel: R. F. C. Hull." *Philosophy East and West* Vol. 5, No. 3 (1955): 263–264.

Oakeshott, Michael. *What Is History? And Other Essays*. Exeter, UK and Charlottesville, VA: Imprint Academic, 2004.

Reder, Lynne M., Xiaonan L. Liu, Alexander Keinath, and Vencislav Popov. "Building Knowledge Requires Bricks, Not Sand: The Critical Role of Familiar Constituents in Learning." *Psychonomic Bulletin & Review* (2015): 1–7.

Schonbrun, Zach. *The Performance Cortex: How Neuroscience Is Redefining Athletic Genius*. New York: Dutton, 2018.

Shōji, Yamada. "The Myth of Zen in the Art of Archery." *Japanese Journal of Religious Studies* Vol. 28, No. 1/2 (2001): 1–30.

Sor, Fernando. *Method for the Spanish Guitar*. Translated by A. Merrick. London: R. Cocks & Co., n.d. Reprint, New York: Da Capo Press, 1971.

Syed, Matthew. *Bounce: Mozart, Federer, Picasso, Beckham, and the Science of Success*. New York: Harper Perennial, 2011.

Tashman, L. S. "The Development of Expertise in Performance: The Role of Memory, Knowledge, Learning, and Practice." *Journal of Multidisciplinary Research* Vol. 5, No. 3 (2013): 33–48.

Thistleton, Frank. *The Art of Violin Playing for Players and Teachers*. London: The Strad, 1924.

Tocqueville, Alexis de. *Democracy in America*. New York: Knopf, 1951.

Tocqueville, Alexis de. *Democracy in America: Historical-Critical Edition of De La Démocratie en Amérique*. Vol. 4. Edited by Eduardo Nolla. Translated from the French by James T. Schleifer. Indianapolis: Liberty Fund, 2010.

Wallace, David Foster. "How Tracy Austin Broke My Heart." In *Consider the Lobster and Other Essays*. New York: Little, Brown, 2005.

2

A FOUNDATION OF KNOWLEDGE AND SKILL

The authors of *Make It Stick* write that "all new learning requires *a foundation of prior knowledge.*"[1] When practicing music, one must know not simply what to do but *what* knowledge needs to be applied and how.[2] It is a false choice to pit the learning of basic knowledge against creative thinking and activity. The use of pieces or passages from pieces as the principal means of technical study exposes this false choice because creative thinking is dependent upon having developed a solid foundation of knowledge and skill. As Brown and colleagues write, "The stronger one's knowledge about the subject at hand, the more nuanced one's creativity can be in addressing a new problem."[3] The less nuanced one's creativity is, the more lost one's individuality becomes. With apologies to Tolstoy: Bad practicers are alike in their lack of artistry; good practicers each express artistry in individual ways.

Information and Knowledge

Pedagogical works don't usually make a distinction between "information" and "knowledge" or make clear how knowledge is developed, other than through "deliberate," "mindful," "deep," "purposeful," or "exceptional" practice, the usual adjectives used to clarify that practice is not the simple-minded repetition of material. Most studies that explore the acquisition of expert performance are centered around the relationship between knowledge and skill.

In good practice, we develop the skills to transform *information into knowledge.* Too often the words "information" and "knowledge" are used interchangeably as though they were synonyms, but they're not. Information can be given and learned. Knowledge is earned.

If information is learned well, it may be *available* but not effortlessly *accessible*. The ways in which one works with information, that is, practices, create the possibility of transforming information into knowledge. After a process of consolidation, this knowledge becomes instantly accessible. This consolidation is the beginning of the development of a solid foundation of knowledge and skill.

Information is any inert fact: key signatures, the notes of a scale, practice procedures, the notes of a piece, or interpretive ideas. Keep these distinctions in mind as you continue reading as I will not be interjecting comments every time I think "knowledge" is used in place of "information" in the sources I discuss. Knowledge is always earned, and this is the purpose and measure of good practice.

Novices and Experts

The high-level skill that experts have is made possible by the development and existence of a formidable body of well-organized knowledge and superior cognitive processes. Lauren Tashman summarizes the difference between experts and novices: Novices lack knowledge about expectations for situations, what actions should be taken in a situation, and when that action is best taken. Novices haven't developed a relationship between knowledge and situation, and they often aren't able to identify what information is relevant and what is not.[4] An example of this in music training is when inexperienced students assume that because they're able to play a piece in the practice room, they should be able to perform it before a live audience.

Citing the research of psychologist Robert Sternberg, past President of the American Psychological Association, Tashman writes that experts have a large and well-organized store of knowledge of their discipline and are more efficient in their problem-solving. They've developed high-levels of creativity in their problem-solving because they can quickly distinguish between relevant and irrelevant information and have gained insight because they can combine and compare solutions to current problems by recognizing similarities and differences in other problems they've encountered.[5] Experts are also more adept at problem-*recognition*, which is necessary for problem-solving.

If one wishes to reach a high level of expertise, the development of a foundation of knowledge and skill should be the primary and overriding goal of initial practice. But Daniel Coyle, author of *The Talent Code*, writes, "One of the interesting things about deep practice is that *it feels indistinguishable from shallow practice*, something [Robert] Bjork calls the 'illusion of competence.'"[6] Having access to a teacher who can guide you through this process is indispensable.

Anders Ericsson makes this clear:

> To reach the status of an expert in a domain it is sufficient to master the existing knowledge and techniques. To make an eminent achievement

one must first achieve the level of an expert and then in addition surpass the achievements of already recognized eminent people and make innovative contributions to the domain. In sum, the belief that a sufficient amount of experience or practice leads to maximal performance appears incorrect.[7]

The legendary pianist Vladimir de Pachmann (1848–1933) gives an example: "Why does Busoni produce inimitable results at the keyboard? Simply because he was not satisfied to remain content with the knowledge he had obtained from others."[8] Busoni explains that even though he had been accepted as a virtuoso in Europe and America, he was dissatisfied with his playing. He devoted two years to technical study "along the individual lines [he] had devised."[9]

The Center

Alan Watts (1915–1973), British philosopher and writer, writes in the forward to Chungliang Al Huang's *Embrace Tiger, Return to Mountain: The Essence of Tai Ji*, about Huang's teaching:

> He begins from the center and not from the fringe. He imparts an understanding of the basic principles of the art before going on to the meticulous details. The traditional way is to teach by rote, and to give the impression that long periods of boredom are the most essential part of training. In that way a student may go on for years and years without ever getting the feel of what he is doing. This is as true of theology, law, medicine, and mathematics as it is of tai ji, so that we have many "masters" of these disciplines who are plainly incompetent, no more than well-contrived imitations of the real thing.[10]

Pablo Casals wrote about beginning from the center fifty years earlier. Casals compared good instruction to the ever-widening circles created by the dropping of a stone into a pond. One begins with fundamentals and works outward:

> The stone is the "basis" or starting point of instruction. If we examine an object of small dimensions we are able to look at it from all sides. Could we do the same with a more voluminous one? Evidently not, as our minds would follow "diverging lines" so that certain things, except by a miracle, would certainly be missed. Therefore, the best method to follow in the study of technique is to trace a spiral, starting from a sound basis and ending at the extreme limit of physical possibilities.[11]

When pianist Wilhelm Bachaus (1884–1969) spoke with James Francis Cook, he was hesitant to mention a simple exercise he had devised to focus on a specific technical movement. But he added, "However, elemental processes lead to large structures sometimes."[12] Once one understands and can apply basic principles and is not distracted by diverging lines, one can begin to build increasingly complex structures of knowledge and skill.

Structure Building

The more developed our foundation of knowledge and skill, the more adept we become at what psychologists call "structure building," defined by Brown as "the act, as we encounter new material, of extracting the salient ideas and constructing a coherent mental framework out of them."[13] High-structure builders can filter out irrelevant "noise" through a process of selective encoding. John Briggs in *Fire in the Crucible: The Alchemy of Creative Genius*, his landmark study of creativity, describes this process as identified by Sternberg: "Here the creator sifts the relevant information from the irrelevant. Significant artistic and scientific problems have considerable information or 'noise' and the creator has to be able to 'recognize what is important.'"[14] The noise that distracts musicians in practice are symptoms mistaken for problems and ends mistaken for means. One can never solve a symptom without addressing the underlying problem(s), and one can never reach an end without a well-designed series of means to get there.

One of the ways in which problems are solved is that an insight, or a creative idea, connects with a body of preexisting knowledge and skill. Guy Claxton, the author of *Hare Brain, Tortoise Mind*, writes that "studies of conspicuous innovators suggest that this pre-existing body is most fecund when it is full of rich experience—but not to the point where it has become so familiar that it is automated and fixed."[15] Knowledge must be effortlessly accessible, and one must have "the conceptual understanding of how to use it."[16] Claxton is suggesting that one's body of knowledge and skill not become mind-numbingly routine and inert.

Pianist Emil Sauer (1862–1942) describes what happens if one doesn't have a solid foundation. Great artists of the past were always looking for metaphors and analogies to get their points across to their students. Sauer insists that students must learn to draw and make "correct designs" before they can paint:

> They will persist in trying to apply colors before they learn the art of making correct designs. This leads to dismal failure in almost every case. Technic first—then interpretation. The great concert-going public has no use for a player with a dirty, slovenly technic no matter how much he strives to make morbidly sentimental interpretations that are expected to reach the lovers of sensation. For such players a conscientious and exacting study of Czerny, Cramer, Clementi and others of similar design is good musical soap and water. It washes them into respectability and

technical decency. The pianist with a bungling, slovenly technic, who at the same time attempts to perform the great masterpieces, reminds me of those persons who attempt to disguise the necessity for soap and water with nauseating perfume.[17]

Violinist Demetrius Constantine Dounis (c. 1894–1954) gives an example of high-structure building in *The Artist's Technique of Violin Playing* from 1921: "[W]hat we call technique is nothing but a series of brain-reflected movements. The secret lies in building up these movement pictures into a rational, logical whole—namely, technique."[18]

Mindless repetition and rote learning calcify knowledge and skill, leaving one unable to recognize a good idea, or as Claxton suggests, "the grooves of thought become so worn that they do not allow a fresh perception, or a mingling of different currents of ideas, to occur."[19] The creation of fresh perspectives is one reason why variety in practice is so important as one is learning new skills and refining previously developed skills.

Building Structures

It's no coincidence that the word "building" is so often used as a metaphor to describe the incremental process involved in developing ability. Dounis used it above; Ivan Galamian called the part of practice devoted to technique work "building time"; Peter Brown writes "that creativity absent a sturdy foundation of knowledge builds a shaky house";[20] violinist Frank Thistleton wrote in 1924 that a house must first be built before one can decorate it. "Stick to the foundations," he wrote, "until you are quite sure they are well and truly laid, then you will have something upon which to build."[21] Predating all these remarks is Theodor Leschetizky, quoted in 1906: "Your house still remains to be built when the foundations are laid."[22]

Building as a metaphor for what happens in practice is hardly original and is not difficult to come up with on one's own. A pianist known as Dr. Wullner looked out his studio window in 1902 and saw a large building under construction and compared the precision, detail work, and polishing comparable to what's needed for a pianist to bring a work to perfection:

> Learning a solo is really building up a work which is to be of service and is expected to last a reasonable length of time. Each measure may be looked upon as a block to be shaped and polished by the chisel of patience, the hammer of repetition, the rule and level of self-criticism. One hundred separate measures learned perfectly are of no use. They must be properly combined. When each one fits into its place easily and in due proportion, the effect is a beautiful ensemble. And, as one ill-shaped, improperly polished block will destroy the beauty of an entire

structure, so one imperfectly learned measure will spoil the effect of a page—if not of the whole composition. The pupil is the stone-cutter as well as the stone-mason, and must see to it that his work in both capacities is just right.[23]

Building metaphors, however overwrought, also reveal the importance of chunking, exemplified by Dr. Wullner's blocks "to be shaped and polished," and its relationship to a foundation of prior knowledge, which is made explicit in articles like "Building Knowledge Requires Bricks, Not Sand: The Critical Role of Familiar Constituents in Learning"[24] from 2015. Pianist Josef Lhévinne (1874–1944) foreshadowed the title of this article in a 1913 conversation with James Francis Cooke about why Russian pianists had become so famous: "[They] have earned fame for their technical grasp because they give adequate study to the matter. Everything is done in the most solid, substantial manner possible. *They build not upon sands, but upon rock.*"[25]

There is something that precedes building that is not mentioned explicitly by those using building metaphors: *Buildings must be designed.* Frank Thistleton writes that "Almost every would-be violinist has suffered innumerable setbacks during his or her weary climb to the top rung of the ladder, merely because *the steps were so imperfectly designed.*"[26] Geoffrey Colvin points out in *Talent Is Overrated* that if something can be designed well, it can also be designed poorly.[27]

Practice by Design or Waste Your Time

After the Commons Chamber of Parliament was destroyed during the Blitz in May of 1943, Winston Churchill thought the chamber should be rebuilt with the same design, which he thought was responsible for the vitality of the two-party system. "We shape our buildings and afterwards our buildings shape us," he said as he addressed the House of Commons the following October.

Almost twenty-five years later, Father John Culkin, a Professor of Communication at Fordham University in New York, wrote in "A Schoolman's Guide to Marshall McLuhan" in *The Saturday Review:* "We shape our tools and thereafter they shape us."[28]

Something similar can be said of practice: *We design our practice, and afterwards our practice designs us.*

Sergei Rachmaninoff (1873–1943) also used the metaphor of building: "A technic must be built, just as a house must be built. It takes years to do this. There are no real short cuts."[29] Rachmaninoff went beyond metaphor, however. He presented a design for how this work was to be was done.

Rachmaninoff thought that two hours of daily scale and arpeggio practice was necessary for students to prepare themselves for the "great tasks of performing the masterpieces of the art."[30] The best teachers, Rachmaninoff says, do this work with their students as early as possible. The process takes about five years. He would not have thought much of the advice given by guitarist Andrés Segovia (1893–1987) that we'll look at later, at least as usually represented.

Rachmaninoff was convinced that the rigorous routine he outlines below "may be one of the reasons why some of the Russian pianists have been so favorably received in recent years."[31]

You can see the scope of this work by seeing what Rachmaninoff says about the examination students must pass when they reach their "sixth class" if they are to be allowed to continue their studies. Students are expected to know their scales and arpeggios as well as "the average child knows the multiplication tables."[32] No hesitation is allowed for one to gather one's wits. The knowledge and skill to perform the exam are expected to be readily accessible:

> The student on coming into the examination room is told that he will be examined upon the scales and arpeggios centered, as it were, upon a given note, "A" for example. He does not know in advance what note he will be examined upon. First come the scales. The metronome is set and the pupil is directed to play eight notes to a beat, or any given number, *in any rhythm the examiner determines upon*. First, he would possibly be asked to play the scale of A major, then that of A minor, in the different forms. Then he might be asked to play the scale of G major, starting with A, then C major, then F major, then D major, then B flat, then E major; in fact any major or minor scale containing A. The examiner notes at once whether the student has the fingering of the scales at his finger tips, whether he employs the right fingers for each scale. It is comparatively simple to play the scales in a given key from octave to octave; but, when you think of it, they rarely appear in such form in actual compositions. Rather does one find a snatch of a scale here and there.[33]

Example 2.1 applies Rachmaninoff's outline for major scale practice starting on the note C (without metric and rhythmic variations). This practice was also done for harmonic and melodic minor scales, although there are only five possibilities using the melodic minor scale because the sixth and seventh degrees vary depending on whether the scale is ascending or descending.

Note that Rachmaninoff says that the examiner can ask for these to be played in any rhythm and any number of notes per beat, meaning the accents could be anywhere. Rachmaninoff outlines a similar method for the practice of arpeggios.

Did the rigorous technical regimen Rachmaninoff describes stifle his artistic freedom and creativity? If anything, it *contributed* to his freedom. In the November 1997 issue of *Early Music*, pianist Malcolm Bilson relates a discussion that took place at the 1991 Mozart Conference in New York City.

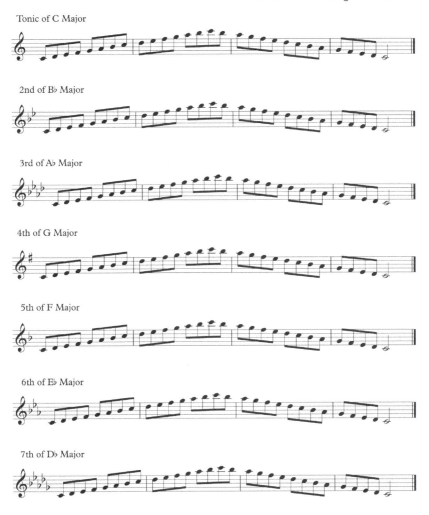

Tonic of C Major

2nd of B♭ Major

3rd of A♭ Major

4th of G Major

5th of F Major

6th of E♭ Major

7th of D♭ Major

EXAMPLE 2.1   Major scale practice beginning on C, per Rachmaninoff's instructions.

After listening to a recording of Rachmaninoff playing the first movement of Mozart's A major sonata, K. 331, some conference participants became quite agitated. Bilson wrote:

> To describe Rachmaninoff's performance as not heeding the text would be superfluous; it was so free in this regard that the penultimate Adagio variation was actually faster than the Allegro that followed it. This gave rise to a great deal of controversy among the participants; there were those who were outraged at the "utter lack of respect for the composer

and the text," while others proclaimed, "But who today plays as flexibly and gorgeously as Rachmaninoff?"[34]

To suggest that Rachmaninoff wasn't heedful of the composer's intentions misses the point. Timothy Day writes of an extended passage in a 1919 Chopin recording of Rachmaninoff's in which he plays sixteenths and eighths all as sixteenth notes. Day adds that "it would be absurd to suggest that Rachmaninoff would have been unable to make the distinction clear if he had wished to."[35]

Part of Rachmaninoff's 1923 article anticipated the research of Anders Ericsson by seventy years. In Ericsson's article "The Role of Deliberate Practice in the Acquisition of Expert Performance," which appeared in the journal *Psychological Review*, he writes,

> [E]lite performers rarely experience problems from long periods of inactivity because once they take up systematic practice they continue practicing at a uniformly high level, and we assume that the amount of deliberate practice necessary to specifically maintain earlier attained levels of performance is negligible for active young experts.[36]

Rachmaninoff's words add weight to Ericsson's observation: "[I]f the hand and mind are trained in youth, it is possible after a lapse of years, to build again. *The technic acquired in youth seems to remain as a kind of musical capital.*"[37] Rachmaninoff clearly assumes that the mind is trained as well as the hands. This is not mindless drilling.

This way of studying scales is not a relic of some halcyon time now lost. Pianist Boris Berman writes in *Notes from the Pianist's Bench* from 2002 that he is

> accustomed to playing scales and arpeggios as I learned them during my school years in Moscow. Since the collapse of the Soviet Union, this technical regimen is no longer regarded as 'the secret weapon' of the Russian school. Many Russian-trained pianists, teaching all over the world, have passed it on to their students or have referred to it in print.[38]

This type of scale work has remained part of Berman's practice routine.

Josef Lhévinne gives a brief description of this secret weapon:

> The scales should be known so well that the student's fingers will fly to the right fingering of any part of any scale instinctively. One good way of fixing them in the mind is to start to play the scales upon the different tones of the key consecutively.[39]

Ivan Galamian describes something similar for violin scale practice in 1962: "[T]he scale should be started on notes other than the tonic. This is another way of saying that each scale may be practiced with many different signatures."[40]

Many guitar students—I can't speak for students of other instruments—do not approach their foundational studies with this type of rigor and have fallen in thrall to what I call the "technique-from-pieces fallacy."

The Technique-From-Pieces Fallacy

I looked at several fallacies in chapter 1 but have reserved a detailed exploration of the technique-from-pieces fallacy for this chapter on foundations because it is sometimes used by teachers in lieu of providing their students with a rigorous foundational study, which betrays an impoverished understanding of their responsibility to those under their tutelage.

An approach based on this fallacy is easy for teachers to apply and for students to remember, and it has an appeal to impatient students because it leads them to believe they are *playing music*. But it takes students farther from being able to *make music* and probably does more damage in the long run, either when they quit in discouragement because they're unable to recognize problems, when they realize they can't reach the level of expressivity and freedom in performance they'd like, or when things start going wrong with their technique. Many of these things won't become apparent until years after serious study has begun, and if students never received helpful feedback, it will be impossible to connect cause with effect. There's a double curse here: Teachers who use this approach most likely can only give feedback about a far-off goal not reached. F. M. Alexander shows that working directly for an end ensures that the student will be caught in a vicious cycle: A striving for the end precludes a consideration of the means, and the lack of consideration of the means ensures continued unsuccessful striving.

Part of the problem is the legacy of the self-taught musician who sees a straight line where there is none and confuses the means with the ends. Pianist Andor Földes wrote in 1948: "That ancient axiom, 'the shortest distance between two points is a straight line,' does not hold true in piano playing."[41] Pablo Casals also recognized the danger of this approach:

> It would be a mistake to neglect the perusal of that of which one believes to have complete knowledge, for one rarely works one's way through difficulties otherwise than by a "straight line." *The result is that many things are passed by.*[42]

To Casals, a straight line is in opposition to beginning at the center, which is where one starts to build a solid foundation.

Perhaps the oft-repeated words of Andrés Segovia (1893–1987) have encouraged guitar students to discount the need for foundational technical work:

> Out of difficult passages I made a new exercise. Often I ceased to regard the motif I had chosen as part of a specific work and elevated it to a

superior level of studies in which was latent the promise of victory over more general difficulties.[43]

   Much of the pedagogical advice that Andrés Segovia dispensed to students throughout his career is probably unknown to guitar students today, and many guitarists who came of age in the later years of Segovia's life consciously rejected his approach, but the ambiguity of this remark has quietly infiltrated guitar study and many have chosen an easy and less-imaginative interpretation of it.

   Christopher Parkening, Segovia's protégé, gives similar advice in *The Christopher Parkening Guitar Method*, although his advice is less ambiguous and points to acquiring technique through pieces:

> I developed technique by playing pieces which involved technical exercises. This method encouraged me to practice by making practice enjoyable. Of course, I also played exercises which concentrated on specific techniques that needed developing, but for the most part I learned the guitar by playing pieces I loved and trying to perfect them. This method seems to me by far the best; it is the method I've used since I began to teach and is the principle I've applied to this book.[44]

I don't think that "pieces which involved technical exercises" can mean anything other than "pieces that contained passages of technical difficulty." Segovia, like Parkening, was also speaking about how he developed his technique when he was younger, not how he maintained it in later years. And although I know what most people think Segovia meant—which Parkening makes explicit—I don't think it necessarily means that he selected difficult passages from pieces and practiced them repeatedly. Segovia also said, "Build a technique to cover all the difficulties of the piece, slowly with efficiency,"[45] although he only gave mere hints about how one is to do this.

   In the preface to his *Diatonic Major and Minor Scales* from 1953, Segovia writes that the guitar lacks "a practical system of studies and exercises coordinated in such a way as to permit the faithful student to progress continuously from the first easy lessons to real mastery of the instrument."[46] He recommends that students practice scales for two hours a day. I've written elsewhere about the defects of Segovia's edition of major and minor scales,[47] but his preface makes clear that he saw the drawback of students studying only repertoire pieces. He illustrates this with criticism of Dionisio Aguado's (1784–1849) method:

> The beginner who tries to learn from Aguado's book will find himself floundering helplessly. The beautiful, useless lessons which comprise one part of the method please his ear without limbering his fingers, and the others will be far beyond his capabilities.[48]

Segovia doesn't say much about how to practice the scales, other than slowly and vigorously at first and then faster and lighter. He does recommend that the scales be played with a variety of right-hand fingerings, but he doesn't mention rhythmic variations or variety that incorporates musical nuance.

By itself, Segovia's remark about making exercises out of difficult passages is vague: Does it mean he created a new exercise modeled after the technique needed for a passage (extracting the salient ideas and constructing a coherent mental framework, as mentioned by Peter Brown), or does it mean he extracted a passage from the piece and *the passage itself*—unchanged—was the exercise? Or could it mean something else? "Ceasing to regard the motif . . . as part of a specific work" implies that he only changed the way he thought about the passage. Did this change in thinking cause the passage to become "elevated," or did he elevate it in some other way? Did he extract the underlying technical problem to focus on it in a concentrated way, or was the passage elevated by playing it repeatedly?

Something that might clarify and bring context to Segovia's influential remark is to look at what other musicians said about the relationship between repertoire and the act of developing technique and solving problems in a work.

In 1915, around the time Segovia was probably still developing and refining his technique, pianist Germaine Schnitzer (1887–1982) said, "I take the difficult passages of a composition and make the minutest study of them in every detail, making all kinds of technical exercises out of a knotty section, sometimes *playing it in forty or fifty different ways*."[49] Note that she does not say the passage itself became the exercise; she transformed it. We'll explore in chapter 6 what forms the playing of the passage in "forty or fifty different ways" might have taken.

Pianist Teresa Carreño (1853–1917), a child prodigy, describes a series of five hundred exercises her father wrote out for her when she was young. Some were drawn from difficult passages from the piano literature. Carreño says, "Everything must be played in all keys, and with every possible variety of touch—legato, staccato, half-staccato, and so on; also, with all kinds of shading."[50] This cannot be called mechanical repetition. All the shadings of articulation, tone, voicings, and dynamics would have led to a refined and artistic technique.

Alfred Cortot (1877–1962) writes in the forward to his *Rational Principles of Pianoforte Technique* from 1928 (English version, 1930):

> One of the most significant points in the progress of instrumental teaching during the last few years, is that the mechanical and long-repeated practice of a difficult passage has been replaced by the reasoned study of the difficulty contained therein, reduced to its elementary principle.[51]

Busoni said the same: "In playing, always note where your difficulties seem to lie. Then, when advisable, isolate those difficulties and practice them separately.

This is the manner in which all good technical exercises are devised."[52] Michael Stembridge-Montavont states that Jean-Jacques Eigeldinger, author of *Frederic Chopin: Esquisses pour une Méthode de Piano*, finds that "this axiom of practising—trying to isolate the inherent difficulty in a passage rather than repeating it *ad nauseam*—is reminiscent of Chopin's teaching."[53]

It appears that Chopin anticipated the research of psychologists: "When you're adept at extracting the *underlying principles* or *'rules'* that differentiate types of problems, you're more successful at picking the right solutions in unfamiliar situations. This skill is better acquired through *interleaved and varied practice* than massed repetition."[54] We'll discuss interleaved and varied practice shortly.

Pianist Rafael Joseffy (1852–1915) also made difficult exercises out of passages in pieces, which is defined as "selecting the hard parts and then *turning them about in different ways*, for one hand or the other."[55] In her 1917 book, *Piano Mastery: Talks with Master Pianists and Teachers*, Harriette Moore Brower explains that Joseffy learned this from Carl Tausig (1841–1871) and Franz Liszt, with whom he studied. She continues, "It is also [Moriz] Rosenthal's plan; he doubtless got it from his teacher, Joseffy."[56] We see again that this "turning them about in different ways" means creating variety.

There are more recent expressions of this practice technique. Ivan Galamian writes in his *Principles of Violin: Playing & Teaching* from 1962: "A student practices a difficult passage from a piece. He analyzes it properly, *transforms it into well-devised exercises,* and finally masters it technically."[57] Again, note the word *transform* and that Galamian writes "exercises" and not "exercise."

The authors of *Miraculous Teacher Ivan Galamian* explain further the reasons behind Galamian's approach:

> "Practice means repetition, but repetition means monotony." Therefore, "repetition must be accompanied by variety, and the variety must be challenging enough *to entice the mind to stay active.*" In the case of advanced students, they can create new and more difficult combinations of rhythms and bowings based on his suggestions in his exercises. Consequently, while practicing, whether on an etude or bothersome passage in the repertoire, the whole general level of the playing could achieve new heights. With Galamian, "an etude is not just a piece of music to be learned. Instead, it becomes a vehicle for building a whole mass of pertinent techniques."[58]

The mind "staying active" means that more mental effort is needed, which creates more durable learning.[59]

If Segovia meant that he simply played a difficult passage *ad nauseam*, then he was clearly at odds with the practices of his contemporaries who played other instruments. No notable artists or authors who wrote about violin or piano playing advocated playing a difficult passage repeatedly to acquire technique unless they first extracted the underlying principle or difficulty of the passage or modified the passage in a variety of ways. *That the practice did exist among bad teachers and students is clear by the frequent prohibitions issued against it.*

If Segovia meant what Cortot, Joseffy, Galamian, and others meant, then he performed a disservice to guitarists who came after him by obfuscating his practices. Those who represent Segovia's remark as meaning all one need do to learn technique is to repeat difficult passages as they appear in one's repertoire, do injury to themselves, to those they teach, and to music.

Rule Learners and Example Learners

The musicians cited above were successful using parts of a piece for practice, with modifications, because they were adept at extracting the underlying principles or "rules" that a technical or musical problem presented. Peter Brown makes a distinction between "rule learners" and "example learners." Rule learners can take underlying principles they've abstracted and can apply these principles to unfamiliar situations; example learners simply memorize the examples—or as is the case for musicians, repeat a passage without gaining a knowledge of the underlying rules and have difficulty when faced with unfamiliar situations.[60] This is reminiscent of Fernando Sor's "rules given from authority" as opposed to the "reasons for which they were established" that we saw in chapter 1. Stembridge-Montavont quotes a saying of Cortot's: "One must be intelligent to use an example as a source of inspiration; and very stupid to copy it."[61] Rote learners, or those who repeat things mindlessly, have little chance of understanding the underlying principles of what they're doing.

A Dreadful Muddle

In a 1934 article in *The Musical Times* about violin teacher Ottakar Ševčík (1852–1934), M. Montagu-Nathan writes that before the appearance of Ottakar Ševčík and his method, violin teaching was in a "dreadful muddle." In the absence of method, students were not taught technique and faced "technical difficulties as and when they were confronted with them in whatever music they were studying."[62] Montagu-Nathan maintains that Ševčík "seems to have been the first to realise that the practising of difficult passages as they presented themselves simply would not do."[63]

Even if students are successful in acquiring some level of technique through repertoire pieces alone, they still will only have gained the minimum technique required to play the piece or passage. Carl Flesch maintains that the

> more complete and unbroken our technical armor, the better able will we
> be able to transfer our efforts to the purely artistic field, without danger

of losing the real essential in our solicitude for the daily bread of technique. In the interests of fruitful activity on the concert platform a certain *surplus* of technical power even is necessary.[64]

Andor Földes offers a way out of this muddle, which involves knowing how to build the foundation of prior skill needed for a piece:

> It will help us a great deal in our piano practice if we know that certain technical passages are more characteristic of certain composers. For instance, about eighty percent of Mozart's piano works are built around scales and rapid, pearly passages. The best preparation for successful Mozart playing, as far as technique is concerned, can be made by studying some of the easier Czerny Etudes, such as the first volume of the School of Velocity, Opus 299, which I cannot recommend too heartily to every young piano student.[65]

More Than I Can Express in Words . . .

K. Anders Ericsson and his colleagues stress that the acquisition of domain-specific knowledge is essential to becoming an expert in a field and that "with mere repetition, improvement of performance was often arrested at less than maximal levels, and *further improvement required effortful reorganization of the skill.*"[66] This "effortful reorganization" of skill *expands* the skill. This is a fundamental tenet of the Feldenkrais Method and has been developed by Feldenkrais's student, Yochanan Rywerant: "[M]ere repetition involves going through, again and again, the same well-known pattern. Improvement, however, involves something quite different: a change in our patterns of functioning."[67]

Experts, or those working with teachers who know the path to becoming an expert, are adept at recognizing and making the changes they need. It's not simply that experts have a greater body of knowledge and skill in their field, but "the superior organization (i.e., representation in memory) of this knowledge also impacts their performance."[68]

Vladimir Nabokov, writing about verbal and written expression, offers a compact and eloquent statement about the importance of cultivating more than you think you need: "I know more than I can express in words, and the little I can express would not have been expressed had I not known more."[69]

A Hateful Habit?

I know of no written words more overtly antagonistic to the study of technique as proposed by great artists than the words of Michel Savary in his *Encyclopedia of Guitar Virtuosity* from 1987, a collection of 210 difficult passages to be used for technique practice:

The examples chosen directly from the repertory will enable the teacher to show the pupil numerous aspects of virtuosity to be found in musical reality. *Perhaps this will put a final stop to the hateful habit of having to study scales, for example, a practice which belongs to a form of sterile teaching devoid of rhythm, phrasing, bars or dynamics.*[70]

This is a mechanistic approach to study masquerading as an artistic one. Savary says nothing about how to practice these passages other than to play them. He seems unaware of the ways in which great artists transformed passages by adding varieties of rhythm, dynamics, voicings, and accents in their movement toward mastery. Savary's desire to make practice more interesting went in the wrong direction: Instead of starting from the center, as described by Alan Watts and Pablo Casals, he has made the common error of starting at the end. Violinist Max Rostal (1906–1991) observed in the same year as Savary that "In recent times, meaning the 1980s, there have been doubts as to the purpose and necessity of practising scales, a view stemming partly from an addiction to originality and a lack of insight."[71] Rostal continues by referring to the value placed upon scale work by great violinists such as Jascha Heifetz (1901–1987), Joseph Szigeti (1892–1973), and Eugène Ysaÿe (1858–1931).

Thinking one must "put a final stop to the hateful habit of having to study scales" represents "a crippled epistemology," which legal scholar Cass Sunstein defines as occurring when one knows only "a sharply limited number of (relevant) informational sources."[72] A crippled epistemology such as this is an example of the worst of the guitar world's misunderstanding of how best to acquire high-level skill and artistry—a process that has been transparent to high-level artists for well over a century.

The process of how best to achieve a high level of skill isn't always clear to students. Vladimir de Pachmann complained that "the young pupil will literally turn up his nose at the scale of C Major and at the same time claim that he is perfectly competent to play a Beethoven Sonata."[73] De Pachmann despaired of trying to convince students otherwise:

> But what is the use of saying all this? To tell it to young pupils seems to be a waste of words. They will go on making their mistakes and ignoring the advice of their teachers and mentors until the great teacher of all—experience—forces them to dive for the hidden riches.[74]

Wilhelm Bachaus said of de Pachmann:

> The ultra-modern teacher who is inclined to think scales old-fashioned should go to hear de Pachmann, who practices scales every day. De Pachmann, who has been a virtuoso for a great many years, still finds daily practice necessary, and, in addition to scales, he plays a great deal of Bach.

To-day his technic is more powerful and more comprehensive than ever, and he attributes it in a large measure to the simplest of means.[75]

Putting "the cart before the horse," as John Dewey described the flaws of imitation,[76] and what F. M. Alexander has called "end-gaining" has been a shortcoming of music students at all levels, the harmful effects of which high-level artists and teachers describe in this book. But it has fallen to those working outside of music, like Dewey and Alexander, to explain in a reasonable way why this is so. We'll go into detail in chapter 5.

Spaced, Interleaved, and Varied Practice

What is sometimes called "massed practice" or "massed repetition," that is, playing the same thing repeatedly, is the preferred practice strategy of students at all levels, but Peter Brown calls it "among the *least productive*."[77] It's preferred by the self-taught and by those under the instruction of incurious teachers because it seems to make intuitive sense and has consistency to it, but here we have a foolish consistency.

Brown has a section in his book titled "The Myth of Massed Practice." Simply put, "Practice that's spaced out, interleaved with other learning, and varied produces better mastery, longer retention, and more versatility."[78] One of the reasons, though, why massed practice is used so much is because students become increasingly familiar with material, which creates the "illusion of mastery."[79]

George Kochevitsky suggests putting at least a few seconds between repetitions to assess what one has done and to dismount from what I call "the hamster wheel of massed repetition":

> We should point out that pupils are often inclined to repeat a passage in fast succession, starting the next repetition when the preceding one is hardly finished. In correct practicing, a slight pause (several seconds) must be inserted between repetitions, to give the pianist time to check whether everything just performed was correct and the results were musically satisfactory, and to prepare himself mentally for the next repetition.[80]

There are firm condemnations of massed practice in the pedagogical literature for the piano and violin. Marie von Unschuld (1871–1965), a pupil of Theodor Leschetizky and author of *The Pianist's Hand*, wrote in 1903:

> To rattle down one and the same passage ten times,—a hundred times, till it is familiar to the fingers, what foolish practice, what waste of time, what boundless suffering for fellow-creatures, and what injury to the physical constitution of the person concerned![81]

Unschuld also sees the superficiality of the assumption that exercises, so necessary to building a foundation, mean one must practice mechanically: "However much 'mechanical exercises' have been elucidated in the preceding chapters, just so little is it permitted to confound them with 'mechanical practising.'"[82] It's interesting that Unschuld connects mechanical practice to physical injury. Although beyond the scope of this book, might this be one of the first acknowledgments of physical problems associated with overuse or misuse?

Violinist Frank Thistleton describes a form of massed practice laced with inattention to detail in 1924:

> Many pupils throw away hours of their time in needless labour which might be more profitably spent did they but know how to utilise the time at their disposal. For instance, we have a study to prepare. The usual method is to begin at the beginning and carry on, regardless of mistakes, to the conclusion. We then begin again and perpetrate the same fiasco once more; repeating it until the time at our disposal has gone by.[83]

Violinist Achille Rivarde (1865–1940) calls for constant mental effort in practice but notices that massed practice is easier because it doesn't require much mental effort, like Dewey's "refuge of the timid." That it is easier may account for why many students and teachers think it is intuitive: "It is easy to understand how the far less wearisome method of physical practice commends itself to all but the most courageous spirits, on account of the minimum of mental effort involved."[84] Rivarde was a rising star of the violin world in the nineteenth century. *The New York Times* wrote of his Carnegie Hall debut in 1895, "His style is one of remarkable elegance and is full of poetry."[85] The great Eugène Ysaÿe put Rivarde at the head of the younger school of violinists.[86] Two months prior to Rivarde's New York debut, he was on the cover of *The Musical Courier*.

To Rivarde, thought and imagination were prerequisites to quality playing, although he acknowledged the difficulty of getting students to realize that "thinking must come before playing."[87] Without thought and imagination, the repeated playing of a work will never rise above the mechanical level, no matter how accurate.[88] Trying to acquire too many skills simultaneously also blocks thought and imagination, like Leopold Auer's student who "was too much absorbed in the playing of the notes." We'll return to Rivarde's ideas in chapter 8 when we discuss "phrase-storming."

Daniel Coyle shares Rivarde's antipathy to easy practice and notes that practice strategies that create beneficial struggles can facilitate improvement.[89]

What These Strategies Are

Spaced practice means leaving time between practice and study sessions.[90] This is especially effective for memory work that involves visualization and the techniques I discuss in chapter 4. Instead of trying to burn something into memory through massed repetition, the effort involved in trying to retrieve material mentally after an interval of time solidifies learning and makes it more secure and accessible.

Interleaved practice is the study and practice of two or more skills. Learning may feel slower, and the long-term advantages may not be clear to students, but Brown writes, "research shows unequivocally that mastery and long-term retention are much better if you interleave practice than if you mass it."[91] There's also a physiological benefit as muscles used for one type of technique—right-hand arpeggios for guitarists, for example—will receive rest when one interleaves that with work of another technique, say, left-hand slurs.

Varied practice means adding variety to whatever it is you're working on. What this means for musicians is practicing exercises or passages from a piece with various rhythmic formulae, different accents and articulations, and a variety of dynamics and voicings. (There are examples in chapter 6.) Massed repetition is not a good method for building a foundation of knowledge and skill.

Pianist Wassili Safonoff[92] (1852–1918), who taught Alexander Scriabin (1872–1915), Josef Lhévinne, and Rosina Lhévinne[93] (née Bessie; 1880–1976), concludes his *New Formula for the Piano Teacher and Piano Student* from 1916 with practice advice about spaced and varied practice, although not by those names:

- Never practise in the same order, starting with the exercises, then proceeding to the studies, and finally to the pieces, but always change the order of practice every day. One day a week rest completely from the technical practising.
- In practising, change the order of the technical exercises every day, so as not to allow the hands to get accustomed to the same series, of movements.
- When many repetitions of an exercise are necessary, do not always make the same number of repetitions, and choose by preference the odd (3, 5, 7, 9, 11, etc.) rather than the even numbers.[94]

How These Strategies Help

Peter Brown and his coauthors present reasons why spaced, interleaved, and varied practice produce better mastery, longer retention, and more versatility than massed practice: Interleaved and varied practice creates improved powers of discrimination;[95] spaced practice and recall are much better for developing long-term memory, but massed practice favors short-term memory;[96] interleaved and varied practice make it easier to extract the underlying principles from a problem, which allows one to recognize and solve unfamiliar problems;[97] and the challenges created by adding variety to practice engages the part of the brain that is linked with the learning of high-level motor skills.[98]

Pianist Andor Földes describes spaced practice almost by name in 1948: "The secret of memorizing is slow learning, a good understanding of what we want to memorize, many repetitions *spaced over a long period of time.*"[99]

He also touches upon the value of interleaved practice:

> Working on several pieces at the same time, the student will have a much larger repertoire. Often there are certain passages of a difficult composition which, in spite of long and conscientious practice, don't seem to yield. By working on other pieces at the same time, suddenly the "tough spot" will be smoother and difficulties will disappear, for *everything is interrelated on the keyboard*, and one piece helps the other.[100]

Földes also gives a good description of encoding and consolidation as given by Brown[101] and which is important in initial learning:

> Nothing can be learned immediately. Learning is a slow process and should not be forced. When studying new works, it often proves helpful to lay them aside after several weeks of intense study and start new ones. In the meantime, the player's subconscious mind will keep on working on them, and when he returns to them after a period of time, he will find that his conception of the work has matured, and he brings to it more understanding than ever before. Even technical difficulties may yield after such resting periods, provided the pianist keeps on practicing other pieces.[102]

Pianist Ludwig Deppe (1828–1890) also recommends setting a piece aside to ripen after it has been learned. This ripening, though, won't happen if the piece has been learned by rote. Here is Deppe on interleaved practice as described by Elizabeth Caland in 1903:

> Deppe made his pupils practice *very slowly*, and frequently with each hand separately; thus there was ample opportunity for the heedful attention which alone can insure that one tone shall not predominate over another, but that all shall be equally pure and clear. When the pupil, after some weeks of this slow, single-handed practice, had assimilated the composition to such a degree that each tone and movement had special reference to the musical content thereof, then he was allowed to use both hands simultaneously, *but still in the same slow tempo*. Once the piece was fairly well learned, it was laid aside "to ripen," and another took its place and was treated in precisely the same manner. Through this progressive activity, physical and mental, the growth of musical sense and perception was

wonderfully stimulated, and musical ideas rendered clear and coherent. After four to six weeks of retirement, the pieces laid [aside] were brought again to the light of day, and polished into readiness for performance.[103]

Ivan Galamian wrote about interleaved and spaced practice: "Mixing the material and not dwelling too long on a single item will often help to keep the mind fresh longer."[104]

Freeing the Future

Beyond the prosaic work of practice, the interleaving of various interests and projects that seem unrelated "can pry loose insights that might have been otherwise impossible to obtain."[105] Arthur Kornberg, biochemist and Nobel Laureate, said that a creator "needs intense motivation or focus, but he also needs a certain restlessness. That may sound like a contradiction."[106] Psychologist Howard Gruber (1922–2005), who specialized in the study of creativity, said that it only *sounded* like a contradiction.

John Briggs discusses Gruber's work on creativity: Darwin moved about among many projects; William James was interested in areas that bridged science and philosophy; Sergei Eisenstein was a filmmaker, a teacher, and theoretician of film; and Leonardo da Vinci's free-range genius roamed among science, painting, architecture, medicine, urban planning, and engineering.[107]

All this may seem more relevant to a polymath than a player of polyphony, but what Gruber calls a creator's "network of enterprises" allows creative people to "explore their visions from a number of different angles."[108]

Why discuss this in a chapter devoted to foundations? Because foundations need to be built with a fluid and flexible intelligence and not through a process that coats skills with an impenetrable veneer of mindlessness. When we're beginning our study, we have no idea where it may lead or what we're capable of. We're drawn to study music because of a creative vision, although the ways of realizing that vision may be inchoate and unclear. We need to have begun our work in a way that will help us clarify and set free that vision in the future.

Notes

1. Brown, *Make It Stick*, 5.
2. Ibid., 18.
3. Ibid., 30.
4. Tashman, "The Development of Expertise," 37.
5. Ibid., 39.
6. Coyle, *The Talent Code*, 224.
7. Ericsson, "The Role of Deliberate," 366.
8. Cooke, *Great Pianists on Piano Playing*, 193.
9. Ibid., 101.

10. Chungliang Al Huang, *Embrace Tiger, Return to Mountain: The Essence of Tai Chi* (Moab, Utah: Real People Press, 1973), 1, 2.
11. Alexanian, *Traité Théorique et Pratique du Violoncelle*, 4.
12. Cooke, *Great Pianists on Piano Playing*, 59.
13. Brown, *Make It Stick*, 153.
14. John Briggs, *Fire in the Crucible: The Alchemy of Creative Genius* (New York: St. Martin's Press, 1988), 186.
15. Guy Claxton, *Hare Brain, Tortoise Mind: How Intelligence Increases When You Think Less* (New York: Harper Perennial, 1998), 72.
16. Brown, *Make It Stick*, 18.
17. Cooke, *Great Pianists on Piano Playing*, 240–241.
18. Quoted in Gwendolyn Masin, "Violin Teaching in the New Millennium: In Search of the Lost Instructions of Great Masters: An Examination of Similarities and Differences between Schools of Playing and How These Have Evolved: Or Remembering the Future of Violin Performance" (PhD diss., Dublin: Trinity College, 2012), 63.
19. Claxton, *Hare Brain, Tortoise Mind*, 72.
20. Brown, *Make It Stick*, 30.
21. Thistleton, *The Art of Violin Playing,* 13–14.
22. Hullah, *Theodor Leschetizky*, 52.
23. Ludwig Wullner, "Solo Building Is Structure Building," *The Musical Standard*, September 13, 1902, 162.
24. Reder and Liu, "Building Knowledge Requires Bricks," 1–7.
25. Cooke, *Great Pianists on Piano Playing*, 176. [Italics added].
26. Thistleton, *The Art of Violin Playing*, 9. [Italics added].
27. Geoffrey Colvin, *Talent Is Overrated: What Really Separates World-Class Performers from Everybody Else* (New York: Portfolio Trade, 2010), 80.
28. John M. Culkin, "A Schoolman's Guide to Marshall McLuhan," *Saturday Review* Vol. 50, No. 11 (1967): 70.
29. Sergei Rachmaninoff, "New Lights on the Art of the Piano," *The Etude* Vol. 41, No. 4 (April 1923): 223–224.
30. Ibid.
31. Cooke, *Great Pianists on Piano Playing*, 210.
32. Rachmaninoff, "New Lights on the Art of the Piano," 223–224. [Italics added].
33. Ibid.
34. Malcolm Bilson, "The Future of Schubert Interpretation: What Is Really Needed?" *Early Music* Vol. 25, No. 4 (November 1997): 715.
35. Timothy Day, *A Century of Recorded Music: Listening to Musical History* (New Haven, CT: Yale University Press, 2000), 157.
36. Ericsson, "The Role of Deliberate Practice," 388.
37. Rachmaninoff, "New Lights on the Art of the Piano," 223–224. [Italics added.]
38. Boris Berman, *Notes from the Pianist's Bench* (New Haven, CT: Yale University Press, 2002), 48–49.
39. Josef Lhévinne, *Basic Principles in Pianoforte Playing* (Philadelphia: Theo. Presser Company, 1924), 10.
40. Ivan Galamian, *Principles of Violin: Playing & Teaching* (Englewood Cliffs: Prentice Hall, 1962), 102.
41. Andor Földes, *Keys to the Keyboard, a Book for Pianists: With Explanatory Music* (New York: E.P. Dutton, 1948), 53.
42. Alexanian, *Traité Théorique et Pratique du Violoncelle*, 3–4. [Italics added]. I have modified the published translation from the French for clarity.
43. *The Guitar and I* LP (Decca DL 710182; MCA S 30 020). The quote is also given in Graham Wade, *Maestro Segovia* (London: Robson Books Ltd., 1986), 47.
44. Christopher Parkening, *The Christopher Parkening Guitar Method* (Milwaukee: Hal Leonard Corporation, 1998), 7.

45. Wade, *Maestro Segovia*, 47. Wade's book has an extensive bibliography, but he doesn't connect quotations with their sources.
46. Andrés Segovia, *Diatonic Major and Minor Scales* (Washington, DC: Columbia Music Co, 1953), 1.
47. Berg, *Mastering Guitar Technique*, 144.
48. Segovia, *Diatonic Major and Minor Scales*, 1.
49. Harriette Moore Brower, *Piano Mastery* (New York: Frederick A. Stokes Company, 1915), 221. [Italics added].
50. Ibid., 161–162.
51. Alfred Cortot and Métaxas Le Roy, *Rational Principles of Pianoforte Technique* (Paris: M. Senart and Boston: Oliver Ditson Company, 1930), 1.
52. Cooke, *Great Pianists on Piano Playing*, 102.
53. Michael Stembridge-Montavont, "Variations on a Theme of Chopin," *Piano* (September/October 2004): 34.
54. Brown, *Make It Stick*, 4.
55. Brower, *Piano Mastery: Second Series* (New York: Frederick A. Stokes Company, 1917), 251. [Italics added].
56. Ibid., 251.
57. Galamian, *Principles of Violin: Playing & Teaching*, 101.
58. Elizabeth A. H. Green, Judith Galamian, and Josef Gingold, *Miraculous Teacher: Ivan Galamian & the Meadowmount Experience* (Bryn Mawr, PA: Theodore Presser, 1993), 94. The internal quotations are from Galamian's, *Principles of Violin: Playing & Teaching*.
59. Brown, *Make It Stick*, 3.
60. Ibid., 155–157.
61. Stembridge-Montavont, "Variations on a Theme of Chopin," 35.
62. M. Montagu-Nathan, "Ottakar Ševčík," *The Musical Times* Vol. 75, No. 1093 (1934): 217.
63. Ibid.
64. Flesch, *The Art of Violin Playing, Book Two*, 65.
65. Földes, *Keys to the Keyboard*, 49.
66. Ericsson, "The Role of Deliberate Practice," 365–366. [Italics added].
67. Yochanan Rywerant, *The Feldenkrais Method: Teaching by Handling: A Technique for Individuals* (San Francisco: Harper & Row, 1983), 215.
68. Tashman, "The Development of Expertise in Performance," 37.
69. Vladimir Nabokov, *Strong Opinions*, Reissue ed. (Vintage, 1990), 65.
70. Michel Savary, ed., *Encyclopedia of Guitar Virtuosity* (Heidelberg: Chanterelle Verlag, 1987), iv. [Italics added].
71. Carl Flesch, *Flesch Scale System a Supplement to Book 1 of the Art of Violin Playing*, ed. Max Rostal (New York: Carl Fischer Music, 1987), viii.
72. Cass R. Sunstein and Adrian Vermeule, "Conspiracy Theories: Causes and Cures," *Journal of Political Philosophy* Vol. 17, No. 2 (2009): 204.
73. Cooke, *Great Pianists on Piano Playing*, 188.
74. Ibid.
75. Ibid., 54–55.
76. John Dewey, *Democracy, and Education*, 41.
77. Brown, *Make It Stick*, 3.
78. Ibid., 47.
79. Ibid., 15.
80. Kochevitsky, *The Art of Piano Playing*, 28.
81. Marie von Unschuld, *The Pianist's Hand*, trans. Henry Morgan Dare (Leipzig: Breitkopf & Härtel, 1903), 58.
82. Ibid.

83. Thistleton, *The Art of Violin Playing*, 143.
84. Achille Rivarde, *The Violin and Its Technique as a Means to the Interpretation of Music* (Musician's Library) (London: Macmillan, 1921), 40.
85. "A Young Violinist Makes a Successful First Appearance in America," *The New York Times*, November 18, 1895.
86. Marc C. Blumenberg, ed., "Achille Rivarde," *The Musical Courier* Vol. 31, No. 12 (1895): 8.
87. Ibid., 46.
88. Ibid.
89. Coyle, *The Talent Code*, 18.
90. Brown, *Make It Stick*, 203.
91. Ibid., 50.
92. Safonoff's name also appears as "Vasily Safonov" and "Wassily Safonov." I am using his name as it appears on the cover of his 1916 publication of *New Formula for the Piano Teacher and Piano Student*.
93. Rosina Lhévinne assumed her husband's teaching duties at The Julliard School upon his death in 1944 and taught there until her death at age 96 in 1976. Her students included Van Cliburn, James Levine, John Browning, Mischa Dichter, Edward Auer, Garrick Ohlsson, and composer John Williams.
94. Wassili Safonoff, *New Formula for the Piano Teacher and Piano Student* (London: J. & W. Chester, 1916), 28.
95. Brown, *Make It Stick*, 53.
96. Ibid., 49.
97. Ibid., 4.
98. Ibid., 51.
99. Földes, *Keys to the Keyboard*, 67. [Italics added].
100. Ibid., 98.
101. Brown, *Make It Stick*, 72–73.
102. Földes, *Keys to the Keyboard*, 100.
103. Elizabeth Caland, *Artistic Piano Playing as Taught by Ludwig Deppe*, trans. Evelyn Sutherland Stevenson (Nashville, TN: The Olympian Publishing Co., 1903), 48–49.
104. Galamian, *Principles of Violin: Playing & Teaching*, 94.
105. Briggs, *Fire in the Crucible*, 206.
106. Ibid.
107. Ibid., 207.
108. Ibid., 206.

Sources

Alexanian, Diran, and Frederick Fairbanks. *Traité Théorique et Pratique du Violoncelle; Theoretical and Practical Treatise of the Violoncello*. Paris: A. Z. Mathot, 1922.

Berg, Christopher. *Mastering Guitar Technique: Process & Essence*. Pacific, MO: Mel Bay Publications, 1997.

Berman, Boris. *Notes from the Pianist's Bench*. New Haven, CT: Yale University Press, 2002.

Bilson, Malcolm. "The Future of Schubert Interpretation: What Is Really Needed?" *Early Music* Vol. 25, No. 4 (1997): 715–722.

Blumenberg, Marc A., ed. "Achille Rivarde." *The Musical Courier* Vol. 31, No. 12 (1895): 8.

Briggs, John. *Fire in the Crucible: The Alchemy of Creative Genius*. New York: St. Martin's Press, 1988.

Brower, Harriette Moore. *Piano Mastery: Talks with Master Pianists and Teachers, and an Account of a Von Bülow Class, Hints on Interpretation*. New York: Frederick A. Stokes Company, 1915.

Brower, Harriette Moore. *Piano Mastery: Second Series; Talks with Master Pianists and Teachers*. New York: Frederick A. Stokes Company, 1917.

Brown, Peter C., Henry L. Roediger, III, and Mark A. McDaniel. *Make It Stick: The Science of Successful Learning*. Cambridge, MA: Belknap Press, 2014.

Caland, Elizabeth. *Artistic Piano Playing as Taught by Ludwig Deppe*. Translated by Evelyn Sutherland Stevenson. Nashville, TN: The Olympian Publishing Co., 1903.

Claxton, Guy. *Hare Brain, Tortoise Mind: How Intelligence Increases When You Think Less*. New York: Harper Perennial, 1998.

Colvin, Geoffrey. *Talent Is Overrated: What Really Separates World-Class Performers from Everybody Else*. New York: Portfolio Trade, 2010.

Cooke, James Francis. *Great Pianists on Piano Playing*. Philadelphia: Theodore Presser Co., 1913.

Cortot, Alfred, and Métaxas Le Roy. *Rational Principles of Pianoforte Technique*. Paris: M. Senart; Boston: Oliver Ditson Company, 1930.

Coyle, Daniel. *The Talent Code: Greatness Isn't Born: It's Grown. Here's How*. New York: Bantam, 2009.

Culkin, John M. "A Schoolman's Guide to Marshall McLuhan." *Saturday Review* Vol. 50, No. 11 (1967): 51–53, 70–72.

Day, Timothy. *A Century of Recorded Music: Listening to Musical History*. New Haven, CT: Yale University Press, 2000.

Dewey, John. *Democracy and Education: An Introduction to the Philosophy of Education*. New York: The Macmillan Company, 1916.

Ericsson, K. A., R. T. Krampe, and C. Tesch-Römer. "The Role of Deliberate Practice in the Acquisition of Expert Performance." *Psychological Review* (1993): 363–406.

Flesch, Carl. *The Art of Violin Playing, Book Two*. New York: Carl Fischer, Inc., 1930.

Flesch, Carl. *Carl Flesch Scale System a Supplement to Book 1 of the Art of Violin Playing*. Edited by Max Rostal. New York: Carl Fischer Music, 1987.

Földes, Andor. *Keys to the Keyboard, a Book for Pianists: With Explanatory Music*. New York: E.P. Dutton, 1948.

Galamian, Ivan. *Principles of Violin: Playing & Teaching*. Englewood Cliffs, NJ: Prentice-Hall, 1962.

Green, Elizabeth A. H., Judith Galamian, and Josef Gingold. *Miraculous Teacher: Ivan Galamian & the Meadowmount Experience*. Bryn Mawr, PA: Theodore Presser, 1993.

Huang, Chungliang Al. *Embrace Tiger, Return to Mountain: The Essence of Tai Ji*. Moab, Utah: Real People Press, 1973.

Hullah, Annette. *Theodor Leschetizky*. London and New York: J. Lane Company, 1906.

Kochevitsky, George. *The Art of Piano Playing: A Scientific Approach*. Princeton, NJ: Summy-Birchard, 1967.

Lhévinne, Josef. *Basic Principles in Pianoforte Playing*. Philadelphia: Theo. Presser Company, 1924.

Masin, Gwendolyn. "Violin Teaching in the New Millennium: In Search of the Lost Instructions of Great Master: An Examination of Similarities and Differences Between Schools of Playing and How These Have Evolved, Or Remembering the Future of Violin Performance." PhD diss., Dublin: Trinity College, 2012.

Montagu-Nathan, M. "Ottakar Ševčík." *The Musical Times* Vol. 75, No. 1093 (1934): 217–218.

Nabokov, Vladimir. *Strong Opinions*. New York: Vintage, 1990.

Parkening, Christopher, Jack Marshall, and David Brandon. *The Christopher Parkening Guitar Method*. Milwaukee, WI: Hal Leonard, 1997.

Rachmaninoff, Sergei. "New Lights on Piano Playing." *The Etude* Vol. 41 (1923): 223–224.

Reder, Lynne M., Xiaonan L. Liu, Alexander Keinath, and Vencislav Popov. "Building Knowledge Requires Bricks, Not Sand: The Critical Role of Familiar Constituents in Learning." *Psychonomic Bulletin & Review* (2015): 1–7.

Rivarde, A. *The Violin and Its Technique as a Means to the Interpretation of Music*. London: Macmillan, 1921.

Rywerant, Yochanan. *The Feldenkrais Method: Teaching by Handling: A Technique for Individuals*. 1st ed. San Francisco: Harper & Row, 1983.

Safonoff, Wassili. *New Formula for the Piano Teacher and Piano Student, Chester Edition*. London: J. & W. Chester, 1916.

Savary, Michel. *Encyclopedia of Guitar Virtuosity: 210 Difficult Passages*. Heidelberg: Chanterelle Verlag, 1987.

Segovia, Andrés. *Diatonic Major and Minor Scales*. Washington, DC: Columbia Music Co, 1953.

Segovia, Andrés, Napoléon Coste, Fernando Sor, and Mauro Giuliani. "The Guitar and I: My Early Years in Granada and Córdoba." (1970): 2 s. 12 in. 33 1/3 rpm. microgroove. stereophonic.

Stembridge-Montavont, Michael. "Variations on a Theme of Chopin." *Piano* (September/October 2004): 34–45.

Sunstein, Cass R., and Adrian Vermeule. "Conspiracy Theories: Causes and Cures." *Journal of Political Philosophy* Vol. 17, No. 2 (2009): 202–227.

Tashman, L. S. "The Development of Expertise in Performance: The Role of Memory, Knowledge, Learning, and Practice." *Journal of Multidisciplinary Research* Vol. 5, No. 3 (2013): 33–48.

Thistleton, Frank. *The Art of Violin Playing for Players and Teachers*. London: The Strad, 1924.

Unschuld, Marie von. *The Pianist's Hand*. Translated by Henry Morgan Dare. Leipzig: Breitkopf & Härtel, 1903.

Wade, Graham. *Maestro Segovia*. London: Robson Books, 1986.

Wullner, Ludwig. "Solo Building Is Structure Building." *The Musical Standard* (September 13, 1902): 162.

"A Young Violinist Makes a Successful First Appearance in America." *The New York Times*, November 18, 1895.

3

CHUNKING

"Chunking is a strange concept," writes Daniel Coyle in *The Talent Code*. "The idea that skill—which is graceful, fluid, and seemingly effortless—should be created by the nested accumulation of small, discrete circuits seems counterintuitive, to say the least."[1] The concept was written about often by great musicians of the past, although they never used the term "chunking," but it's the word psychologists, neurologists, and physiologists use.[2]

Chunking is the recognition of the constituent parts of a skill, a piece of music, or perception and then focusing on them individually and mastering them. Then they are combined into a unified and secure whole. How the combination takes place will be the subject of chapters 5 and 7.

A 1946 study by Adriaan de Groot (1914–2006) had no immediate impact but years later proved crucial to the understanding of the acquisition of expert skill. De Groot, who was a psychologist and amateur chess player, wanted to explore the chess skills of friends who were like him in many ways, but they were better at chess. The assumption at the time was that great chess players had phenomenal memories and an innate aptitude for the game.

De Groot's experiment was simple. He arranged chess pieces on the board as they might occur in a real game and had experts and novices look at the board for five seconds. When their memory was tested, the "master players recalled the pieces and arrangements four to five times better than the ordinary players did. (World-class players neared 100 percent recall.)"[3]

Then de Groot varied his experiment and set up the chess pieces in configurations *that would never occur in a chess game*. When the players' recall was tested, master players performed no better than the novices. Coyle explains that de Groot showed that the success of the master players in the first test was because they recognized *patterns* (or chunks), made possible through their accumulated knowledge and experience, while novices saw individual pieces and squares.[4] Think of how a trained musician can look at a group of notes and see it immediately as a fragment of an ascending melodic minor scale while a beginner only sees individual notes. The masters' skill consisted of "identifying important elements and grouping them into a meaningful framework."[5] The first test was more difficult for the novices because they had not yet constructed a meaningful framework; the second test was difficult for the masters because it didn't reflect any meaningful framework related to chess.

The ability to identify relevant elements and group them together speaks directly to the importance of solid, well-designed training. Regarding scale practice as a hateful habit, as did Michel Savary, doesn't consider that the study of scales helps one build structures that can be grouped into meaningful frameworks. The frameworks constructed by scale work have to do with a high-level understanding of music theory and fluency with how this relates to the guitar fingerboard, to say nothing of developing the structures of skill needed for a high-level technique. A superficial view of scale practice belies one of the most important reasons for studying scales. The notes on a fingerboard or keyboard are more than isolated geographic locations, much like chess is more than a bunch of separate squares and chess pieces. Notes have meaning in their varied relationships to other notes. The more clearly these relationships are seen, that is, the more detailed the structures are, the easier it will be to read, study, memorize, and interpret literature.

In 1994, the U.S. Army Research Institute for the Behavioral and Social Sciences published "A Review of the Literature on Part-Task and Whole-Task Training and Context Dependency," a paper that reviewed and summarized two popular methods of training. The report defined whole-task training as consisting of "presenting a complete task to learners so that they are able to practice the task as a single unit,"[6] which is the same as massed or blocked practice. Part-task practice consists of "splitting a task into sub-tasks for presentation to the learner. Part training allows the learner to practice subsets of a task, in isolation from the whole."[7] Part-task practice is the same as chunking. A 1963 paper in the *Journal of Experimental Psychology* found that the greater the interdependency of the internal components of a larger skill, the more effective part-task training was.[8] Virtuoso technique is, in part, a set of highly developed interdependent and interlocking skills.

The U. S. Army has a life-and-death interest in designing superior training methods. Their report found that "if a task is highly complex and can easily be divided into sub-tasks, part-task training is the better choice."[9]

The Magical Number Seven

People remember roughly the same number of chunks of information—five to nine items. These numbers exactly fit what George Miller proposed in his famous 1956 paper, "The Magical Number Seven, Plus or Minus, Two."[10] The difference between experts and novices lies in what those chunks contain. Geoffrey Colvin also mentions de Groot's chess experiment and says, "For the novices, a particular piece on a particular square was a chunk. But for the masters, who had studied real positions for years, a chunk was much larger, consisting of a whole group of pieces in a specific arrangement."[11]

Chunking is an efficient way to maintain a reserve of mental energy. If one thinks in terms of chunks, a C-major chord rather than the individual notes C-E-G, to give a simple example, there's more time and energy available for other things. Some of these other things might be delicate shadings of tone, dynamics, rubato, and other artistic nuances.

Mental, Physical, and Perceptual Chunking

Chunking, as the building of these structures came to be called by psychologists, applies not only to mental pursuits but also to physical skills. Mastering the right chunks in the correct order, that is, in a hierarchical manner, and then combining them into a fluid skill is the essence of purposeful practice. A 2015 article found that the strength of individual chunks matters if they are to be effectively incorporated into a new skill or structure of knowledge. The implication is that practicers and their teachers need to be mindful of the amount of *new* information they try to digest. The authors of "Building Knowledge Requires Bricks, Not Sand: The Critical Role of Familiar Constituents in Learning" write, "[T]he components must be introduced slowly so that the lower level elements become strong chunks before instruction that requires many new elements to be combined."[12]

Howard Austin uses the ungainly term "subprocedurization" to describe the building of a complicated skill by focusing separately on its individual components. He adds that "beginners frequently try to solve all the problems at the same time and as a result fail to solve any."[13] Unless they have a skilled guide, beginners have no way to understand the most effective hierarchical order of skill acquisition for consistent-circuit skills.

Matthew Syed writes in *Bounce* that had you seen tennis star Roger Federer while he was acquiring technique, you would have seen movements practiced under conscious control. His playing would seem sluggish compared to today because his skills had yet to be integrated into a larger, flexible structure.[14]

Alan Walker reports that Franz Liszt "sometimes practiced for ten or twelve hours a day, and much of this labour was expended on exercises—scales, arpeggios, trills, and repeated notes."[15] He was isolating and strengthening the elements that would become constituent parts of a greater whole. Geoffrey Colvin writes about Jerry Rice, one of the NFL's greatest wide receivers: "Of all the work Rice did to make himself a great player, practically none of it was playing football games."[16] In chapter 1, we saw that when Busoni and Arthur Rubinstein decided they needed to overhaul their technique, they withdrew from performing for a time. Federer, Rice, Liszt, etc. all designed their practice to focus on strengthening various chunks and then combining them.

Syed continues by noting that the development of skilled movements "is inseparable from the development of perceptual expertise."[17] It's not that high-level musicians have faster reflexes than others, it is that they perceive and understand more of what they see and hear and can initiate a response or the next step more quickly.

Great sight-readers, or expert typists, read farther ahead than average sight-readers or typists. Amy Fay (1844–1928), an American concert pianist who traveled to Europe to study, remarked how difficult it was to turn pages for Liszt because he looked so far ahead and took in five bars at a glance.[18] When prevented from looking ahead, experts perform scarcely better than novices.[19] Here's Syed:

> When Roger Federer returns a service, he is not demonstrating sharper reactions than you and I; what he is showing is that he can extract more information from the service action of his opponent and other visual clues, enabling him to move into position earlier and more efficiently than the rest of us, which in turn allows him to make the return.[20]

Rather than possessing superior memories, or sharper reaction time, top performers "possess enhanced awareness and anticipation."[21] Syed quotes Janet Starkes, a professor of kinesiology: "The exploitation of advance information results in the time paradox where skilled performers seem to have all the time in the world. Recognition of familiar scenarios and the chunking of perceptual information into meaningful wholes and patterns speeds up processes."[22] This accounts for the effortless artistry outstanding performers have achieved. But how does one set oneself on a course wherein separate motor processes can be executed as one or, as mentioned in chapter 1, transcend the limits of serial reaction time?

Motor Programs and the Time Paradox

Virtuoso violin, guitar, or piano technique—or advanced technique for any instrument—comprises numerous high-level and interdependent skills. How could neurologists study the development and execution of these interlocking skills? The problem becomes more daunting if one tries to account for the subtle and minute variations that contribute to artistic nuance.

Relatively simple skills or easy movements have been the usual subjects of motor control studies. Activities such as cigar making or simple positioning tasks can be guided by sensory feedback as they occur,[23] but actions that need to arise quickly are of short duration, and those for which there is no time to receive and act upon feedback, such as commonly occur in virtuoso instrumental performance, present challenges to those trying to form theories about motor control. The thought that initiates an action does not result in an instantaneous movement, regardless of how it appears. This won't be seen as a problem—except to a trained ear and eye—until one attempts to reach the high speeds required to play virtuoso literature or needs to perform complex interdependent skills simultaneously.

Neurologists have observed that "complex sequences of learned movements can be executed at a rate too fast to be guided be sensory feedback, or for the individual components to each be under conscious control."[24] Movements need to have been "preprogrammed" because "feedback loops aren't fast enough."[25] Neurologists call these preprogrammed movements "motor programs." (This is another way of describing the process of explicit skills becoming implicit skills, which we'll explore shortly.) These motor programs "permit movement sequences to be executed rapidly, as a single movement."[26] If one has not learned to integrate a movement that is a constituent part of a larger skill into a motor program, and the time to perceive the need for a movement and to initiate it is greater than response latency, one's development will be constrained by the limits of serial reaction time.

George Kochevitsky recognized these limits: "If we try to play a scale or passage without dividing it into several groups with regular accents, then for each movement of each single finger a separate will-impulse must be sent from the central nervous system."[27] Kochevitsky views this as a metric problem. By uniting a series of notes into a metric grouping, "many volitional impulses, each directed to a single action, would be replaced by a few directed to the compound action."[28] Kochevitsky's uniting of many notes into a group is a motor program.

If the individual movements required for a skill have not been learned, or have not been learned well, as may happen if one's first encounter with a new technique is in a piece of music, these movements will not be successfully integrated into a motor program, which will hinder technical progress and artistic expression. Students won't be able to see this as the cause of delayed progress and will either think they're not practicing enough or they're not talented. It's usually neither; they're not working in a way that can help them transcend the problems of latency.

Latency varies depending on the type of stimuli: Kinesthetic reaction time is about 119 milliseconds while visual latency is 190 milliseconds.[29] The response time for auditory stimuli is about 160 milliseconds.[30] These stimuli allow one to receive feedback and are essential while learning and practicing a skill, but trying to initiate corrections at the note level during virtuoso performance at fast *tempi* is impossible. Richard Schmidt of the University of Southern California writes that "the processes involving the generation of sensory error information, perceiving it, and initiating corrections in response to those errors was quite slow, requiring from 120–200 msec."[31]

Motor programs are probably best understood by musicians as amalgams of interdependent chunks of skill that are constituent parts of a greater whole. This greater whole, in turn, becomes a larger chunk as it is assimilated into one's technique. Although the development of these initial chunks, or micro skills, is *necessary*, having developed these skills-within-a-skill is not *sufficient* for the development of high-level technique in service to an artistic vision. What renders their development sufficient lies in finding a way to transcend any latency connected with the initiation of a movement. But first, a digression on milliseconds.

Milliseconds by Any Other Name

Musicians work with milliseconds every day and already know how much time, for example, 250 milliseconds take, even if they don't know they do: It's a sixteenth-note played at ♩ = 60 BPM (beats per minute). Consider table 3.1:

TABLE 3.1 Notes and Milliseconds

When playing ♩♪♪♪ notes at ♩=:				
60 BPM	80 BPM	100 BPM	120 BPM	140 BPM
		one ♪ equals:		
250 MS.	187 MS.	150 MS.	125 MS.	107 MS.

Although we shouldn't go about the business of practicing and making music thinking about milliseconds, milliseconds need not be unfathomable abstractions that have no meaning to us. The implications of the numbers in the above table are striking when compared to the latency times of various stimuli and point to why some ways of working are effective and others are not. If you're playing a scale in sixteenth notes at ♩ = 120 BPM and rely on visual feedback at the instant it's time to make a change of position on the guitar, you'll always be straggling because the time required for visual feedback is more than the time required for an individual sixteenth note.

When neurologists write about motor control and use the term "response latency," they're considering how one *responds* to external stimuli by initiating a movement or correcting a movement. For example, a batter at home plate needs to wait to perceive the ball thrown by the pitcher before initiating a swing of the bat. Experts, however, quickly extract more information from a stimulus—in the case of a batter, it could be the way the ball left the pitcher's hand—and can initiate a response more quickly. High-level solo musicians understand more of what they're doing (perceptual chunking) and don't need to wait for external stimuli; they have learned the most efficacious time to initiate a movement, *and it's never at the instant the movement is required*. There is about a 100-millisecond delay between brain activity and the onset of a movement.[32]

Transcending Latency

Although high-level solo musicians don't rely upon external stimuli before initiating movements—such as an athlete needs to do before responding to an action by an opponent—many students and amateurs create their own virtual external stimuli by making a "cue" from where they are in the piece. This cue—created by either default or intention—is often the instant a movement is needed. Once one reaches a certain speed, cues like this will be too late because of the limits hard-wired into the central nervous system.

An example of how one comes to develop these late cues can sometimes be found in instructions given in an instrument's basic pedagogical literature. In 1843, guitarist Dionisio Aguado writes about an arpeggio study:

> The Allegro tempo makes this study more difficult than the last because the movements of the left hand must be very rapid in order to take up each new position in time *after the last note of each group* [by which he means 'chord'] in the accompaniment has been clearly heard.[33]

Aguado's tempo marking for the piece is ♩ = 104 BPM, and the piece consists of continuous sixteenth notes, which means the last note of a group is 144 milliseconds long.

Aguado is, in effect, recommending that students wait for the feedback (or cue) of clearly hearing the last note before initiating the next movement. The emphasis on making rapid movements at the last instant—at the expense of learning to think ahead and choreograph movements of individual fingers—is an unmerciful recipe for adding tension to one's playing and obstructing the possibility of legato phrasing. Advice like this prevents students from learning how to transcend latency for a skill within a skill and will stunt development because students will wait to *respond* to something—the end of a note's duration—before they *initiate* the next thing. Experts develop advance cues to prepare physical movements and bypass the limits novices have when it comes to executing a series of movements.[34]

Developing advanced cues is only part of it, though: Experts transcend the limits of executing movements serially through hierarchical chunking. Jörn Diedrichsen, a researcher at the University of Western Ontario, and Atushi Yokoi, a Japanese colleague, presented the first neural evidence of hierarchical chunking at a conference for the Society for Neuroscience in 2016.[35] It is the *way* in which one combines these chunks that contributes to or detracts from fluency. As Diedrichsen says, "Some ways of chunking are biomechanically better, can lead to better performance,"[36] something great musicians understand well.

Hierarchical chunking accounts for a higher quality of skill and helps skills become more quickly assimilated, which in turn helps one transcend the limits of serial reaction time. The problems posed by recognizing and transcending latency in virtuoso playing can best be explained by analogy.

The 100-millisecond delay between brain activity and the onset of a movement is hard-wired into our central nervous system and is consistent from person to person. Zach Schonbrun writes that this is "why the International Association of Athletics Federations, which governs track events, considers a false start in the 100-meter dash to be any jump off the blocks that occurred within a tenth of a second after the firing of the gun."[37] Runners off the blocks within 100 milliseconds had to have initiated their movement *before* the gun fired and are penalized. The problem that penalized runners have is that they're anticipating a cue that is meant to be the signal to *initiate* their movement off the blocks, not a signal to *move* off the blocks.

But imagine if the object *is* to move at the instant the gun fired. You would certainly want to give yourself the message, or cue, to move before then, but how would you know when? You couldn't know exactly. But you could know if there were a *series* of shots in succession, and you need to move on, say, the fourth one. If the shots were steady and predictable, you could learn the best time to initiate your movement off the blocks so that the movement would be timed with the fourth shot. Now imagine the four shots as musical notes that have rhythmic values. With practice, you would be able to learn the best time to initiate your movement so it would line up with the fourth note. This illustration has limitations, of course, but it shows the difference between intention and movement. This distinction is relevant only to movements that are a feature of the highest levels of virtuoso playing or training that has as its object to develop to these levels.

Developing virtuosity is not usually discussed in these terms. There are plenty of times when the message to move off of a note at rapid *tempi* is best given the instant that note has sounded, not after it has completed its full duration, as recommended by Aguado. This is an example of criteria changing as one reaches higher levels of skill, or, to put it another way, what if there were a "pedagogy of virtuosity"? If there were, it would help one distinguish between the limits of a skill's development and the limits of the central nervous system. Knowing how to transcend the latter will decrease the limits of the former.

Great teachers incorporate this advanced knowledge in their teaching of students at all levels. Some great teachers of the past had a sense of these types of problems and touched upon them in their writings—as we saw in Kochevitsky's awareness of serial reaction time and as we will see below in Galamian's recognition of the importance of mentally anticipating a physical action—but they didn't have the advantage of modern research that has helped clarify what goes on "under the hood."

I can only give a practical example of transcending latency from my own discipline, concert performance of virtuoso literature on the guitar. I don't know the technical limits of other instruments and how these relate to the limits of the central system, but I hope other instrumentalists are stimulated to imagine examples from their own disciplines.

The following scale passage in measure 121 of J. S. Bach's famous chaconne in d minor for violin, fingered in example 3.1 for solo guitar, illustrates this problem. I prefer to slur the two notes of each group of thirty-second notes, except for the final one.[38] This musical choice necessitates that all the notes in the second beat be fingered on the third string, which means one must shift from the fifth position to the second position. Assuming a tempo of ♩ = 64 BPM, this shift must occur between notes that last 117 milliseconds each, but about 100 milliseconds will pass before the neuronal message *even gets to the hand*. The shift will be more fluid if initiated mentally *as one strikes* the d" that occurs before the b-flat, which is the first note played in the new position (the Roman numerals indicate positions and the circled numbers indicate the string):

EXAMPLE 3.1   m. 121 of J. S. Bach's chaconne in d minor fingered for guitar.

Without this anticipatory initiation, movements will be late, rushed, and tenser than they need to be, even if the movement itself is anticipatory, such as the left elbow moving to anticipate a shift in guitar and bowed string playing. If one has mastered the technique of shifting as a separate skill and learns when to initiate it within a larger context, one can execute the shift seamlessly at high speed; if one follows the "move-after-the-last-note-has-been-clearly-heard" advice, one will learn to make movements at the instant they're needed. Beyond a certain tempo, the limits of the central nervous system will emerge as a significant barrier to progress, and one will not have time to make a musically sensitive shift at fast *tempi*. If working this way is habitual, it will cumulatively add to one's general level of tension. I'm not recommending cutting note values short and playing staccato; the point is that although a movement might be *initiated* during a portion of the previous note's value, the movement itself can occur at the right time and players maintain control over their artistic intentions.

Galamian sees the correlation between mental preparation and all types of practice to be of critical importance. He writes that "the mind always has to anticipate the physical action that is to be taken and then to send the command for its execution."[39] Other teachers imply this when they speak about "thinking ahead." Of course, if one hasn't mastered the constituent components of a complex skill, no amount thinking ahead will help.

If the components of a complex skill have not been worked out meticulously in early training, students end up relying on short-term memory and short-term skill acquisition, both of which have built-in limitations because a complex skill will exist as a series of separate processes executed in succession.[40] The shifting example given above illustrates the importance of developing the right kind of advance cues to initiate movements at high speeds. The development and timing of these cues allows players to perform multiple interlocking skills simultaneously. This meticulous work is one of the purposes of well-designed early training, although this purpose won't be clear to novices because they can't experience its advantages until they are no longer novices.

It's not necessary for virtuosos to know that they've discovered ways to transcend latency or how they do it—they may think of it as "being relaxed" or "thinking ahead"—unless they're responsible for training students.

Explicit and Implicit Skill

As one masters the components, or discrete chunks, of a skill and assimilates these chunks into a larger whole—which in turn becomes another larger chunk—one eventually turns an *explicit skill*, a skill that must be consciously controlled, into an *implicit skill*, a skill that feels natural and reflexive.

Syed gives an excellent description of this. He's writing about sports, but it's the same thing that happens with musicians:

> This migration from the explicit to the implicit system of the brain has two crucial advantages. First, it enables the expert player to integrate the various parts of a complex skill into one fluent whole (this "motor chunking" is akin to the perceptual chunking described [earlier]), something that would be impossible at a conscious level because there are too many interconnecting variables for the conscious mind to handle. And second, it frees up attention to focus on higher-level aspects of the skill such as tactics and strategy.[41]

This is another way of describing what had yet to happen with Leopold Auer's violin student in chapter 1. Explicit skill had yet to become an implicit skill, and there was no conscious attentiveness left over for the higher-level aspects of the skill. For musicians, the higher-level aspects of a skill comprise the subtle physical gestures that are requisite for the expression of a nuanced and artistic interpretation.

Choking and Other Curses

Sometimes events occur during a performance that cause a performer to panic and try to move implicit skill back to explicit skill. The results are always disastrous because explicit skill functions more slowly. Athletes call it choking, and musicians call it "a train wreck" or "crash and burn." The consequences of trying to move an implicit skill back to an explicit skill may be the origin of the unhelpful advice, "Don't think so much," which is especially pernicious when it spreads to all aspects of study. Matthew Syed describes choking as

> a neural glitch that occurs when individuals are under pressure; when they find themselves explicitly monitoring skills that would be better executed automatically. We have also seen that this is a deeply confusing and often surreal experience for the performer—unable to execute the smooth and refined actions he or she has spent a lifetime mastering.[42]

Syed's description of choking centers around a "glitch" that happens in the event. In chapter 1, Zack Schonbrun suggested that thinking about the plan in the moment will take one out of the flow of time. But only Leschetizky (also in chapter 1) connected the problem to the way in which one studied. The tenets of good practice discussed in this book can serve to keep one in the flow of time required by implicit skills during performance.

Before we explore the parallels between what great musicians have written about practice and chunking, we must mention a concealed and detrimental byproduct of an explicit skill having become an implicit skill. Psychologists have even devised terms for it: *expert-induced amnesia* and the *curse-of-knowledge effect*.[43] These byproducts account for the inability experts have in explaining to a novice how they acquired the ability to do something, rather like what David Foster Wallace called "blindness and dumbness." Experts' skills have become so deeply encoded that they're usually incapable of offering any insight unless they have studied the development of skill in their discipline from a pedagogical standpoint, as did Claudio Arrau.

An understanding of the way an explicit skill becomes an implicit skill also helps one understand the plateau mentioned in chapter 1 and the slight decline that precedes it. George Leonard writes about tennis:

> What you really need is to hit thousands of balls under fairly controlled circumstances at every step along the way: forehand, backhand, footwork, serve, spin, net play, placement, strategy. And the process is generally incremental. You can't skip stages. . . . With the introduction of each new stage, you're going to have to start *thinking* again, which means things will temporarily fall apart.[44]

Prototypical Chunking, or Dr. Wullner's Blocks

None of the tenets of good practice I discuss in this book exist alone. They overlap one another to varying degrees but can only be discussed one at a time. For example, foundation studies are a form of chunking as is practicing variety in repetition. Daniel Coyle observed students at the famed Meadowmount School of Music (a seven-week intensive summer school founded by Galamian in 1944) practicing difficult spots in dotted rhythms and saw that as a way of chunking pairs of notes.[45] Mental work, so important for secure memorization, is dependent upon the high-level structures created in early study. The development of continuity is dependent upon having mastered the constituent parts of the whole and having developed the sustained focus that results from mental practice. The freedom required for creative phrase-storming depends on mastery of all the tenets of good practice.

Chunking in practice is implied by the description given in chapter 2 by Dr. Wullner of successive blocks to be shaped and polished before they can be used in a larger structure. Coyle gives a good description of chunking in action: "The goal is always the same: to break a skill into its component pieces (circuits), memorize those pieces individually, then link them together in progressively larger groupings (new, interconnected circuits)."[46]

In the previous chapter, violinist Frank Thistleton described a method of practice that wasted time and perpetuated a fiasco. Instead of continuing to barrel through a piece, he recommends a form of chunking: correct the mistake and practice it separately from the piece. He suspects there will be more errors in other spots, and this procedure should be applied again as needed.[47]

The recognition and correction of errors is critical. All modern writers on improving performance speak to the importance of corrective feedback. Ideally, this would first be given by a good teacher then internalized by the student. The presence of feedback in the recognition and quick correction of errors helps strengthen neural connections, in addition to having fixed the mistakes and attended to any underlying causes.

Thistleton notes that the different techniques for the two hands in violin playing must be mastered separately:

> It is impossible for the beginner to concentrate on both the left and the right hand at the same time. Therefore, if the difficulties that present themselves in bowing are mastered *first*, we are able to give all the attention to the left hand.[48]

Three decades earlier, Carl Courvoisier (1846–1908) issued a warning to students in his book, *The Technics of Violin Playing on Joachim's Method* from 1894,[49] about why the violin is so difficult:

> [T]he actions of the two hands, or rather of the entire two sides of the body, are so utterly unlike each other as to require the player's attention to be continually divided. A very large amount of time and exercise must be spent, under the control of unflagging presence of mind, in order to obtain mastery over the combined action of both sides.[50]

Unlike Thistleton, Courvoisier doesn't say anything about working on hands separately. Guitarists are similar to bowed string players in this respect: *They have separate techniques for each hand.*[51]

Rachmaninoff doesn't say anything explicit that could be taken as a description of chunking, but while speaking about the essentials of artistic playing, he says that the

> technical ability of the performer should be of such a nature that it can be applied immediately to all the artistic demands of the composition to be interpreted. Of course, there may be individual passages which require some special technical study, but, generally speaking, technic is worthless unless the hands and the mind of the player are so trained that they can encompass the principal difficulties found in modern compositions.[52]

One can safely infer, given Rachmaninoff's description of the five-year course of scale and arpeggio practice in the April 1923 issue of *The Etude*, that technique would be built bit by bit.

Carl Flesch was of a similar opinion: "The technical level of ability demanded for the reproduction of a work should *already* have been attained by means of *general* technical studies."[53] Flesch describes general technique as the raw materials; applied technique is the finished goods.[54] Certainly, raw materials must be ready before one can create finished goods.

Violinist Benjamin Cutter writes in 1903 that he has noticed that time and effort are wasted when trying to get a piece up to tempo "because the powers of attention and of observation are dissipated by the playing of *too many consecutive measures*."[55] He suggests that students divide the music into smaller groups of notes: "The brevity of such a group allows close attention in a slow tempo to the pitch of each tone, and to the adjustment, the tempering, of all the tones."[56] Cutter then describes knitting the smaller groups into a larger unit: "After several groups have been treated in this way and each goes in tune, put two, then three, together at the increased rate of speed."[57] Cutter is concerned with intonation in his example, but the procedure he outlines is helpful for any facet of technique.

Violinist Achille Rivarde describes five or six different movements upon which left-hand technique is built. After describing them, he writes, "In order to gain complete mental control of these movements it is necessary to study them separately and in the simplest forms."[58]

Rivarde gives timeless advice about repetition:

> There should be no repetition in good practice. I do not mean that the same passage or movement should never be repeated. I mean that it should never be repeated without adding at least that touch of improvement to its performance which means that each time it will be done better and

therefore differently from the last.[59] Nothing is more stupid and lifeless than repetition, and nothing grows upon us more easily.[60]

He writes that one can get in a groove—and he doesn't mean the groove where everything is working great; he means more of a rut—and that our minds go to sleep. Rivarde uses the term *automata* for this.

Automaticity

Both Geoffrey Colvin and Daniel Coyle use the term "automaticity" but mean different things by it. Colvin equates the term with an "arrested-development stage,"[61] and it is something to be avoided. He acknowledges that great performers use much less mental energy to execute their skill, but that "ultimately, the performance is conscious and controlled, not automatic."[62] He continues in agreement with Rivarde: "Avoiding automaticity through continual practice is another way of saying that great performers are always getting better. This is why the most devoted can stay at the top of their field for far longer than most people would think possible."[63]

Coyle thinks of "automaticity" as something that happens when a skill becomes so well learned it seems unconscious and second nature, although this "naturalness" is illusory: "a skill, once gained, feels utterly natural, as if it's something we've always possessed."[64] This is the origin of the curse-of-knowledge effect and expert-induced amnesia mentioned earlier.

The two uses of the term can be reconciled by realizing that Coyle's use of the word "automaticity" refers to the process of an explicit skill having become an implicit skill; Colvin's use (and Rivarde's) has more in common with the "worn grooves of thought" mentioned by Guy Claxton in the previous chapter.

The More You Master the Chunks, the More You Master the Whole

Before presenting what amounts to a textbook definition of chunking, pianist Mark Hambourg (1879–1960) gives an injunction against the common practice of rushing headlong into the repetition of difficult passages:

> [T]he student should not then just play them; over and over again, as so many do, hoping that by much repetition the difficulties will finally be surmounted. He must rather play his passages once or twice, then stop and think, about them for a minute, and try to get a clear definition of them in his mind.[65]

Hambourg was an advocate of mental work, as we'll see in the next chapter.

I can't use today's all-too-common term "problem-solving skills" to describe what Hambourg wants students to do because many students and teachers set about trying to solve the wrong problem. The lack of what are quaintly referred to as "problem-solving skills" is really a lack of "problem-*recognition* skills." It is the mental structures that are created in early training that create a point of view with which one can accurately recognize a problem. If one has not built those structures, one won't see the real problem.

Hambourg then states:

> It is also a very good thing when first learning a piece to divide it, taking, say, each eight bars or so at a time to work at, and thus getting to know the component parts well before reviewing the work as a whole.[66]

Several chapters later, Hambourg lays out a procedure for memorization that follows the precepts set down by Peter Brown, Daniel Coyle, and some of the other modern authors we've discussed, but Hambourg's articulation of the ideas was seven decades earlier.

Josef Lhévinne, who had a lot to say about building a solid foundation, connects foundational training with technical mastery of a piece *and* interpretation:

> A knowledge of the keys, the common chords, and the seventh chords, should be as familiar to the student as his own name. This would not be mentioned were it not for the fact that I have repeatedly had students come for instruction who have after great effort prepared one, two, or at the most three show pieces, even pieces as far advanced as the Tchaikowsky or the Liszt Concerto, who barely knew what key they were playing in. As for understanding the modulations and their bearing upon the interpretations of such complicated and difficult master works, they have been blissfully ignorant.[67]

If one can see multiplication as a prerequisite for calculus or trigonometry, then here is Lhévinne's take on chunking: "[T]he trouble with many students is that they attempt difficult problems in what might be termed musical calculus or musical trigonometry without even ever mastering the multiplication table. Scales are musical multiplication tables."[68]

Violinist Sydney Robjohns is another who sees the problems of using "blind repetition in the hopes that sufficient repetition will alone make the most difficult passage easy!"[69] Robjohns sees this as an illogical idea and notes that it will simply solidify any errors. "No," he continues, "you must first examine the passage in every minutest detail, musical and technical. You must analyse the difficulty and see exactly what it is; then you are ready to devise ways of overcoming it." Isolating and solving the problem and reincorporating it into the whole is implied by this description.

Pianist Karl Leimer (1858–1944), the teacher of Walter Gieseking (1895–1956), writes in the same year as Robjohns,

> It is not advisable to play the whole [Bach] invention straight through, when studying. In fact, this should be forbidden. Only small parts should be practiced at a time; and these should be repeated over and over again, so that irregularities and unevennesses may be immediately corrected. It is much more difficult, if not impossible, to do this when longer parts are played.[70]

This is preceded by a discussion of mental practice.

Carl Flesch makes an explicit connection between massed practice and the dulling of one's ear. He writes that "the great majority of violinists draw the erroneous conclusion that purposeful *practising*, and the incessant repetition of the passage in question, until one is 'able to play it,' are identical."[71] Flesch goes as far as to call this a "fatal error" and adds, "habitual, thoughtless and endless repetition invariably destroys a player's capacity for musical feeling, and at the same time robs him of that which makes the artist—his *personality*"[72]

Alfred Cortot insists upon "the complete assimilation of the principle of each difficulty taken separately."[73]

Pianist Seymour Bernstein gives an example of applied chunking, which he calls "practicing pyramid fashion," for the study of a difficult passage in his 1981 book, *With Your Own Two Hands: Self Discovery Through Music*:

> Practice the passage pyramid fashion: that is, start to play a few measures before the difficult passage begins and stop on the first note of it; start once again from the same place, but this time stop after the second note; continue to add one note at a time until you have played through the entire passage. This is perhaps one of the most useful approaches to mastering a technically difficult passage.[74]

Here Bernstein is building chunks note by note as the first step of a multi-step process. The next step is building chunks in reverse order: start on the last note, add the next-to-last note, and play from there, then play from the note before that, and so on. Later the difficult passage is carefully incorporated back into the piece.

Ivan Galamian stresses the importance of mental preparation in practice and sees the correlation between the mind and physical action as the key to building technique and overcoming problems. "The basic procedure," he writes, "is to present to the mind, for transmission to the muscles, problems that progress from the simple to the ever more complicated."[75] In other words, hierarchical chunking. His assertion that the mind must "anticipate the action" is a precondition for transcending initiation latency. He describes how this is done:

> Each difficulty should be isolated and reduced to its simplest terms so that it will be easier to devise and to apply a practice procedure for it. The mind, which has to be able to anticipate the action, must have a clear picture of the motion involved, of its technical timing, and of the anticipated sound in order to give its commands with clarity and precision.[76]

We looked at the technique-from-pieces fallacy in chapter 2, and although mastery of repertoire pieces doesn't come solely from the practice of exercises, mastery of well-designed exercises helps one build increasingly complex technical structures that make the study of repertoire easier. There also exists the possibility of developing a more artistic technique. Kochevitsky writes that according to Liszt, "technique does not depend on exercise, *but on the technique of exercise.*"[77]

The Technique of Exercise

Liszt wished to ensure that virtuosity be pursued within musical contexts and that it not become a mechanical end in itself,[78] but this doesn't mean that the practice of exercises is synonymous with a mechanical end. Liszt's idea of musical context was to study well-designed technical exercises that incorporate the artistic nuances one must master to animate and bring life to the notes, rather than to bring an undeveloped technique to a repertoire piece. A piece of music is never music until we can make it so. In the preface to the *Technical Studies,*[79] Liszt writes:

> It will be useful to exercise the fingers, the ears and the intelligence simultaneously and to study, together with the mechanism, the dynamics and rhythm inherent in the music. Consequently, these first exercises should be practiced with every degree of intensity: *crescendo*, from *pianissimo* to *fortissimo* and *diminuendo*, from *fortissimo* to *pianissimo.*[80]

Michael Stembridge-Montavont quotes Thomas Tellefeson (1823–1874), one of Chopin's most important students, on the purpose of exercises: "It is not the exercise, per se, that one practices, but the development of the hand by means of it."[81]

Julio Esteban, a piano professor at the Peabody Conservatory while I was a student, writes that Liszt "worked on this project for twelve years, from 1868 to 1880, and the result was a monumental work, filled with new concepts and new forms of practice, that had no comparison with any other system or method written before."[82] Below are the contents of each of the twelve books, as given in an early edition of the exercises edited by Alexander Winterberger (1834–1914), a student of Liszt's. The volumes comprise an extensive and organized means to acquire technique through well-paced chunking:

- Book I: Exercises for gaining strength and independence of each individual finger with quiet hand, and chord-studies
- Book II: Preparatory studies for the major and minor scales
- Book III: Scales in thirds and sixths. Arpeggios, or broken scales
- Book: IV: Chromatic scales and exercises. Scales in contrary motion
- Book V: Repeated thirds, fourths, and sixths, with various fingerings. Exercises in thirds (formed from scales) in parallel and contrary motion. Exercises in fourths and sixths
- Book VI: Major, minor, and chromatic scales in double-thirds and -sixths
- Book VII: Scales in chords of the sixth with various fingerings. Arpeggios, or broken scales in double-thirds and -sixths, and chords of the sixth. Chromatic thirds, fourths, and sixths. Octave scales, major, and minor
- Book VIII: Broken octaves. Arpeggiated, or broken octave scales. Chord-studies. Shakes [Trills] in thirds, sixths, fourths, and octaves
- Book IX: Chords of the diminished seventh. Exercises with quiet hand. Arpeggios, or broken chords
- Book X: Broken chords with various fingerings throughout all major and minor scales
- Book: XI: Arpeggios in thirds and in sixths with various fingerings
- Book XII: Octave-studies with various fingerings and chord-studies[83]

It's not simply the mechanical aspects of technique that are to be acquired—teachers had students drill exercises well before Liszt came along. Esteban, who published his own edition of the exercises in 1971, notes that before Liszt, the main criterion when practicing exercises had been "absolutely even rhythm, with a full round tone. This was basically all."[84] Esteban describes the significance of what Liszt meant by "the technique of exercise":

> Liszt's idea is different. Following the same method of firmly holding down four fingers the remaining finger is made to use a full range of dynamics, all kinds of accents and, what was positively new then, different types of rhythms. By doing this, one gains in every aspect and perhaps most important of all, in the question of mental concentration. As one is involved with the continuous changes, the boredom of the long, even repetition is avoided. . . . And this is only the first page. Later, he goes on with free five-finger exercises *using all possible combinations of articulation and dynamics.*[85]

In the first exercise of Book I of the Winterberger edition (example 3.2), note the application of accents to acquire finger independence and the variety of rhythmic and dynamic nuance:

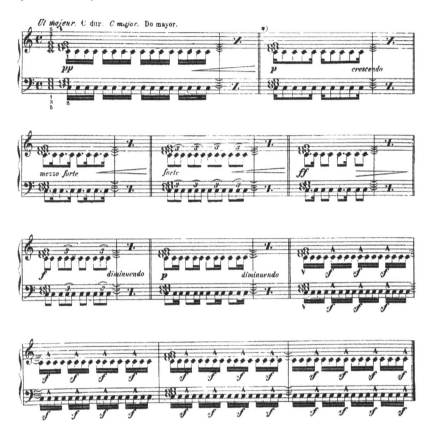

EXAMPLE 3.2 The first exercise from Book I of the Winterberger edition of the Liszt exercises (1887).

Liszt wanted exercises to be played with every kind of nuance, and he wanted the ability to execute expressive nuances to be second nature. The refined skills necessary to express these nuances would be assimilated into one's technique as would any other technical skill. Liszt recommended that students have a plan to bring artistic nuance to their technical practice. Below is an example of how he told Valérie Bossier to practice crescendos:[86]

EXAMPLE 3.3 Liszt's example of *crescendo* and *diminuendo*.

An exercise early in the second volume of Rudolph Breithaupf's 1909 *Natural Piano Technique* is designed to enhance one's tactile sense, which Breithaupf connects with musical nuance. He writes:

> The object is the culture and refinement of the muscular or tactile sense, concentration of the mental perception of tone, awakening of a keen sense for all that concerns the dynamic value of the single tone, to render the feeling in the finger-tips more acute, and refine the sense of touch, i. e., the harmonic connection between brain and tone.[87]

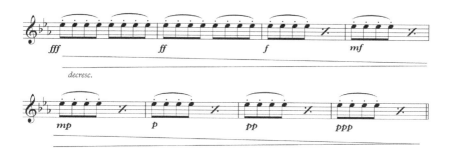

EXAMPLE 3.4 Exercise from R. M. Breithaupf's *Natural Piano Technique* (1909).

Claudio Arrau had a high opinion of Breithaupf's books and mentions them in a 1972 interview in *Clavier*.[88] In the same article, he talks of hearing Teresa Carreño perform many times when he was a child. He adds that she "changed her entire way of playing through Breithaupf " when she was around fifty years old.[89]

An exercise from Alfred Cortot's *Rational Principles of Pianoforte Technique* shows an example of his attention to voicing:[90]

EXAMPLE 3.5 Exercise from Alfred Cortot's *Rational Principles of Pianoforte Technique* (1928).

What these exercises have in common is that they allow one to study the extracted principles, rules, or formulae required to solve technical and artistic problems. We saw in chapter 2 that this way of working allows one to build stronger and more reliable structures of skill. The extracted skills then can become mastered as chunks, with wide-ranging applications and easily applied to new situations.

The more familiar individual chunks are, the easier they are to combine with other chunks to build a cohesive whole as one moves forward to the ever more complicated.[91] In chapters 5 and 6, we will touch upon the type of practice procedures to which Galamian, Liszt, Tellefson, Esteban, and Cortot refer, but first, why do they work?

Myelin

The "code" referred to in Daniel Coyle's book *The Talent Code* is practicing in such a way that one taps into "a neurological mechanism in which certain patterns of targeted practice build skill."[92] This "code" involves *myelin*, a neural insulator that wraps nerve fibers and makes signals stronger and faster. Coyle describes the process of building myelin:

> When we fire our circuits in the right way—we practice swinging that bat or playing that note—our myelin responds by wrapping layers of insulation around that neural circuit, each new layer adding a bit more skill and speed. The thicker the myelin gets, the better it insulates, and the faster and more accurate our movements become.[93]

Those who practice well have "cracked the talent code."[94]

Coyle goes as far as to offer a new definition of skill: "*Skill is a cellular insulation that wraps neural circuits and that grows in response to certain signals.*"[95] Good practicers develop their neural circuitry—effectively changing the brain—by growing more myelin. Growing myelin at an early age through a process of rigorous training probably accounts for Rachmaninoff's description of "a kind of musical capital." A detailed discussion of myelin is beyond the scope of this book, but Coyle's book is the one to read if you want to dive deeper. It should be obvious that *practice must target the right patterns*. Myelin doesn't know what nerve impulses it's strengthening—it can just as well strengthen poor technique and confused thought processes as good ones.

Neurologists' awareness of myelin is recent, although great musicians have always worked in a way that took advantage of what myelin could do. In 1988, John Briggs described the work of Marian Diamond, a neuroanatomist at the University of California Berkeley, who examined Einstein's brain in 1985, thirty years after Einstein's death. Einstein had more glial cells in his brain than other brains that were examined.[96] No conclusive inferences were drawn, however, and researchers puzzled over whether these extra glial cells were developed by Einstein or if they were present at birth. As recently as 1998, Guy Claxton described the purpose of glial cells—which are necessary for myelin to grow—as being "responsible for housekeeping: they mop up chemical waste."[97] No one knew how important these cells were.

We now know that glial cells "produce and support myelin."[98] One can't help wonder whether Einstein's famous thought experiments were responsible for building myelin and the cells necessary for its support. The production of myelin has significant ramifications for procedures like visualization, which we'll explore in the next chapter.

Notes

1. Coyle, *The Talent Code*, 78.
2. The earliest description I've seen of something that could be viewed as "chunking" for studying a piece of music comes from lutist Jean Baptiste Besard's "Necessarie Observations Belonging to the Lute and Lute Playing," which were included in Robert Dowland's 1610 *Varietie of Lute Lessons*. Besard advises students to choose a piece appropriate their level and then to "examine each part of it diligently, and stay upon any one point so long (though thou play it over a thousand times) till thou get it in some sort. The like you shall do in all parts of the said Song, till you shall find yourself prettily seen in it." (Robert Dowland, *Varietie of Lute Lessons* (London: Schott, 1958), 6.) Besard's "Necessarie Observations" were a translation from Latin of material that was first published in his *Thesaurus Harmonicus* in 1603. "Prettily" would have been understood as meaning "skillful" or "artful" to an early seventeenth-century reader.
3. Coyle, *The Talent Code*, 76.
4. Ibid., 76–77.
5. Ibid., 77.
6. Ross C. Teague, Stuart S. Gittelman, and Ok-choon Park, "A Review of the Literature on Part-Task and Whole-Task Training and Context Dependency," *United States Army Research Institute for the Behavioral Sciences*, Technical Report 1010 (October 1994): 2.
7. Ibid.
8. J. C. Naylor and G. E. Briggs, "Effects of Task Complexity and Task Organization on the Relative Efficiency of Part and Whole Training Methods," *Journal of Experimental Psychology* Vol. 65 (1963): 217–224.
9. Teague, "A Review of the Literature on Part-Task and Whole-Task Training and Context Dependency," i.
10. G. A. Miller, "The Magical Number Seven, Plus or Minus Two: Some Limits on Our Capacity for Processing Information," *Psychological Review* Vol. 63 (1956): 81–97.
11. Colvin, *Talent Is Overrated*, 99.
12. Reder and Liu, "Building Knowledge Requires Bricks," 5–7.
13. Austin, "A Computational Theory," 349.
14. Syed, *Bounce*, 36.
15. Alan Walker, *Franz Liszt: The Virtuoso Years, 1811–1847*, Vol. 1 (New York: Cornell University Press, 1987), 297.
16. Colvin, *Talent Is Overrrated*, 54.
17. Ibid.
18. Amy Fay, *Music-Study in Germany* (Chicago: A. C. McClurg, 1886), 216.
19. Colvin, *Talent Is Overrated*, 87.
20. Syed, *Bounce*, 31.
21. Ibid.

22. Ibid.
23. K. M. Newell, "Motor Skill Acquisition." *Annual Review of Psychology* Vol. 42 (1991): 216, 219.
24. Robert D. Rafal, Albrecht W. Inhoff, Joseph H. Friedman, and Emily Bernstein, "Programming and Execution of Sequential Movements in Parkinson's Disease," *Journal of Neurology, Neurosurgery, and Psychiatry* Vol. 50 (1987): 1267. [Italics added].
25. Austin, "A Computational Theory," 104.
26. Rafal, et al. "Programming and Execution of Sequential Movements," 1268.
27. Kochevitsky, *The Art of Piano Playing*, 45.
28. Ibid.
29. Richard Schmidt, "A Schema Theory of Discrete Motor Skill Learning," *Psychological Review* Vol. 82, No. 4 (July 1975): 231.
30. Aditya Jain, Ramta Bansall, Avnish Kumar, and K. D. Singh. "A Comparative Study of Visual and Auditory Reaction Times on the Basis of Gender and Physical Activity Levels of Medical 1st Year Students." *International Journal of Applied and Basic Medical Research* Vol. 5, No. 2 (2015): 125.
31. Schmidt, "A Schema Theory," 231.
32. Schonbrun, *The Performance Cortex*, 112.
33. Dionisio Aguado, *New Guitar Method*, ed. Brian Jeffry, trans. Louise Bigwood (London: Tecla Editions, 1981), 126. [Italics added].
34. Ericsson, "The Role of Deliberate Practice," 397.
35. Schonbrun, *The Performance Cortex*, 206.
36. Ibid., 210.
37. Ibid., 68.
38. There are, of course, many ways this passage could be fingered on the guitar, and some of them need no shifting at all. My choice of articulation imposes some constraints on where the passage can be played. For the sake of the example, the only thing that matters is to show a shift in a scale passage that's played at a rapid tempo. Bach's chaconne happened to be something I was practicing while writing this book.
39. Galamian, *Principles of Violin: Playing & Teaching*, 95.
40. Ericsson, "The Role of Deliberate Practice," 383.
41. Syed, *Bounce*, 191.
42. Ibid., 198.
43. L. L. Jacoby, R. A. Bjork, & C. M. Kelley, "Illusions of Comprehension, Competence, and Remembering," in *Learning, Remembering, Believing: Enhancing Human Performance*, ed. D. Druckman and R. A. Bjork (Washington, DC: National Academy Press, 1994), 57–80.
44. Leonard, *Mastery*, 10.
45. Coyle, *The Talent Code*, 84.
46. Ibid.
47. Thistleton, *The Art of Violin Playing*, 144–145.
48. Ibid., 26.
49. Joseph Joachim (1831–1907) was the reigning violinist of the nineteenth century. A letter from him to Courvoisier appears as the preface of the book, but Joachim didn't have a hand in writing the book.
50. Carl Courvoisier, *The Technics of Violin Playing on Joachim's Method* (London: The Strad, 1894), 2.
51. Not only are the techniques for the two hands complicated and different from one another, the guitar and other fretted, plucked strings, such as lute and vihuela, are the only instruments capable of complex textures (polyphony, melody with accompaniment, for example) that have a *different* technique for each hand.
52. Cooke, *Great Pianists on Piano Playing*, 209–210.
53. Flesch, *The Art of Violin Playing, Book One*, 106–107.
54. Ibid., 104.

55. Benjamin Cutter, *How to Study Kreutzer: A Handbook for the Daily Use of Violin Teachers and Violin Students, Containing Explanations of the Left Hand Difficulties and of Their Solution, and Directions as to the Systematic Acquirement of the Various Bowings, Both Firm and Bounding* (Boston: O. Ditson Co., 1903), 15. [Italics added].
56. Ibid.
57. Ibid.
58. Rivarde, *The Violin and Its Technique*, 24.
59. Compare Rivarde's comment to what Moshe Feldenkrais wrote in 1972: "Action must improve a living and developing body at least to the extent that the same action will be carried out more effectively the next time," (quoted in Berg, *Mastering Guitar Technique*, 21).
60. Rivarde, *The Violin and Its Technique*, 40.
61. Colvin, *Talent Is Overrated*, 83.
62. Ibid.
63. Ibid.
64. Coyle, *The Talent Code*, 36–37.
65. Hambourg, *How to Play the Piano* (New York: George H. Doran Company), 25.
66. Ibid.
67. Lhévinne, *Basic Principles in Pianoforte Playing*, 9.
68. Ibid., 10.
69. Sydney Robjohns, *Violin Technique: Some Difficulties and Their Solution* (London: Oxford University Press and H. Milford, 1930), 8.
70. Karl Leimer and Walter Gieseking, *Piano Technique Consisting of the Two Complete Books the Shortest Way to Pianistic Perfection and Rhythmics, Dynamics, Pedal and Other Problems of Piano Playing* (New York: Dover Publications, 1972), 26.
71. Flesch, *The Art of Violin Playing, Book One*, 105.
72. Ibid.
73. Cortot and Le Roy, *Rational Principles of Pianoforte Technique*, 2.
74. Seymour Bernstein, *With Your Own Two Hands: Self Discovery Through Music* (New York: G. Shirmer, 1981), 104.
75. Galamian, *Principles of Violin: Playing & Teaching*, 95.
76. Ibid., 99.
77. Kochevitsky, *The Art of Piano Playing*, 7.
78. Neil L. Goodchild, "Liszt's *Technical Studies*: A Methodology for the Attainment of Technical Virtuosity." Goodchild is a professor at the University of New South Wales. This paper is undated and doesn't appear to be published.
79. Liszt gave a manuscript of his exercises to his student, Valerie Bossier, in 1831–1832, and they have been published several times. When the exercises appeared, they comprised twelve volumes.
80. Hilda Gervers, "Franz Liszt as Pedagogue," *Journal of Research in Music Education* Vol. 18, No. 4 (Winter 1970): 390.
81. Stembridge-Montavont, "Variations on a Theme of Chopin," 34.
82. Franz Liszt, *Technical Exercises for the Piano*, ed. Julio Esteban (Van Nuys, CA: Alfred Publishing Co., 1971), 5.
83. Franz Liszt, *Études Techniques Pour Le Piano, Books I–XII*, ed. A. Winterberger. Vol. I of XII (Leipzig: J. Schuberth & Co., 1887).
84. Liszt, *Technical Exercises*, 5.
85. Ibid. [Italics added].
86. Walker, *Franz Liszt: The Virtuoso Years, 1811–1847*, 311. This diagram is also given in Gervers, "Franz Liszt as Pedagogue," where it is presented as a plan for practicing technique. It originates in Madame Auguste Bossier, *Liszt Pédagogue* (Paris, 1832).
87. R. M. Breithaupf, *Natural Piano Technique*, Vol. 2 (Leipzig: C. F. Kahnt Nachfolger, 1909), 18.
88. Quoted in von Arx, *Piano Lessons with Claudio Arrau*, 7.

89. Ibid.
90. Cortot, *Rational Principles of Pianoforte Technique*, 89. This exercise could be practiced as written by guitarists to great advantage. The key is not to let the repeated ***p*** notes overwhelm the longer ***f*** notes.
91. Reder and Liu, "Building Knowledge Requires Bricks," 2.
92. Coyle, *The Talent Code*, 5.
93. Ibid.
94. Ibid.
95. Ibid., 6.
96. Briggs, *Fire in the Crucible*, 140.
97. Claxton, *Hare Brain, Tortoise Mind*, 134.
98. Coyle, *The Talent Code*, 73.

Sources

Aguado, Dionisio. *New Guitar Method*. Edited by Brian Jeffry. Translated by Louise Bigwood. London: Tecla Editions, 1981.

Arx, Victoria A. von. *Piano Lessons with Claudio Arrau: A Guide to His Philosophy and Techniques*. New York: Oxford University Press, 2014.

Austin, Howard. "A Computational Theory of Physical Skill." PhD diss., Massachusetts Institute of Technology, 1976.

Berg, Christopher. *Mastering Guitar Technique: Process & Essence*. Pacific, MO: Mel Bay Publications, 1997.

Bernstein, Seymour. *With Your Own Two Hands: Self Discovery through Music*. New York: G. Shirmer, 1981.

Breithaupf, R. M. *Natural Piano Technique*. Leipzig: C. F. Kahnt Nachfolger, 1909.

Briggs, John. *Fire in the Crucible: The Alchemy of Creative Genius*. New York: St. Martin's Press, 1988.

Claxton, Guy. *Hare Brain, Tortoise Mind: How Intelligence Increases When You Think Less*. New York: Harper Perennial, 1998.

Colvin, Geoffrey. *Talent Is Overrated: What Really Separates World-Class Performers from Everybody Else*. New York: Portfolio Trade, 2010.

Cooke, James Francis. *Great Pianists on Piano Playing*. Philadelphia: Theodore Presser Co., 1913.

Cortot, Alfred, and Métaxas Le Roy. *Rational Principles of Pianoforte Technique*. Paris: M. Senart; Boston: Oliver Ditson Company, 1930.

Courvoisier, Karl. *The Technics of Violin Playing*. London: The Strad, 1894.

Coyle, Daniel. *The Talent Code: Greatness Isn't Born: It's Grown: Here's How*. New York: Bantam, 2009.

Cutter, Benjamin. *How to Study Kreutzer: A Handbook for the Daily Use of Violin Teachers and Violin Students, Containing Explanations of the Left Hand Difficulties and of Their Solution, and Directions as to the Systematic Acquirement of the Various Bowings, Both Firm and Bounding*. Boston: O. Ditson Co., 1903.

Dowland, Robert. *Varietie of Lute Lessons*. A Lithographic Facsimile of the Original Edition of 1610. London: Schott, 1958.

Ericsson, K. A., R. T. Krampe, and C. Tesch-Römer. "The Role of Deliberate Practice in the Acquisition of Expert Performance." *Psychological Review* (1993): 363–406.

Fay, Amy, and Fay Peirce. *Music-Study in Germany, from the Home Correspondence of Amy Fay*. Chicago: A. C. McClurg, 1886.

Flesch, Carl. *The Art of Violin Playing, Book One.* New York: Carl Fischer, Inc., 1924.

Galamian, Ivan. *Principles of Violin: Playing & Teaching.* Englewood Cliffs, NJ: Prentice-Hall, 1962.

Gervers, Hilda. "Franz Liszt as Pedagogue." *Journal of Research in Music Education* Vol. 18, No. 4 (1970): 385–391.

Goodchild, Neil L. "Liszt's Technical Studies: A Methodology for the Attainment of Technical Virtuosity." Unpublished.

Groot, Adrianus Dingeman de. *Thought and Choice in Chess.* The Hague: Mouton, 1965.

Hambourg, Mark. *How to Play the Piano.* New York: George H. Doran Company, 1922.

Jacoby, L. L., R. A. Bjork, and C. M. Kelley. "Illusions of Comprehension, Competence, and Remembering." In *Learning, Remembering, Believing: Enhancing Human Performance*, edited by D. Druckman and R. A. Bjork, 57–80. Washington, DC: National Academy Press, 1994.

Jain, Aditya, Ramta Bansall, Avnish Kumar, and K. D. Singh. "A Comparative Study of Visual and Auditory Reaction Times on the Basis of Gender and Physical Activity Levels of Medical 1st Year Students." *International Journal of Applied and Basic Medical Research* Vol. 5, No. 2 (2015): 124–127.

Kochevitsky, George. *The Art of Piano Playing: A Scientific Approach.* Princeton, NJ: Summy-Birchard, 1967.

Leimer, Karl, and Walter Gieseking. *Piano Technique Consisting of the Two Complete Books the Shortest Way to Pianistic Perfection and Rhythmics, Dynamics, Pedal and Other Problems of Piano Playing.* New York: Dover Publications, 1972.

Leonard, George. *Mastery: The Keys to Success and Long-Term Fulfillment.* New York: Plume, 1992.

Lhévinne, Josef. *Basic Principles in Pianoforte Playing.* Philadelphia: Theo. Presser Company, 1924.

Liszt, Franz. *Études Techniques Pour Le Piano.* Edited by A. Winterberger. 12 bks. Leipzig: J. Schuberth & Co., 1887.

Liszt, Franz. *Technical Exercises for the Piano.* Edited by Julio Esteban. Van Nuys, CA: Alfred Publishing Co., 1971.

Miller, G. A. "The Magical Number Seven, Plus or Minus Two: Some Limits on Our Capacity for Processing Information." *Psychological Review* Vol. 63 (1956): 81–97.

Naylor, J. C., and G. E. Briggs. "Effects of Task Complexity and Task Organization on the Relative Efficiency of Part and Whole Training Methods." *Journal of Experimental Psychology* Vol. 65 (1963): 217–224.

Newell, K. M. "Motor Skill Acquisition." *Annual Review of Psychology* Vol. 42 (1991): 213–237.

Rafal, Robert D., Albrecht W. Inhoff, Joseph H. Friedman, and Emily Bernstein. "Programming and Execution of Sequential Movements in Parkinson's Disease." *Journal of Neurology, Neurosurgery, and Psychiatry* Vol. 50 (1987): 1267–1273.

Reder, Lynne M., Xiaonan L. Liu, Alexander Keinath, and Vencislav Popov. "Building Knowledge Requires Bricks, Not Sand: The Critical Role of Familiar Constituents in Learning." *Psychonomic Bulletin & Review* (2015): 1–7.

Rivarde, A. *The Violin and Its Technique as a Means to the Interpretation of Music.* London: Macmillan, 1921.

Robjohns, Sydney. *Violin Technique: Some Difficulties and Their Solution.* London: Oxford University Press and H. Milford, 1930.

Schmidt, Richard. "A Schema Theory of Discrete Motor Skill Learning." *Psychological Review* Vol. 82, No. 2 (1975): 225–260.

Schonbrun, Zach. *The Performance Cortex: How Neuroscience is Redefining Athletic Genius.* New York: Dutton, 2018.

Stembridge-Montavont, Michael. "Variations on a Theme of Chopin." *Piano* (September/October 2004): 34–45.

Syed, Matthew. *Bounce: Mozart, Federer, Picasso, Beckham, and the Science of Success.* New York: Harper Perennial, 2011.

Teague, Ross C., Stuart S. Gittleman, and Ok-choon Park. "A Review of the Literature on Part-Task and Whole-Task Training and Context Dependency." *United States Army Research Institute for the Behavioral Sciences* Technical Report 1010 (October 1994): 1–33.

Thistleton, Frank. *The Art of Violin Playing for Players and Teachers.* London: The Strad, 1924.

Walker, Alan. *Franz Liszt: The Virtuoso Years, 1811–1847.* Vol. 1. Ithaca, NY: Cornell University Press, 1988.

4

MENTAL WORK

Study methods *away* from the instrument that were used by some of the great pianists and violinists of the past—specifically mental work and the use of recall—anticipate and confirm current research about learning and memory. Research by sports psychologists has established that visualizing a physical act can have a beneficial impact on performance. Zach Schonbrun writes that "cognitive processes seem to share, to some degree, representations, neural structures and mechanisms with the *seeing* and *doing* aspects of the motor system."[1] Many great musicians of the past intimated that they knew this empirically and practiced it.

Saved From Unprofitable Blundering

Not all great musicians wrote about their process of learning, but those who did credited mental work as an essential ingredient of their success. In Frederick G. Shinn's *Musical Memory and its Cultivation* from 1898, we learn:

> Quite distinct from the method of rehearsing a piece at the piano is the method of mentally rehearsing it, that is, of thinking it carefully through away from the instrument. To do this successfully requires not merely a greater degree of concentration but a reliance on forms of memory other than Muscular memory, which, when rehearsing at the instrument we may unconsciously rely upon to an extent that is unsafe unless other forms are able to rigorously control it. Passages which resemble one another as wholes but differ in details . . . are only absolutely secure if they can be accurately rehearsed away from the instrument.[2]

Shinn quotes the great pianist and conductor Hans von Bülow (1830–1894):

> I once played a piece in public for the first time, which I learned from the notes. This seems impossible, yet for once it is true. A friend of mine had put down a piece of his own in my next concert, and I had not the time even to play it through. I therefore took the copy with me in the train, studied it in the carriage, and played it in the evening.[3]

Bülow's phrase "learned from the notes" means "learned from the score."[4]

In *Great Pianists on Piano Playing* (1913), a book containing conversations with the foremost virtuosi of the time, Franz Xaver Scharwenka (1850–1924) states, "*Before you place your fingers on the keyboard* you should have formed your ideal mental conception of the proper rhythm, the proper tonal quality, the aesthetic values and the harmonic content."[5]

Ernest Schelling (1876–1939) agrees:

> In studying a new musical composition experience has revealed to me that the student can save much time and get a better general idea of the composition by reading it over several times before going to the instrument. While this is difficult for very young pupils to do before they have become accustomed to mentally interpreting the notes into sounds without the assistance of the instrument, it is, nevertheless, of advantage from the very start. *It saves the pupil from much unprofitable blundering.*[6]

Olga Samaroff (1880–1948) says:

> Successful concentration is a mental process *attained only after much intellectual effort.* There is unfortunately a tendency among certain American students to look upon anything intellectual connected with music with more or less contempt. They do not hesitate to criticize certain great artists in such a way that one readily discovers that the students make "intellect" synonymous with inferiority. One realizes how absurd this is when one remembers that all higher musical work is based upon a development of the individual's intellectuality.[7]

Samaroff seems to have recognized that peculiar strain of American anti-intellectualism that we saw in chapter 1. She is adamant that it not infiltrate music study:

> The precious divine spark, which the artist must keep flaring on his high altar, is not to be dimmed by higher mental culture. But the emotional content of the artist's interpretation will not be lessened because he uses his brain every second during his study hours. It is true that we often hear music performed with a kind of technical coldness which many ascribe to

a superior intellectual attitude, the divine spark quite extinct. We can but say that the warmth of emotion, the fervor of interpretative genius, never existed in the soul of the performer. If it had, no amount of so-called "intellectual effort" would have done away with it.[8]

Samaroff wasn't a haughty Russian émigré looking down upon Americans; she was born Lucy Hickenlooper in San Antonio. She was the second pianist in history to perform all thirty-two Beethoven piano sonatas in public—after Bülow—and joined the faculty of the Julliard School in 1924. Samaroff continues by noting that a disdain for the intellect has misled students into thinking that musical success is possible without mental effort. She maintains that those who are capable of the highest level of artistic expression are not lacking in intellect and have reached one of the highest levels of intellectual achievement.[9]

Violinist Theodore Spierling (1871–1925) was concertmaster of the New York Philharmonic under Gustav Mahler (1860–1911) from 1909 to 1911 and conducted the orchestra for the last eleven concerts of the 1910–1911 season during Mahler's final illness. Spierling later was a member of the Chicago Symphony and Director of the Chicago Musical College, now part of Roosevelt University. Spierling made a direct link between mental work and technique: "*Mental preparedness* (Marcus Aurelius calls it 'the good ordering of the mind') is the keynote of technical control."[10]

Violinist Frank Thistleton writes in 1913: "Difficulties, with few exceptions, are mental."[11] He stresses the importance of understanding the smallest details: "The fingers cannot execute that which the brain does not thoroughly comprehend."[12] Thistleton is aware that mental work alone is not all that is required; one must constantly reinforce the association of the mental with the physical.[13]

Mark Hambourg says simply, "I do my best practice away from the keyboard. That is, I work out the musical problems and get them straight in my mind so that no time is lost in fumbling over keys."[14]

Pianist Arthur Shattuck (1881–1951), a pupil of Theodor Leschetizky, said,

> Study your music away from the piano; it is amazing how quickly you get at the form and shape; you can hear it mentally, undistracted by physical contact with keys. Form a decided idea of passage or piece, though it may vary from time to time.[15]

Based on comments by Leschetizky's students and his amanuensis, Malwine Brée, mental work was an important part of Leschetizky's teaching and certainly contributed to his success. Harriette Moore Brower summarizes his approach. Note the use of chunking:

> It is a well-known fact that Leschetizky advises memorizing away from the instrument. This method at once shuts the door on all useless and thoughtless repetition employed by so many piano students, who repeat

a passage endlessly, to avoid thinking it out. Then they wonder why they cannot commit to memory! The Viennese master suggests that a short passage of two or four measures be learned with each hand alone, then tried on the piano. If not yet quite fixed in consciousness the effort should be repeated, after which it may be possible to go through the passage without an error. The work then proceeds in the same manner throughout the composition.[16]

As noted in chapter 1, the way Leschetizky taught students to learn a piece was the only aspect of his teaching that he considered "a method."

Josef Hofmann (1876–1957), one of the giants of early twentieth-century piano playing, was clear about the role of the mind in developing secure memory. He writes in *Piano Playing with Piano Questions Answered* from 1920 (originally published in 1907):

> If you wish to strengthen the receptivity and retentiveness of your memory you will find the following plan practical: Start with a short piece. Analyse the form and manner of its texture. Play the piece a number of times very exactly with the music before you. Then stop playing for several hours and try to trace the course of ideas mentally in the piece. *Try to hear the piece inwardly.* [Italics added.] If you have retained some parts, refill the missing places by repeated reading of the piece, away from the piano . . . . If you still fail, resume your silent reading of the piece *away from the piano.* [Hofmann's italics.] Under no circumstances skip the unsafe place for the time being, and proceed with the rest of the piece.[17]

Hofmann presents a rough outline of his preferred approach to memorization after one can accurately sight-read a piece. Note his use of spaced practice by letting the piece rest for a day:

> Now let the piece rest for a whole day and try to *trace in your mind* the train of thoughts in the piece. Should you come to a dead stop be satisfied with what you have achieved. Your mind will keep on working, subconsciously, as over a puzzle, always trying to find the continuation. If you find that the memory is a blank, take the music in hand, look at the particular place—but only at this—and, since you have now found the connection, continue the work of *mental tracing.* At the next stop repeat this procedure until you have reached the end, not in every detail, but in large outlines. Of course, this does not mean that you can now play it from memory. You have only arrived at the point of transition from the imagined to the real, and now begins a new kind of study: to transfer to the instrument what you have mentally absorbed.[18]

Andor Földes recommends that before a student plays a new work, he should read it away from the instrument: "By doing so he will be able to get a clear mental picture of the music he is about to study without being distracted by the physical aspects of its playing."[19] Földes thought that this reading away from the instrument could stimulate the imagination.[20]

Jorge Bolet (1914–1990), who studied with Leopold Godowsky, Hofmann, and Moriz Rosenthal, said, "[W]hen it comes to memorizing the music, I do perhaps ninety-five to ninety-eight percent of it away from the piano. I look at the score, study it, go through it in my mind, and piece it all together."[21] Bolet credits mental work with his ability to solve musical and technical problems:

> I never solved a major mechanical or interpretive problem at the keyboard, only away from it. Even when I sometimes become so completely baffled that I am utterly stuck for a direction in which to go, I return to the music and piece it out. I don't know about others but I do know that I have never solved a major mechanical or interpretive problem at the keyboard. I have always solved it in my mind.[22]

Violinist Sydney Robjohns suggests testing one's memory by "simply thinking the music through note by note without playing it at all on the instrument."[23]

Karl Leimer and Visualization

Theodor Leschetizky may have been the first to use the word "visualize" for mental work. Annette Hullah, one of Leschetizky's assistants, described in 1906 what Leschetizky required of a student:

> [H]e shall study every piece of music so thoroughly that he knows every detail in it, can play any part of it accurately, beginning at any point, and that he can *visualise* the whole without the music—that is, see in his mind what is written, without either notes or instrument.[24]

But Karl Leimer wrote about mental work more than anyone who preceded him. He presents a procedure for visualization in 1932:

> By this method of visualization, this careful thinking through of the piece of music in question, the pupil will be capable of writing down the whole exercise from memory. After intense concentration, most of my pupils have been, to their great astonishment, able *in a few minutes* of time to play the entire exercise *from memory*. Visualized reading at the same time affords the pupil the best insight into the form of the composition under study.[25]

Leimer's work anticipated that of sports psychologists, as we'll see later. Leimer writes that by practicing visualization, one can acquire the ability to prepare the piece from a technical standpoint,

> without studying at the instrument itself . . . The piece can be perfectly performed and this in a most astonishingly short time. By many this is thought to be impossible, but in fact it has been done not only by Gieseking but also by other pupils of this method.[26]

Leimer makes clear that success is dependent upon a strong foundation in theory and the development of prior skill. It is nothing like Bonpensiere's Ideo-Kinetic approach.

Leimer writes that

> In order to acquire a perfect technique through brain work, an exact impression of the note picture upon the mind is the first problem which we must solve. Thereafter we should busy ourselves with the study in question, as to fingering, touch, note value, etc., to achieve perfection along these lines in the broadest sense. This occurs quickest and completely through intensive concentration of all intellectual powers and is, therefore, *strenuous brain work.*[27]

This strenuous brain work enhances learning through the continuous reconstruction of the skill or memory.

Leimer, like many others, condemns the practice of playing through a piece or a difficult section many times with little concentration. Even if a student does get the piece "in the fingers," most will never achieve the results they hope for. They work this way because "it is more convenient than the intensive mental way of studying, and therefore preferred."[28]

Leimer says that interpretation should be studied "only after the technical work is well advanced."[29] He avoids the danger of the interpretation being affected by monotonous drill because the *student has learned the piece quickly.* This explains the almost doctrinal divide between those who think interpretation should be incorporated into the study of a work at the outset and those who prefer to gain a sense of the whole before fashioning an interpretation. The former are afraid of the piece growing stale; the latter spend less time learning the piece, and their ears are still fresh by the time the piece is learned and memorized.

Echoing Leopold Auer's complaint that his student couldn't interpret the piece because he was "too much absorbed in the actual playing of the notes," Leimer writes:

> I think it harmful to pay attention to the interpretation of a piece while it is being studied, as the pupil is at first too much taken up with technical

problems. If the interpretation is incorrect, a false impression is made upon the ear of the pupil, and the tiring business of correcting mistakes has to begin all over again. The pupil should first study a small part thoroughly, and then he should go on a bit farther (it is not necessary to play to the end of a phrase) and practice this in exactly the same manner. Three or four short parts may be now practiced together.[30]

Note Leimer's use of chunking and then the act of combining the smaller parts. As with any technique, visualization becomes easier and better with practice, which Leimer also acknowledges.

Myelin . . . Again

The mental recall required for visualization supports the production of myelin. As more is created, the easier visualization becomes. It's the difficulty of it that makes for more secure learning, which in turn makes learning easier because we've changed the brain.[31]

The number of musicians in the past who wrote about mental work is stunning. The higher-level practices that these artists have in common are the importance of understanding the components of a piece before diving in, the importance of mental work *away from the instrument*, the intellectual effort involved, and how these allow the subconscious mind to work as it assimilates the piece in a secure manner.

Let the Future In

The authors of *Make It Stick* set out to disprove many widely accepted teaching and study practices that they maintain are not effective, although these practices may seem intuitively correct. Chief among these is massed repetition, whether rereading and obsessively highlighting texts in an academic class or sight-reading a piece over and over on the assumption that the material will etch itself into memory. We've seen how massed repetition can slow one's technical progress and dull one's ear, but it's especially unproductive and harmful when it comes to developing memory. It is time-consuming; it feels like progress but doesn't result in reliable retention, and it gives the illusion of mastery.

Make It Stick opens with a dozen or so claims the authors maintain are backed up by recent neurological and psychological research. All of their claims have relevance to high-level music study, but there are six that have direct relevance to developing secure memorization: Learning is stronger and longer-lasting when it requires effort; we cannot reliably assess whether we're learning well or not, especially in initial work; massed practice is often the default strategy for all sorts of learners, but it has been shown to be unfruitful when it comes to developing mastery; retrieving material from memory is more effective in developing memory than is reading through material repeatedly; the idea that one learns better by having material presented in one's preferred learning style is unsupported by research; and all new learning requires a foundation of prior knowledge.[32]

We tend to be poor judges of our progress, in part because of what is known as the Dunning-Kruger Effect. As David Dunning and his coauthors state,

> People fail to recognize their own incompetence because that incompetence carries with it a double curse. In many intellectual and social domains, the skills needed to produce correct responses are virtually identical to those needed to evaluate the accuracy of one's responses.[33]

David Dunning told Errol Morris in *The New York Times'* Opinionator Blog, "The road to self-insight really runs through other people. So it really depends on what sort of feedback you are getting."[34] Giving valuable feedback is one of the important responsibilities of a teacher; it reflects back to the student the truth of where that student is, and it serves as a model for the student's self-criticism.

Retrieval practice is akin to Shinn's "mentally rehearsing," Scharwenka's "ideal mental conception," von Bülow's "learned from the notes," Schelling's "reading it over several times before going to the instrument," Hambourg's "practice away from the keyboard," Hofmann's "mental tracing," and Leimer's "visualization." Retrieval practice changes the brain and expands our capabilities. Recall is far more effective than mere repetition when trying to develop long-term memory. Effective here means that learning can eventually be quicker, more durable, and more secure, which will engender a higher level of artistic freedom in performance and may allow one to embrace Artur Schnabel's (1882–1951) famous dictum, "Safety Last!"[35] Schnabel's advice, offered to his advanced pupils, stands as a testament to his goal of giving himself over with passion and freedom to the full artistic potential of a piece.[36]

Massed practice is to assiduously repeat the same thing over and over. The problem with repetition, as seen in the oft-proffered advice to read a piece over and over until it's memorized, is that students become *familiar* with the material yet mistake this for having become *fluent* with the material.[37] Familiarity can create the illusion of mastery, which may not reveal itself as an illusion until the pressure of performance is brought to bear.

The authors of *Make It Stick* not only *did not* find empirical evidence that one learns better having received instruction in one's preferred learning style, they found that the concept of learning styles caused students' perceptions of their abilities to contract rather than expand.[38] It turns out that having developed critical-thinking skills, whatever way information and experiences come to you is more important than staying within your perceived learning style:

> Each of us has a large basket of resources in the form of aptitudes, prior knowledge, intelligence, interests, and sense of personal empowerment

that shape how we learn and how we overcome our shortcomings. Some of these differences matter a lot—for example, our ability to abstract underlying principles from new experiences and to convert new knowledge into mental structures. Other differences we may think count for a lot, for example having a verbal or visual learning style, actually don't.[39]

Annette Hullah reports that Leschetizky would consciously force students to learn in opposition to what would later be known as a preferred learning style. In one case, he made a student who relied heavily on her ear learn unfamiliar music by studying the score away from the keyboard. In another case, he played a piece bar by bar for a student whose ear was undeveloped, requiring the student to learn the music by ear alone.[40]

We saw in chapter 3 that experts can rapidly chunk or group together bits of new material because they can relate the new material to a foundation of prior knowledge. The authors of *Make It Stick* are under the impression that musicians have this all figured out, but it's easy to come to an incorrect conclusion looking at a discipline outside one's own. They write, "Concert soloists are skilled memorizers. Any musician will recognize that chunking occurs—that notes can be organized into familiar patterns such as scales, arpeggios, and harmonic progressions."[41] (But see what the authors of *Practicing Perfection: Memory and Piano Performance* have to say about the *teaching* of memorization later in this chapter.) Consequently, they're able to retain more while learning and do so quickly; for beginners, every piece of information is perceived as discrete and separate. The foundation of prior knowledge that every musician needs to become a more effective learner comprises basic musical structures: scales, harmony, cadences.[42] To paraphrase novelist Graham Greene, "There is always a moment when a door opens and lets the future in."[43] Learning to study better is that moment.

Daylight Upon the Magic

Had the authors of *Make It Stick* expanded their study to include the learning of physical and technical skills, they might have discovered that mental work not only changes the brain, *but it affects physical functioning as well*. This process is largely opaque, even to articulate, high-level concert musicians, and is rarely mentioned directly when they discuss their teaching and study practices, although Jorge Bolet and Karl Leimer made explicit connections between mental work and solving technical problems.

Physical skill can be developed to a certain extent through mental work. Mental work is why Bülow could learn a piece on the train and perform it that evening in concert without having played it before.

While doing his research on jugglers, Howard Austin pondered the question of the roles of physical and mental practice in learning a skill. Austin found that "the weight of evidence so far tends to be surprisingly heavy in favor of the mental point of view"[44] and that "learning a new physical skill requires a great deal of purely mental activity."[45] Austin's conclusion that a combination of physical and mental work was best was corroborated by the research of Jack Augustine a decade and a half later.

In his 1990 doctoral dissertation, "Combining Physical and Mental Practice with Muscle Memory Training to Improve a Motor Skill," Jack Augustine looked at fifteen studies that explored the relationship between mental practice and the acquisition of motor skills. The studies occurred between 1943 and 1985, and although the researchers studied athletic skills (basketball free throws, baseball pitching), Augustine's work has ramifications for high-level music study:

- Directed mental practice was almost as effective as physical practice in dart throwing and basketball free-throw shooting.
- Mental practice was *as effective* as physical practice in his study on improving the basketball free throw.
- It was possible for male university students, without previous experience, to learn skills of a gymnastic nature by mentally practicing the skill.
- A study made by the Russians [found] that those athletes who combined twenty-five percent physical practice and seventy-five percent mental practice did better in the Winter Olympics than did athletes using other combinations of physical and mental practice.[46]

All the studies agreed that mental practice was as effective, or almost as effective, as physical practice alone. A combination of mental and physical work is a superior way to learn a skill.

The research of Alvaro Pascual-Leone, Professor of Neurology at Harvard Medical School, has added weight to Augustine's work. Augustine and his sources could only study the *results* of athletic performance with and without visualization. Pascual-Leone could scan musicians' brains using functional Magnetic Resonance Imaging (fMRI). He found that pianists who practiced a piece and those who visualized a piece (without moving their hands) showed the same changes in the same region of the brain.[47]

The goals of a musician's physical movements differ significantly from those of an athlete: A musician's movements are a means to an artistic end, and although an athlete's movements are also a means to an end—winning—it is the quality or speed of movement itself that usually determines this end.[48] Nonetheless, the larger point shouldn't be lost: Those who engage in mental practice in addition to their physical practice improve more rapidly and to a greater extent than those who do no mental work.[49]

Research like Augustine's and that of those he studied has informed the field of sports psychology, which has now grown into an industry. In 2014, *The New York Times* reported that the Canadian team came to the Sochi Winter Olympics with eight sports psychologists.[50]

Mental practice is called "imagery" by sports psychologists and athletes and is an important part of an athlete's training. It is now widely acknowledged that imagery helps train the muscles. Nicole Detling, a faculty member at the University of Utah and sports psychologist with the United States Olympic team, said,

> In images, it's absolutely crucial that you don't fail. You are training those muscles, and if you are training those muscles to fail, that is not really where you want to be. So one of the things I'll do is if they fail in an image, we stop, rewind and we replay again and again and again.[51]

Perhaps an unrecognized and unnamed version of this type of preparation was once the purview of great athletes of the past—did Babe Ruth ever visualize himself connecting with the ball and sending it over the fence?—[52]but it is now out in the open, and daylight has fallen upon the magic.

Musicians who have learned to visualize their repertoire will have also learned to develop and refine their kinesthetic sense away from their instruments. Once fluent, they can explore musical ideas and experiment with phrasing and interpretive nuance. Certainly, Bülow's learning of his friend's piece on the train wouldn't have been lacking in artistic shading. Earlier in this chapter Jorge Bolet made the link between mental work and the solving of interpretive problems explicit. And, finally, successful visualization will ameliorate many problems of performance anxiety or prevent them from developing in the first place.

Don't Waste Fine Feeling on Wrong Notes

Malwine Brée, in *The Groundwork of the Leschetizky Method*, makes the point that *thinking* is essential for study and that learning works best when it moves from brain to fingers rather than fingers to brain.[53] Wassili Safonoff wrote the same thing a few years later: "Play always so that your fingers follow your brain, and not your brain your fingers."[54]

Brée outlines a primarily mental procedure for memorization in narrative fashion, which I have reduced to a list of steps with a little paraphrasing:

1. To acquaint yourself with the piece in hand, read (play) it through only once so as not to grow accustomed to a faulty fingering; then—according to the difficulty of the composition or the mental grasp of the student—take up one measure, two measures, or at most a phrase, at a time, analyze it harmonically, and determine the fingering.
2. Except to play the leading parts louder and the secondary parts softer, *abstain for the present from fine shading and emotion*, until Matter is conquered, else it may happen that you waste your finest feelings on wrong notes.

3. Now read your practice-measure or measures through carefully and repeatedly with the eye, until the notes stand out clearly before your mental vision, and name the notes a few times either aloud or mentally; and then—not before—play the measure or phrase from memory, but no faster than memory can dictate the notes.

4. If you forget a note, do not try to find it by groping with the fingers on the keys, or play on by ear, but try to recover the forgotten note in the mind. Should you fail, then glance at the music.

5. When you can play the phrase faultlessly and without hesitation by heart, proceed further exactly in the manner prescribed. Take up each time the portion just learned before, and also try to play the whole by heart from the beginning. This is "memorizing in the form of addition."

6. Next day, should you have forgotten what you learned, do not feel discouraged, but practice it over again as before. You will re-memorize it rapidly, and after a few days of practice you will have made it yours forever.

7. Now proceed to [filling] and shading; impart animation to the phrases and distribute light and shade. Proceed dynamically and technically (as when memorizing), only step by step, suitably dividing long passages, for instance, and practicing each division separately.

8. One never forgets a piece learned by this method, even when it is not often repeated; and neither memory nor fingers are so apt to fail one at critical moments as in the case of players accustomed to practice unreflectingly with the fingers. This latter class, to be sure, will find brain-study hard at first, and must be satisfied to learn two or three lines daily—not at one sitting, but with long intervals between sessions. More advanced students, too, should interrupt study frequently, to prevent overtiring the brain. During such pauses they may busy themselves with technical exercises already well in hand or leave the piano altogether. One finally arrives at the point of being able to think through a piece much faster than the fingers can follow.[55]

Brée's description of mental work applied to memorization is remarkable. She touches upon many of the things we've seen discussed by researchers: mental and physical chunking, spaced practice, interleaved practice, and retrieval.

Note that playing a piece in one's head comes at the end of this process, unlike the descriptions by von Bülow or Leimer. Brée's instructions are designed for one's first forays into "brain-study," as she calls it, while Bülow and Leimer are describing the cultivated application of this work by advanced pianists.

Tips and Hints for Learning by Heart

Marie von Unschuld, also a pupil of Leschetizky, gives less of a process that can be reduced to steps than general comments about the importance of this work. I've freely extracted and paraphrased the salient points from "Tips and Hints for Learning by Heart" in *The Pianist's Hand*.

1. Do not sit down at the piano to thrash the piece out for yourself bar by bar, but read it in smaller sections.
2. Learn the harmonies, sequence of passages, positions, etc. *without* playing.
3. Afterwards, play at the piano *from memory* what has been studied in this way. Repeat this procedure (steps 1 and 2) for that which has escaped the memory, until you are master of the piece. A piece must be as it were *inscribed* in the head, before one can say one possesses it in the repertoire.[56]

Unschuld stresses how quick this process can be, much like Leimer and Gieseking did thirty years later. Unschuld also emphasizes analysis more than is apparent from Brée's procedure. Unschuld writes, "A knowledge of Harmony of course uncommonly facilitates learning and playing by heart, and one will be able to impress the harmonic successions more lastingly upon himself with much greater ease."[57] We know exactly why this helps: a foundation of prior knowledge—in this case, harmony—enables one to build higher-level mental structures. One is not perceiving isolated notes, like the novice chess players in de Groot's experiment could only see squares and chess pieces, but one is recognizing meaningful harmonic relationships, just as the chess masters could see a strategy embedded in the layout of the pieces on the board.

Learning to Memorize

Josef Hofmann thought "memorization indispensable to the freedom of rendition."[58] Although memorization itself does not occur spontaneously, it is a necessary condition for spontaneity in solo performance. The time to develop the conditions for freedom, security, and spontaneity is when the study of the piece *begins*, not after the piece has been learned. The common "sight-read until ready"[59] approach, condemned by pianist Stephen Hough, inculcates a dependency upon rote learning, which leaves the player vulnerable to anxiety[60] and to developing damaging habits, to say nothing of having to waste time later fixing things that were learned incorrectly.

The authors of *Practicing Perfection: Memory and Piano Performance* interviewed or cited scores of concert pianists, historical, and contemporary, to glean successful approaches to memorizing music. Some credited mental work, like those mentioned earlier, many used a variety of different strategies, and some claimed never to think about it.[61] Only high-level concert pianists were canvased or referenced, and none offered a strategy to help students develop or improve this skill. The authors of *Practicing Perfection: Memory and Piano Performance* open their book by stating:

> Given the difficulty of playing long, complicated programs flawlessly from memory, and the public humiliation that attends memory lapses, it might be expected that the pedagogical traditions in music schools and conservatories would include detailed strategies for addressing the

problems involved. *This proves not to be so.* Conservatory training provides plenty of experience with performance, but memorization is seen as a largely idiosyncratic matter.[62]

The research of the authors of *Practicing Perfection* points more to contemporary musicians' lack of knowledge about how best to develop secure memory than it does to the lack of the existence of information that could be transformed into this knowledge. The only historic sources that appear in the bibliography of *Practicing Perfection* are James Francis Cooke's *Great Pianists on Piano Playing* and *Piano Technique* by Karl Leimer and Walter Gieseking.

Guitarist Christopher Parkening outlines an approach uninformed by the practices of outstanding performers on other instruments:

> To start with, play the piece from the beginning and see how far you can go without looking at the music. When you can go no farther, consult the music. If this refreshes your memory, proceed again without the music; otherwise, play only the section you had forgotten until you have learned it. Now continue without the music again until you can go no farther. Repeat the above procedure until the entire piece is memorized.[63]

Frederick Noad, in *Solo Guitar Playing*, recommends that one cultivate a visual image of the printed score, but that seems more of a byproduct of having played from the score than a useful way to understand the score's content. Noad does recognize, though, that repeated playing from the score is not helpful to developing secure memory.[64]

Many legendary musicians had well-described study and practice strategies to secure their memory of a piece so they could attend unfettered to artistic nuance. Even those who never outlined to others how they learned literature practiced a form of visualization. Paderweski said, "I often lie awake the night before a concert going over in my mind each number of a program, and trying to think how its essence may be more fully expressed."[65]

Rather than engage in massed repetition to memorize a piece, I hope readers will be inspired to formulate ways to make memory more secure for themselves or their students based on material in this chapter. The individual steps of such procedures would certainly have to be tailored to accommodate the characteristics of one's instrument and might vary from piece to piece, but the steps would be informed by solid concepts. Everyone's security and span of concentration can be enhanced by working with a small amount of material, learning it well, and then adding to it. The chunking together of bits of information gradually increases the amount of music one can visualize and memorize until one can mentally perform an entire piece and, later, a concert program.

At its highest level, visualization is a mental performance of an entire work. Like any other performance, individual sections must be mastered before they can coalesce into a meaningful whole. Mental performance means seeing and hearing the piece as though on the instrument without an image of the printed page.[66] A mental performance may not include every detail of fingering, although it might in one's initial forays into this type of work. It is similar to thinking in one's language; the spelling and specific meaning of each word is not thought of although it is well known. Most musicians will also have a kinesthetic sense of what their muscles need to do to produce a sound while visualizing. Visualizing correct movements can help develop physical skill.

Andor Földes speaks to the importance of having developed a foundation of prior knowledge and skill: "We memorize more readily music that we understand. If we try to retain pieces that are above our technical ability or musical understanding, we should not be surprised if we experience difficulties."[67] One can't simply start trying to visualize difficult works for which one is not prepared. If one wants to develop this mental skill, it's best to start with material below one's general technical and artistic level. The practices of an advanced artist are different from the procedure a student must use.

In high-level concert playing, the performer shouldn't be thinking of the mechanical details. One of the ways to get to this point, though, is to have thought about the details early on and to have assimilated them, like Max Pauer's act of "achieving a position *through* conscious effort, where one may *dispense* with conscious effort." Only then will it become possible to forget about the mechanics and to think only of your artistic ideas.

One of the best ways to strengthen and maintain memory and to develop a sense of continuity is to play through your pieces extraordinarily slowly, which we'll see in the next chapter was a practice of Busoni's. (This will be challenging for those who have learned their repertoire by rote.)

Most advocates of slow practice use it as a means of increasing accuracy, and in this it is unparalleled, but slow practice can also give one an inviolable sense of continuity and serves to strengthen memory in those spots that may have relied solely on muscle memory. We will explore slow practice in the next chapter and continuity in chapter 7.

Notes

1. Schonbrun, *The Performance Cortex*, 256.
2. Frederick G. Shinn, "The Memorizing of Piano Music for Performance," *Proceedings of the Musical Association* Vol. 25, No. 1 (1898): 59.
3. Relayed by Constance Bache in ibid., 66.
4. "The notes" in the sense of "the score" was a common idiom. Percy Grainger used the term in the same way. See Brower, *Piano Mastery* (1915), 7. Pianist Amy Fay gives another example in 1873: "[Liszt] always teaches Beethoven with notes, which shows how scrupulous he is about him, for, of course, he knows all the sonatas by heart. He has Bülow's edition, which he opens and lays on the end of the grand piano." See Fay, *Music Study in Germany*, 238.
5. Cooke, *Great Pianists on Piano Playing*, 261. [Italics added].

6. Ibid., 267.
7. Ibid., 334.
8. Ibid., 334–335.
9. Ibid., 335.
10. Frederick Herman Martens, *Violin Mastery; Talks with Master Violinists and Teachers, Comprising Interviews with Ysaÿe, Kreisler, Elman, Auer, Thibaud, Heifetz, Hartmann, Maud Powell and Others* (New York: Frederick A. Stokes Company, 1919), 249.
11. Frank Thistleton, *Modern Violin Technique, How to Acquire It, How to Teach It* (London: Longmans, Green, 1913), 3.
12. Ibid.
13. Ibid.
14. Cooke, *Great Pianists on Piano Playing*, 352.
15. Brower, *Piano Mastery: Second Series* (1917), 58.
16. Brower, *Piano Mastery* (1915), 287–288.
17. Josef Hofmann, *Piano Playing with Piano Questions Answered* (Philadelphia: Theodore Presser Co., 1920), 23–24.
18. Ibid., 114–115. [Italics added].
19. Földes, *Keys to the Keyboard*, 26.
20. Ibid., 31.
21. Elyse Mach, *Great Pianists Speak for Themselves*, Vol. 2 (New York: Dodd Mead, 1988), 29.
22. Ibid.
23. Robjohns, *Violin Technique*, 106.
24. Hullah, *Theodor Leschetizky*, 44. [Italics added].
25. Leimer and Gieseking, *Piano Technique*, 18.
26. Ibid., 11.
27. Ibid., 90. [Italics added].
28. Ibid.
29. Ibid., 33.
30. Ibid., 47–48.
31. Brown, *Make It Stick*, 7.
32. *Ibid.*, 3–5.
33. David Dunning, Kerry Johnson, Joyce Ehrlinger, and Justin Kruger, "Why People Fail to Recognize Their Own Incompetence," *Current Directions in Psychological Science* Vol. 12, No. 3 (2003): 84–85.
34. Errol Morris, "The Anosognosic's Dilemma: Something's Wrong But You'll Never Know What It Is" (Part 5), *Opinionator Blog, The New York Times*, June 24, 2010.
35. Konrad Wolff, *Schnabel's Interpretation of Piano Music* (New York: W. W. Norton & Company, 1979), 24.
36. It should be noted that Schnabel had a first-rate technique and an unusually prodigious memory.
37. Brown, *Make It Stick*, 3.
38. Ibid., 147.
39. Ibid., 141.
40. Hullah, *Theodor Leschetizky*, 58–59.
41. Roger Chaffin, "Chapter Four: Expert Memory," in *Practicing Perfection: Memory and Piano Performance*, ed. Roger Chaffin, Gabriela Imreh, and Mary Crawford (New York: Psychology Press, 2012), 70.
42. It is fine for established artists to talk about getting all the scale and harmony practice they need from their study of literature because they already understand scales and harmony; it is misleading for them to offer that advice to those who have yet to develop a foundation of prior knowledge.
43. Graham Greene, *The Power and the Glory* (London: William Heinemann, LTD, 1940), 6, 7.

44. Austin, "A Computational Theory," 87.
45. Ibid., 344.
46. Jack H. Augustine, "Combining Physical and Mental Practice with Muscle Memory Training to Improve a Motor Skill" (Ed.D. diss. The University of Arkansas, 1990), 68–71.
47. Alvaro Pascual-Leone, "The Brain That Plays Music Is Changed by It," *Annals of the New York Academy of Sciences* Vol. 930 (June 2001): 315–319.
48. I realize there may be disagreement here, and I am discounting things like teamwork and strategy and am assuming the work of an individual athlete who competes against the clock or a standard, which requires consistent-circuit skills.
49. Augustine, "Combining Physical and Mental Practice," 85.
50. Christopher Clary, "Olympians Use Imagery as Mental Training," *The New York Times*, February 23, 2014, SP1.
51. Ibid.
52. One could argue that Ruth's famous "called shot" in Game 3 of the 1932 World Series was a form of visualization.
53. Brée and Baker, *The Groundwork of the Leschetizky Method*, 76.
54. Safonoff, *New Formula for the Piano Teacher and Piano Student*, 28.
55. Brée and Baker, *The Groundwork of the Leschetizky Method*, 76.
56. Unschuld, *The Pianist's Hand*, 63.
57. Ibid., 64.
58. Hofmann, *Piano Playing*, 113.
59. Stephen Hough, "The Practice of Practising," *The Telegraph Blogs*, October 14, 2013.
60. The study of performance anxiety has almost become a separate sub-discipline of music study. Remedies for it almost always come *after* material has been learned and include something like, "Perform as much as possible," as though that would permanently inure one to anxiety's effects. (We'll see an example of this approach given by Ernest Hutchinson in chapter 7.) The best first defense against performance anxiety is to have studied the piece well from the start *and to know you have done so*. Then you can trust your work and focus on the music—not the audience and not yourself—while performing.
61. Chaffin, Imreh, and Crawford, *Practicing Perfection*, 49.
62. Ibid., xii. [Italics added].
63. Parkening, *The Christopher Parkening Guitar Method*, 41.
64. Frederick M. Noad, *Solo Guitar Playing*, 3rd ed. (New York and Toronto: Schirmer Books, 1994), 87.
65. Currier, "Some Characteristics of Paderweski the Pianist," 25.
66. A few of the pianists interviewed in *Practicing Perfection* mentioned that they had photographic memories and saw an image of the printed music; others discounted this approach entirely. Even if a student can visualize the printed page (as recommended by Frederick Noad), this is useful only as an *aide de mémoire* and not as the sole basis for an approach to memorizing.
67. Földes, *Keys to the Keyboard*, 62.

Sources

Augustine, Jack H. "Combining Physical and Mental Practice with Muscle Memory Training to Improve a Motor Skill." Ed.D. diss., Fayetteville, AR: The University of Arkansas, 1990.
Austin, Howard. "A Computational Theory of Physical Skill." PhD diss., Massachusetts Institute of Technology, 1976.
Brée, Malwine, and Theodor Baker. *The Groundwork of the Leschetizky Method*. New York: G. Schirmer, 1902.

Brower, Harriette Moore. *Piano Mastery: Second Series; Talks with Master Pianists and Teachers.* New York: Frederick A. Stokes Company, 1917.

Brower, Harriette Moore. *Piano Mastery: Talks with Master Pianists and Teachers, and an Account of a Von Bülow Class, Hints on Interpretation.* New York: Frederick A. Stokes Company, 1915.

Brown, Peter C., Henry L. Roediger, III, and Mark A. McDaniel. *Make It Stick: The Science of Successful Learning.* Cambridge, MA: Belknap Press, 2014.

Chaffin, Roger, Gabriela Imreh, and Mary Crawford. *Practicing Perfection: Memory and Piano Performance (Expertise: Research and Applications Series).* New York: Psychology Press, 2012.

Clary, Christopher. "Olympians Use Imagery as Mental Training." *The New York Times*, February 23, 2014.

Cooke, James Francis. *Great Pianists on Piano Playing.* Philadelphia: Theodore Presser Co., 1913.

Currier, T. P. "Some Characteristics of Paderewski the Pianist." *Modern Music and Musicians. Vol. 1: The Pianist's Guide*, 24–25. New York: The University Society, 1918:.

Dunning, David, Kerry Johnson, Joyce Ehrlinger, and Justin Kruger. "Why People Fail to Recognize Their Own Incompetence." *Current Directions in Psychological Science* Vol. 12, No. 3 (2003): 83–87.

Fay, Amy, and Fay Peirce. *Music-Study in Germany, from the Home Correspondence of Amy Fay.* Chicago: A. C. McClurg, 1886.

Földes, Andor. *Keys to the Keyboard, a Book for Pianists: With Explanatory Music.* New York: E.P. Dutton, 1948.

Greene, Graham. *The Power and the Glory.* London: William Heinemann, 1940.

Hofmann, Josef, and Harriette Brower. *Piano Playing, with Piano Questions Answered.* Philadelphia: Theodore Presser, 1920.

Hough, Stephen. "The Practice of Practising." *The Telegraph Blogs*, October 14, 2013.

Hullah, Annette. *Theodor Leschetizky.* London and New York: J. Lane Company, 1906.

Leimer, Karl, and Walter Gieseking. *Piano Technique Consisting of the Two Complete Books the Shortest Way to Pianistic Perfection and Rhythmics, Dynamics, Pedal and Other Problems of Piano Playing.* New York: Dover Publications, 1972.

Mach, Elyse. *Great Pianists Speak for Themselves.* New York: Dodd Mead, 1988.

Martens, Frederick Herman. *Violin Mastery: Talks with Master Violinists and Teachers, Comprising Interviews with Ysaÿe, Kreisler, Elman, Auer, Thibaud, Heifetz, Hartmann, Maud Powell and Others.* New York: Frederick A. Stokes Company, 1919.

Morris, Errol. "The Anosognosic's Dilemma: Something's Wrong But You'll Never Know What It Is (Part Five)." *The New York Times*, June 24, 2003.

Noad, Frederick M. *Solo Guitar Playing.* 3rd ed. New York and Toronto: Schirmer Books, 1994.

Parkening, Christopher, Jack Marshall, and David Brandon. *The Christopher Parkening Guitar Method.* Milwaukee, WI: Hal Leonard, 1997.

Pascual-Leone, Alvaro. "The Brain That Plays Music Is Changed by It." *Annals of the New York Academy of Sciences* Vol. 930 (2001): 451–456.

Robjohns, Sydney. *Violin Technique; Some Difficulties and Their Solution.* London: Oxford University Press and H. Milford, 1930.

Safonoff, Wassili. *New Formula for the Piano Teacher and Piano Student, Chester Edition.* London: J. & W. Chester, 1916.

Schonbrun, Zach. *The Performance Cortex: How Neuroscience Is Redefining Athletic Genius.* New York: Dutton, 2018.

Shinn, Frederick G. "The Memorizing of Piano Music for Performance." *Proceedings of the Musical Association* (1898): 1–25.

Thistleton, Frank. *Modern Violin Technique, How to Acquire It, How to Teach It.* London: Longmans Green & Co., 1913.

Unschuld, Marie von. *The Pianist's Hand.* Translated by Henry Morgan Dare. Leipzig: Breitkopf & Härtel, 1903.

Wolff, Konrad. *Schnabel's Interpretation of Piano Music.* New York: W. W. Norton & Company, 1979.

5

SLOW PRACTICE

Each of the eight tenets of practice I explore in this book is connected to the other seven. If one is lacking, the others will suffer. We've seen that if one's foundational work is lacking, one will not have built the mental structures necessary to assimilate material quickly. If one is not able to build up a piece bit by bit through chunking, the whole will be compromised. But none of these tenets can be more of a gateway or barrier to success than slow practice. This chapter is to prepare students for the rigors of both the understanding of slow practice and the practice itself.

Great artists and teachers of the past wrote a lot about slow practice, and what they wrote aligns with the results of more modern research—although slow practice is not as relevant to athletes as it is to musicians—but almost everybody leaves out the most important reason for slow practice, which we shall get to presently.

Fitts's Law

One of the obvious benefits of slow practice is accuracy. Daniel Coyle writes that slow practice allows one "to attend more closely to errors, creating a higher degree of precision with each firing—and when it comes to growing myelin, precision is everything."[1] That's not all: When one practices slowly, one gains a deeper knowledge of a skill's "internal blueprints,"[2] which helps build more secure structures.

There's a tradeoff between speed and accuracy, especially as one is learning or applying a new skill. Psychologist Robert Sessions Woodworth first mentioned this in 1899. Psychologist Paul Fitts described it in computational terms in a 1954 paper in the *Journal of Experimental Psychology*. Zach Schonbrun calls Fitts's Law "as firm a neuroscientific doctrine as the field has produced."[3] Pianist Ernest Schelling is straightforward: "The worst possible thing is to start practicing too fast. It invariably leads to bad results and to lengthy delays."[4]

In addition to accuracy, other advantages of slow practice mentioned by artists from the past are memorization, technical refinement, artistic shaping, and enhanced self-criticism. These are all excellent reasons for slow practice. Some artists also make an explicit connection between slow practice and rapid progress, which is difficult for students to grasp because it sounds paradoxical.[5]

Prerequisite for Better Slow Practice

If one has learned a piece by rote, which is usually synonymous with muscle memory, slow practice can prove difficult. Slowing a piece down has the effect of temporarily erasing muscle memory: Z depends on Y, which depends on X, then W, V, and so on back to the beginning of the piece at A. If one of these falters, so goes the whole.

The ability to visualize a piece or a section of a piece will help one to maintain a slow and even concentration, which will aid physical continuity while playing slowly. Mastery of mental work, presented in the previous chapter, expands one's thinking and contributes to the facility to focus on all the benefits of slow work.

Great Artists and Teachers of the Past on Slow Practice

Madame Auguste Boissier, in *Liszt Pédagogue* from 1832, presents a study method outlined by Liszt for how to begin work on a new piece. The student is to read through the piece slowly about five times:

1. The first and second times for accuracy of notes and rhythmic values.
2. The third time paying attention to the dynamics, indicated or implied, as well as details of articulation, accentuation. Liszt wanted the bass and treble studied separately in order to work out the nuances for each.
3. The fourth time looking for points of imitation or hidden themes in the inner parts.
4. The fifth time deciding on the correct speed, and planning *accelerandos* and *ritardandos* where suitable.[6]

This approach assumes well-developed sight-reading skills, which we know Liszt possessed. Note that Liszt is recommending that *this be done slowly*, even the exploration of interpretive nuances. It is not until the fifth run-through, which is devoted to finding the right tempo and its modifications, that one plays at tempo. These suggestions move too quickly for many students but could be helpful to more established artists.

Marie von Unschuld sees slow practice as a means to ensure that one plays the correct notes, can listen better, and reach a higher level of self-criticism. She writes:

- Before all things practise slowly, for only in slow time can each single note be proved [This is an archaic use of the word "prove." It means "to test."]; further accustom yourself after once playing over a phrase or a single passage "to listen to the same mentally."
- This "hearing one's self internally" is the secret of correct practice, of rational working.
- What is not grasped during the playing, is perceived in the quiet listening; mistakes, inequalities, false sound-effects, all this comes first in this way mentally to the ear.[7]

Other artists connect slow practice with providing time for careful thought and control and for securing memory. Fannie Bloomfield Zeisler (1863–1927) speaks of this in 1915:

My pupils are always counseled to practise slowly. If they bring the piece for a first hearing, it must be slowly and carefully played; if for a second or third hearing, and they know it well enough to take it up to time, they can play it occasionally at this tempo before coming to me.[8]

Unless one has worked out the details, she says,

to constantly play a piece in rapid tempo is very harmful; it precludes all thought of analysis, of how you are doing it. When you are playing at concert speed, you have no time to think of fingering, movement or condition—you are beyond all that. It is only in slow practise that you have time and opportunity to think of everything.[9]

Although many see slow practice as the point from which one begins a gradual increase of tempo, Mark Hambourg sees slow practice as a way to bring higher levels of artistry to one's playing. In 1902, he says,

In practising one should play at first very slowly, gradually increasing the speed until the proper tempo is attained. The first point is *to listen* to what one is playing; for it is not a mere matter of tempo that is to be acquired, but tone-production and variety of touch. It is the way that one listens to things that brings the finish and develops the artistic side of the performance.[10]

In her book on Ludwig Deppe's teachings, Elizabeth Caland refers to slow practice as a "Deppean rule," the essence of which is the prohibition that a work "be played even once in its exact tempo unless it has first been faithfully practiced with painstaking slowness,"[11] regardless of the technical level of the player. Caland connects slow practice to interpretation and technique:

> [T]he law holds good that each new piece or etude must, in the beginning, have slow, single-handed study; thus each detail of phrasing and execution can be subjected to strong and perpetual control, and the movement forms characteristic of each particular composition firmly impressed on the memory.[12]

It's hard not to think that someone who has a strict rule named after him could be anything other than the worst sort of pedagogue. But Amy Fay, who worked with Liszt, Carl Tausig, Theodor Kullak, as well as Deppe, regarded Deppe as more than a "mere pedagogue." In her *Music-Study in Germany*, first published in 1880, she contrasted the approach used by Kullak with that of Deppe. In a letter from May 31, 1874, she writes:

> In my study with Kullak when I had any special difficulties, he only said, "Practice always, Fräulein. *Time* will do it for you someday." . . . But Deppe, instead of saying, "Oh, you'll get this after years of practice," shows me how to conquer the difficulty *now*. He takes a piece, and while he plays it with the most wonderful *fineness* of conception, he cold-bloodedly dissects the mechanical elements of it, separates them, and tells you how to use your hand so as to grasp them one after the other. In short, he makes the technique and the conception *identical*, as of course they ought to be, but I never had any other master who trained his pupils to attempt it.[13]

Note that Fay's description of Deppe's "cold-blood dissection" of the technical elements and then working on them one at a time is chunking by another name.

Pianist Andor Földes also thinks of slow practice as a means of mastering elaborate movements and to prevent the errors that occur if one plays too quickly too soon:

> Good practice has to be slow. In order to commit to our nervous system, and to our memory, all the intricate movements that we must make in order to play an even moderately difficult passage, we have to work in a reasonably slow tempo. Otherwise, it will take us three to four times longer to learn the same passage, besides the possibility of memorizing mistakes, which are more likely to creep in during fast practice than when we see to it that everything is exactly right.[14]

Jorge Bolet also doesn't see slow practice as a way of memorizing music or solving technical problems. For Bolet, slow practice ensures mechanical accuracy: "I must have that mechanical accuracy, and for mechanical accuracy the only way to practice is slowly, so as not to miss any of the nuances in the score."[15] This doesn't mean Bolet's playing is mechanical. Note in the previous chapter that he credited work *away from the keyboard* with his ability to solve interpretive problems.

The Slower You Go, the Faster You'll Progress

The examples below apply to the practice of repertoire, but this practice maxim applies equally to exercises. Liszt taught that to achieve speed in scales, they must first be played slowly.[16]

We know from Fitts's Law that the more accurate one's first interactions with a piece, the less time one need spend later to fix things. Harriette Brower writes that Wilhelm Bachaus never works for speed. If he masters the passage slowly, he can play it at tempo: "I seldom practise fast, for it interferes with clearness. I prefer to play more slowly, giving the greatest attention to clearness and good tone. By pursuing this course I find that when I need velocity I have it."[17]

Karl Leimer states that if one avoids mistakes from the outset, progress will be quick; correcting mistakes learned because of practicing too fast is a "difficult and wearisome business." He writes,

> For a pupil, therefore, who wishes to make quick progress, it is of the greatest importance to avoid mistakes, from the very beginning. This can be attained, in the first instance, by playing very slowly, by thorough concentration in regard to rhythm (I would suggest counting aloud), and by the use of correct fingering.[18]

The mention of fingering is especially relevant for guitarists: the many left- and right-hand fingering possibilities can often be narrowed down by context and musical intent, but this filtering process will slow one down if done on the fly. Unless one has decided upon a specific fingering for ambiguous passages, *even if one ends up changing it later*, there will be a moment of indecisiveness as the passage approaches. Indecision is not the same as leaving one's options open; here it is the thin edge of a wedge that can undermine all facets of one's relationship to a piece of music, including the ability to render a fluent performance. If one has developed successful mental strategies in one's work, changing fingerings later is not difficult; if one has learned a piece by rote, it will be difficult.

Tilly Fleischmann (1882–1967) was an Irish pianist who went to the Royal Academy of Music in Munich when she was nineteen. There she worked with Bernhard Stavenhagen (1862–1914) and Berthold Kellermann (1853–1926), former students of Franz Liszt. In 1953, Fleischmann completed a large manuscript documenting the Liszt tradition of piano playing entitled *Tradition and Craft in Piano-Playing*. She offers a perceptive account of how students often go wrong in their practice.

Fleischmann describes how many students dive into a piece and play it at the tempo "at which they can just manage to master its difficulties, and having worked perhaps somewhat more cautiously at the difficult passages, they continue to play the work over and over again as close as possible to the required speed."[19] We know, as Fleischmann notes, that this leads to careless playing.

But Fleischmann also notes that *one's playing of a piece can get worse*: "Sometimes it results in steady deterioration of the work practised, so much so that it is better played after the first few attempts than after it has been played dozens of times."[20] Fleischmann suggests that during one's first forays into a new work, the brain is fully focused because one is working with new material. After many repetitions, movements, and groups of movements become automated, or explicit skills become implicit skills. In this case, however, the explicit skills are not fully developed for the tasks at hand before they become implicit skills.

Fleischmann explains that as one continues to practice at tempo, concentration becomes distributed unevenly and conflicts occur between one's conscious and subconscious response.[21] We saw similar conflicts in the discussion of choking during a performance, *but here they're happening in practice.*

Fleischmann recommends a superior method of practice. Many of her suggestions should be familiar by now. I've paraphrased them slightly and reduced them to a list for clarity. After reading the work through slowly to understand its form and character and fingering it carefully, she recommends:

1. The first phrase (or less, if difficult) is played so slowly that about three seconds can be counted between each successive note or chord. Rhythm and dynamics are eliminated so one can concentrate exclusively on the progression of voices. Students with a knowledge of theory should reflect on tonality, harmonic structure, modulations.
2. The phrase, or portion thereof, is repeated with about two seconds between each note or chord.
3. The next repetition takes time and rhythm into account. The tempo is "exceedingly slow," but note values are proportional.
4. From this point, the tempo is quickened at each repetition, dynamics, phrasing, and interpretation are considered.
5. Succeeding phrases are practised in the same manner.
6. When all the phrases of the first period have been practised, one begins practise of the period as a whole, beginning *moderato* and gradually working up to tempo.[22]

Note the combination of chunking and slow practice *and* the step-by-step approach, similar to what we saw with visualization. Fleischmann concludes her discussion of elemental practice by noting,

> [I]t is by concentrating properly in these slow tempos that one can lay a sure foundation for ultimate technical mastery. The mind has time to

take in the order of the progressions and the muscular movements and the significance of each, as if one were following and studying a slow-motion picture, and the repetition of this close analysis at all times, even when the work is already mastered, will preserve and consolidate one's technique.[23]

Why spend so much time discussing Tilly Fleischmann? The detail and specificity of her advice about practice might be reason enough, but it's her awareness of the conflict between the subconscious and conscious *in the early stages* of learning a work that sets her apart. F. M. Alexander saw this conflict as a "civil war."[24] *The opportunity to resolve this conflict is the most important reason to practice slowly.*

Alexander's Civil War

The relevance and importance of F. M. Alexander's work for those in the performing arts have gained wide acceptance in the last three or four decades. Classes and workshops in the Alexander Technique are now routinely offered in university schools of music and conservatories. His work points the way to a better use of the self, especially when it comes to forming and changing habits.

The term "civil war" was Alexander's favorite way of referring to the conflict between faulty subconscious or instinctive habits—implicit skills gone wrong—and conscious attempts to change these habits. Alexander writes that if we want to change a habit and "proceed in the ordinary way to eradicate it by direct means, we shall fail invariably, and with reason."[25] He presents eight reasons that account for the failure to change a habit:

1. A Defective Kinesthetic System.
2. Erroneous Preconceived Ideas.
3. Defective Sense-Registration and Delusions.
4. Defective Mental and Physical Control.
5. Defective Inhibition.
6. Self-Hypnotism. [Alexander is here referring to a form of self-deception, probably something like the Dunning-Kruger Effect.]
7. Cultivated Apprehension.
8. Prejudiced Arguments and Attempted Self-Defense.[26]

Each of these stands for some degree of contamination of perception or thought. This contamination is most often the result of focusing too much, or too soon, on the ends as opposed to the means whereby one can reach an end. The "means whereby" was a term used frequently by Alexander, and he thought "that in every case the 'means whereby' rather than the 'ends' should be held in mind."[27] Alexander continues, with a nod toward chunking:

As long as the "end" is held in mind instead of the "means," the muscular act, or series of acts, will always be performed in accordance with the mode established by old habits. When each stage of the series essential to the "means whereby" is correctly apprehended by the conscious mind of the subject, the old habits can be broken up, and every muscular action can be consciously directed until the new and correct guiding sensations have established the new proper habits, which in their turn become subconscious, but on a more highly evolved plane.[28]

The process of decontaminating perceptions of action and thought is made possible through a process of inhibition, which in turn is made possible by slow practice.

Inhibition

Everyone who writes in any detail about slow practice writes about *what* to do and, as we saw above, *how* to do it. I mentioned at the start of this chapter that there is a singularly important reason for slow practice that many overlook: Slow practice gives us the opportunity *not to do something* so we can do something better. Slow practice allows us time to resolve the conflict between what Tilly Fleischmann saw as between the subconscious and conscious and what F. M. Alexander saw as between contaminated kinesthetic awareness—he frequently referred to this as a "debauched kinaesthetic system"—[29]and "conscious control." Slow practice helps us *inhibit* the use of a contaminated habit and replace it with something better. This change of habit is only possible, of course, if one knows what is better.

Alexander uses the word "inhibition" to describe the process of consciously inhibiting something that is harmful. He explains this in *Constructive Conscious Control of the Individual* from 1924:

> For if the pupil thinks of a certain "end" as desirable and starts to pursue it directly, he will certainly take the course of action that he has been accustomed to take in like situations. In other words, he will follow his habitual procedure in regard to it, and should that procedure happen to be a bad one for the purpose, he will only strengthen the incorrect experiences in connection with it by using this procedure again. If, on the other hand, the pupil stops himself from going to work in his usual way (inhibition) and proceeds to replace his old subconscious means by the new conscious means which his teacher has given him, he will have taken the first and most important step towards the breaking down of a habit, and towards that constructive, conscious and reasoning control which tends towards a mastery of the situation. It is therefore impressed on the pupil from the beginning that, as the essential preliminary to any

successful work on his part, *he must refuse to work directly for this "end," and keep his attention on the means whereby this end can be achieved.*[30]

Alexander had a three-step approach: *Awareness*, which is awareness of contaminated habits; *inhibition*, which is the shutting down of one's automatic response; and *conscious control*, which is replacing the old habit with one that is better.[31] *An automatic response can only be shut down by proceeding slowly.* The work of a good teacher is essential. First, one must realize that a habit needs inhibiting, but because one's sensations have become contaminated, what feels right will not be trustworthy. Second, one must know what can take its place.

George Kochevitsky makes an explicit connection between inhibition and the need for slow practice. Slow practice "is indispensable, not only for obtaining clear proprioceptive sensations but for strengthening the inhibitory process."[32] Proprioception is one's ability to sense the position and movements of parts of one's body and can become unreliable through misuse. What Kochevitsky calls the "excitatory process," which is the first step in forming neural pathways, forms easily and quickly; the inhibitory process forms slowly and weakens easily.[33] One might think that Kochevitsky's discussions of inhibition may have been the first published use by a musician of concepts developed by F. M. Alexander—Alexander wrote about inhibition in *Man's Supreme Inheritance* in 1910—but Kochevitsky lists no works by or about Alexander in his bibliography. He does, however, list two books by Nobel Laureate Charles Sherrington (1857–1952). Sherrington was a pioneer in the field of motor control, and some of his important work had to do with "inhibition as an active coordinative mechanism."[34]

Stopping-Practice

Kochevitsky recommends slow practice and "stopping-practice" even after mastering a work to preserve what one has learned. Stopping-practice, a term and practice that may have originated with Leschetizky, strengthens the ability to inhibit an impulse for as long as one wants at any time.[35]

The term "stopping-practice" is not entirely satisfactory as a description: The word "stopping" functions as an adjective—known as a deverbal adjective—and not a verb. It describes the *type* of practice, that is, one with many stops. Stopping-practice means working on a passage and stopping every beat, then every two beats, three, and so on. During the stops, one listens, evaluates, and prepares for the next note or chord. Pianist Frank Merrick (1886–1981) notes that the term "stopping-practice" came up in one of his last lessons with Leschetizky, who advised him to stop frequently and listen "when you are practising and then you will find out a great deal for yourself."[36] Merrick, perhaps also sensing the head-scratch that might occur upon encountering the words "stopping-practice," adds that the term " 'delayed continuity' seems to add an explanatory note."[37] (Merrick always presents "stopping-practice" as a hyphenated compound noun; Kochevitsky writes it as two words.) Stopping points should frequently be shifted because the central nervous system tends to fix recurring patterns.[38]

Mark Hambourg offers something that is a combination of stopping-practice and spaced repetition:

> My first advice is not to practise too constantly. Rest between passages, never repeat a thing too often continuously. I would even endorse, after playing a certain passage through once, . . . listening intently until the buzz is out of the ear. . . . The majority play without thinking or listening.[39]

Alexander makes explicit the connection between stopping and the ability to inhibit:

> The pupil *stops himself* from going to work in his usual way (inhibition), and proceeds to replace his old subconscious means by the new conscious means which his teacher has given him, and which he has therefore every reason to believe will bring about the desired result, he will have taken the first and most important step towards the breaking-down of a habit, and towards that constructive, conscious, and reasoning control which tends towards a mastery of the situation.[40]

Kochevitsky's mention of inhibition, along with his discussion of stopping-practice, attest to fine musicians working in a way that anticipates the results of later research. You probably will have observed that we've already seen an example of stopping-practice in Tilly Fleischmann's practice recommendations. Beyond that, might Leschetizky have taught in a way that anticipated the work of neurophysiologist Charles Sherrington?

Very Softly and Not Too Fast

Kochevitsky also suggests practicing *pianissimo* and evenly in slow and fast tempos to make the inhibitory process stronger.[41] Heinrich Neuhaus (1888–1964), the great pedagogue and teacher of Emil Gilels (1916–1985) and Sviatoslav Richter (1915–1995), relays a story about Tausig. After a concert, Tausig would return home and play his program again "very softly and not too fast."[42]

Well, You Get the Idea

As Tausig knew, slow practice isn't simply useful for one's first interactions with a piece. There is no point during one's relationship with a piece of music at which slow practice is not important. Pianist Sara Davis Buechner illustrates this with comments she gave in 2015 at a celebration in honor of her teacher, Reynaldo Reyes (1933–2016). After thanking her teacher for drilling her on scales, arpeggios, Czerny, and Bach, she ended her tribute with these remarks:

- Thank you for phoning me in Brussels at 2:00 a.m. when I made the finals of the *Queen Elisabeth Competition*, just to remind me to practice slowly.
- Thank you for phoning me in Vienna at 2:00 a.m. when I made the finals of the *Beethoven Competition*, just to remind me to practice slowly.
- Thank you for phoning me in Moscow at 2:00 a.m. when I made the finals of the *Tchaikovsky Competition*, just to remind me to practice slowly.
- Thank you for phoning me . . . well, you get the idea.[43]

Notes

1. Coyle, *The Talent Code*, 85.
2. Ibid.
3. Schonbrun, *The Performance Cortex*, 51.
4. Cooke, *Great Pianists on Piano Playing*, 272.
5. Slow practice was also mentioned by lutists. Denis Gaultier wrote in his *Livre de Tablature des Pièces de Luth* (ca. 1680): "One of the most important rules for playing the lute well is to practice the pieces very slowly, lest one fall into the common flaw of muddled performance." In his *Pièces de Luth* from 1684, Jacques Gallot advised students to "Practice all of the pieces slowly to be certain of the notes and to develop the habit of clear playing." [Translations mine].
6. Adapted from Gervers, "Franz Liszt as Pedagogue," 386.
7. Unschuld, *The Pianist's Hand*, 58.
8. Brower, *Piano Mastery* (1915), 194–195.
9. Ibid.
10. Mark Hambourg, "The Making of an Artist," *The Musical Standard* October 25, 1902, 259.
11. Caland, *Artistic Piano Playing*, 54.
12. Ibid.
13. Fay, *Music-Study in Germany*, 318–319.
14. Földes, *Keys to the Keyboard*, 48.
15. Mach, *Great Pianists Speak for Themselves*, 28–29.
16. Gervers, "Franz Liszt as Pedagogue," 386.
17. Brower, *Piano Mastery* (1915), 284.
18. Leimer and Gieseking, *Piano Technique*, 47.
19. Tilly Fleischmann, *Tradition and Craft in Piano-Playing* (Dublin: Carysfort Press, 2014), 21.
20. Ibid.
21. Ibid.
22. Ibid., 21–22. (Freely adapted).
23. Ibid.
24. F. Matthias Alexander, *Man's Supreme Inheritance: Conscious Guidance and Control in Relation to Human Evolution in Civilization* (New York: E.P. Dutton & Company, 1918), 11, 13, 64.
25. Ibid., 65.
26. Ibid., 16–18.
27. Ibid., 128.

28. Ibid.
29. Alexander, *Man's Supreme Inheritance*, 15.
30. F. M. Alexander, *Constructive Conscious Control of the Individual* (Kent: Integral Press, 1986), 97–98.
31. Eleanor Rosenthal, "The Alexander Technique: What It Is and How It Works," *Medical Problems of Performing Artists* (June 1987): 55–56.
32. Kochevitsky, *The Art of Piano Playing*, 26.
33. Ibid., 25.
34. Douglas G. Stuart, "Integration of Posture and Movement: Contributions of Sherrington, Hess, and Bernstein," *Human Movement Science* Vol. 24 (2005): 621.
35. Kochevitsky, *The Art of Piano Playing*, 26.
36. Frank Merrick, *Practising the Piano* (London: Barrie and Rockliff, 1958), 1.
37. Ibid.
38. Kochevitsky, *The Art of Piano Playing*, 26.
39. Hambourg, "The Making of an Artist," 259.
40. F. Matthias Alexander, *Constructive Conscious Control of the Individual* (New York: E.P. Dutton & Company, 1923), 154.
41. Kochevitsky, *The Art of Piano Playing*, 26.
42. Heinrich Neuhaus, *The Art of Piano Playing* (New York: Praeger, 1973), 71.
43. Sara Davis Buechner, "Jeepney Ride: A Tribute to Reynaldo Reyes on the Occasion of His Retirement from 50 Years of Teaching at Towson University" (Talk given at the Reynaldo Reyes Retirement Celebration, Towson University, Towson, MD, April 11, 2015). Ms. Davis Buechner graciously provided me a copy of her address. Sara Davis Buechner won the Gold Medal at the *Gina Bachauer International Piano Competition* in 1984.

Sources

Alexander, F. Matthias. *Constructive Conscious Control of the Individual*. Kent: Integral Press, 1986.

Alexander, F. Matthias. *Man's Supreme Inheritance; Conscious Guidance and Control in Relation to Human Evolution in Civilization*. New York: E.P. Dutton & Company, 1918.

Brower, Harriette Moore. *Piano Mastery: Talks with Master Pianists and Teachers, and an Account of a Von Bülow Class, Hints on Interpretation*. New York: Frederick A. Stokes Company, 1915.

Buechner, Sara Davis. "Jeepney Ride: A Tribute to Reynaldo Reyes on the Occasion of His Retirement from 50 Years of Teaching at Towson University." Talk given at the Reynaldo Reyes Retirement Celebration, Towson University, Towson, MD, April 11, 2015.

Caland, Elizabeth. *Artistic Piano Playing as Taught by Ludwig Deppe*. Translated by Evelyn Sutherland Stevenson. Nashville, TN: The Olympian Publishing Co., 1903.

Cooke, James Francis. *Great Pianists on Piano Playing*. Philadelphia: Theodore Presser Co., 1913.

Coyle, Daniel. *The Talent Code: Greatness Isn't Born. It's Grown: Here's How*. New York: Bantam, 2009.

Fay, Amy, and Fay Peirce. *Music-Study in Germany, From the Home Correspondence of Amy Fay*. Chicago: A. C. McClurg, 1886.

Fleischmann, Tilly. *Tradition and Craft in Piano-Playing*. Dublin: Carysfort Press, 2014.

Földes, Andor. *Keys to the Keyboard, a Book for Pianists: With Explanatory Music*. New York: E.P. Dutton, 1948.

Gallot, Jacques. *Pièces De Luth: Composées Sur Différents Modes.* Edited by François Lesure. Genève: Minkoff Reprint, 1978.

Gaultier, Denis, and Ennemond Gaultier. *Pièces De Luth and Livres De Tablature Des Pièces De Luth.* Genève: Minkoff Reprint, 1975.

Gervers, Hilda. "Franz Liszt as Pedagogue." *Journal of Research in Music Education* Vol. 18, No. 4 (1970): 385–391.

Kochevitsky, George. *The Art of Piano Playing: A Scientific Approach.* Princeton, NJ: Summy-Birchard, 1967.

Leimer, Karl, and Walter Gieseking. *Piano Technique Consisting of the Two Complete Books the Shortest Way to Pianistic Perfection and Rhythmics, Dynamics, Pedal and Other Problems of Piano Playing.* New York: Dover Publications, 1972.

Mach, Elyse. *Great Pianists Speak for Themselves.* New York: Dodd Mead, 1988.

"The Making of an Artist." *The Musical Standard* (October 25, 1902): 259–260.

Merrick, Frank. *Practising the Piano.* London: Barrie and Rockliff, 1958.

Neuhaus, Heinrich. *The Art of Piano Playing.* New York: Praeger, 1973.

Rosenthal, Eleanor. "The Alexander Technique: What It Is and How It Works." *Medical Problems of Performing Artists* (June 1987): 53–57.

Schonbrun, Zach. *The Performance Cortex: How Neuroscience Is Redefining Athletic Genius.* New York: Dutton, 2018.

Stuart, Douglas G. "Integration of Posture and Movement: Contributions of Sherrington, Hess, and Bernstein." *Human Movement Science* Vol. 24 (2005): 621–643.

Unschuld, Marie von. *The Pianist's Hand.* Translated by Henry Morgan Dare. Leipzig: Breitkopf & Härtel, 1903.

6

VARIETY IN REPETITION

The application of different rhythm patterns to a passage to transform it to provide variety and to study it from different angles is frequently mentioned by great artists of the past and those who wrote about them. Applications of this practice technique appear in most serious books on how to develop piano and violin technique written by great artists and outstanding teachers. The use of different rhythms helps create a higher level of finger independence and control; they help one to discover and focus on problems *within* a passage, such as bowings for string players and right-hand fingerings for guitarists; and they foster a higher-level *control over time* (in the sense of rhythm), which will enable one to effect more convincing and elegant rubato when called for.

Many pianists and violinists recommend that when varying rhythm patterns are applied to exercises or portions of a piece that variations in dynamics, accent, and articulation also be practiced. Ivan Galamian presents some of the rhythm patterns in this chapter with numerous combinations of bowing, accent, and staccato.[1] Pianist Alberto Jonás (1868–1943) recommends that exercises be repeated in various ways: *f* and *pp*; accenting every first of two notes and then every second of two notes; staccato *f*; staccato *pp*; legato *f*; legato *pp*.

Displacing the usual metric accents is another useful technique. Ignace Paderewski, arguably one of the finest early twentieth-century pianists and certainly the most famous, said in 1918,

> It is only by playing the scales with strong accent, and the slower the better, that precision and independence of the fingers are acquired. First play the scale through, accenting the notes according to the natural rhythm.

Then, as in speech, let the accent fall upon the weak note instead of upon the strong one, and play the scale, accenting every second note; afterward place the accent upon every third note, then upon every fourth. This gives absolute command of the fingers, and is the only way to acquire it.[2]

Josef Lhévinne, who possessed one of the most formidable techniques of his generation, didn't provide specific rhythm examples for practice in his *Basic Principles in Pianoforte Playing* from 1924, but he did write about variety in repetition:

Variety in practice is most important. Repeating monotonously over and over again in treadmill fashion is the very worst kind of practice. It is both stupid and unnecessary. Take the scale of C. It may be played in hundreds of ways, with different rhythms, with different speeds and with different touches. The hands may be varied. One hand may play legato and the other staccato. Practice in this way, using your brains and your ingenuity, and your practice will not be a bore to you.[3]

Leon Conus (1871–1944) was a classmate of Rachmaninoff and Lhévinne at the Moscow Imperial Conservatory and later taught at the École Normale in Paris before emigrating to the United States where he taught at University of Cincinnati College-Conservatory of Music. He made specific the ways in which the practice of exercises can be varied to obtain the best results in his posthumously published *Fundamentals of Piano Technique: Advanced Technique*:

- Play all exercises at different speeds and keys.
- Use different touches and nuances.
- Change all exercises by utilizing various rhythms and by displacing the accent.
- Invent different figures in addition to the ones illustrated.
- Memorize all exercises.[4]

Conus gave fewer than ten rhythm patterns, which could easily be memorized, but other musicians presented more. I wouldn't make a goal of memorizing all that I present in this chapter, but Conus's other suggestions speak to the amount of variety that can be applied to exercises and which will help develop a player's technique for artistic purposes.

Pianist Andor Földes sees the use of rhythm practice as a way of approaching a difficult passage from various angles:

In trying to transform a difficult passage into an easy one we should work on it from different angles. I find it much harder to master any difficulty 'on the spot,' trying to conquer it by a frontal assault, than to work it out in several different ways. This may take longer, but will lead with more certainty to our goal.[5]

Lhévinne is an example of those who saw this type of practice as a way of relieving boredom; Földes and others saw it as a way of solving technical problems because of the variety of angles with which one could approach a passage; and Alfred Cortot, as we'll see later, made an explicit connection between this type of practice and the ability to effect musical nuance.

Repetition, Repetition, *With Variety*

There's another compelling reason why variety in repetition is so valuable. I wrote in *Mastering Guitar Technique* that misuse of one's technique is often misdiagnosed as overuse.[6] I would write today that "any practice, regardless of the actual quality of one's technique, *that does not incorporate variety*, is misuse." It turns out that by providing variety in repetition, one can still practice a lot and avoid problems associated with overuse.

Guitarist Liona Boyd stopped touring in 2003 after she noticed that her technique had deteriorated so much that she could no longer use her right hand: "My right hand felt so different, I would end up crying every time I picked up the guitar—and it was getting worse."[7] In the January 2011 issue of *Guitar Player* magazine, she described her diagnosis from the National Institute of Health in Washington, DC, of task-specific focal dystonia, a neurological condition:

> Basically, when you've done the same small, precise, motion a billion times over—like arpeggios and tremolo on classical guitar—the neurons in the brain that fire the signals to the fingers are fused together and/ or worn out. It doesn't happen for big motions, say, for example, a golf swing. The condition has nothing to do with the muscles or joints in your hands or fingers—I never felt cramping, for example, but my fingers would involuntarily curl up when I played.[8]

She added, "I was doing a lot of *mindless* practice."[9] Boyd had spent a lot of time doing the same finger exercises while on auto-pilot. "That was the *worst* thing I could have done. I was just burning those neural pathways to my fingers over and over again," Boyd said. "I basically wore out the neuro-receptors in my brain for a specific task."[10]

The authors of "The Neurological Hand," a chapter in *Fundamentals of Hand Therapy*, cite research that shows that motor learning in which there is variability in repetition is better than blocked practice (the same as massed practice: doing the same thing over and over). They advise, "Repetition, repetition, repetition, *with variety*."[11] Neurophysiologist Nikolai Bernstein put it compactly in 1967: "repetition without repetition."[12]

Introducing variety in repetition early in one's training diminishes the chances of wearing out neuro-receptors. If a musician is to develop focal dystonia, it will usually be after years and years of intense practice, but guitarists seem especially vulnerable.[13]

The obstacles created by introducing variety are also desirable because they require more mental effort, which ends up "making you swift and graceful without your realizing it."[14] Robert Bjork explains the reason: Learning that requires effort strengthens connections to previously acquired knowledge and skill. Peter Brown sums this up succinctly:

> [T]he easier knowledge or a skill is for you to retrieve, the less your retrieval practice will benefit your retention of it. Conversely, the more effort you have to expend to retrieve knowledge or skill, the more the practice of retrieval will entrench it.[15]

Bjork gives a recommendation about how Shaquille O'Neal could improve his ability to shoot free throws, which is notoriously inconsistent. He should practice them from a variety of distances: "14 feet and 16 feet, instead of the standard 15 feet."[16] Or as Bjork told Coyle, "Shaq needs to develop the ability to modulate his motor programs. Until then he'll keep being awful."[17]

Howard Austin's research on jugglers anticipated Bjork's comment about the importance of "modulating one's motor programs," although Austin found it counterintuitive that "becoming proficient at a given skill means learning to make better and more sophisticated compensations"[18] and that "the appearance of fluid grace in a skilled athletic performance is an illusion created by computational 'tricks.'"[19] Austin called these computational tricks the "Compensation Phenomenon" and found it unexpected that compensations dominate advanced learning stages.[20] Compensations are made possible through what Austin calls "special case error subroutines," which allow expert performers to adapt when things don't go as planned. Concert artists know that there is always something that doesn't go as planned in live performance.

Variability in practice is not something that has been cultivated by guitarists, much to the detriment of their technique, their musical freedom, and their security in performance. Can it be a coincidence that musicians who recommend this type of work were great artists who possessed a level of interpretive freedom rarely heard today?

Rhythmic Variations

Below are some basic rhythmic variants presented in books by pianists and violinists that can help students apply variety to their practice. This variety can serve to relieve boredom, to prevent aural stagnation from setting in, to help one hear a passage differently, to require one to engage with material mindfully as one mentally reconstructs the skills required, and to provide variety to the muscles involved, which will hasten one's development.

Groups of Two, Four, or Eight Notes

1.

2.

These can also be thought of as:

3.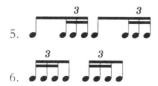

4.

Another variation, grouping three of the four notes together:

5.

6.

The same as variants 1–4 but with sharper rhythmic differentiation:

7.

8.

9.

10.

Some other variations given by Alberto Jonás in 1922:[21]

11.

12.

13.

Numbers 14–17 are notated examples of stopping-practice, which we explored in the last chapter:[22]

Similar patterns given by Jonás (the accents are his):

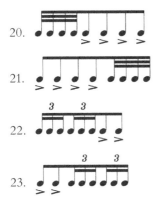

Groups of Three or Six Notes

29.

French pianist Alfred Cortot suggests the following rhythms for Chopin's Prelude, Op. 28, No. 5, which consists of running sextuplets, marked "Allegro motto":[23]

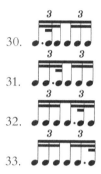

30.

31.

32.

33.

Other Variations

In any rhythm with a dotted note, the dot can be doubled to make the execution more pointed (as done in Nos. 7 & 8).

Sometimes patterns can be tailored to meet the characteristics of specific works. Cortot gives the following rhythms for Chopin's Prelude, Op. 28, No. 16, which consists primarily of sixteenth-note scalar passages marked "Presto con fuoco." The displacement of accents, he says, assures finger independence (he calls it "evenness of finger power"), which in turn makes possible the rapidity and accuracy of a passage and the dynamic control necessary to animate the music with "a constant eddying of intensity and tone."[24]

34.

35.

36.

37.

38.

Cortot had previously given the rhythms in numbers 1, 2, 5, 6 (above) with accents on the eighth or dotted-eighth notes. These rhythms "respect the divisions into which each bar falls." The above rhythm patterns, however, consist of five, six, and eight notes and break the written metric divisions of the prelude at regular intervals, which Cortot says are "more profitable from the point of view of finger independence." Cortot recommends one "practise fragments of four bars according to these rhythms, varying the dynamics of the text each time, *piano* becoming *forte* and vice versa."[25]

Applications of Rhythm Patterns

One can easily apply the above rhythms to scales, and I present a subset of the above in *Mastering Guitar Technique*.[26] Below follow examples of some of the patterns applied to arpeggios, which will be useful for guitarists: the first two measures of Heitor Villa-Lobos's Etude No. 1 for patterns needing four notes and Mauro Giuliani's Etude 5 from Op. 48 for patterns requiring six notes.

Groups of Four Notes

The next pattern requires one to repeat both the note *and* right-hand finger after the fermata:

Groups of Three or Six Notes

The *p-i-m-a-m-i* arpeggio pattern is ubiquitous in guitar music, but composers and publishers don't always make clear whether the resulting sextuplets should be played as two groups of three or three groups of two. Example 6.1, from the third movement of Federico Moreno Torroba's *Sonatina in A*, illustrates this.

Although it's written in $\frac{3}{8}$,

EXAMPLE 6.1 Federico Moreno Torroba: Sonatina in A, Allegro, mm. 49–51.

it usually comes off sounding as though it were written in two:

EXAMPLE 6.2 Federico Moreno Torroba: Sonatina in A, Allegro, mm. 49–51, as often performed.

A guitarist with an unrefined right-hand technique will often unwittingly accent the highest note, which runs counter to the metric accents. The solution is to develop the ability to apply subtly graded metric accents—especially important in the context of the *crescendo*—to make the meter clear:

EXAMPLE 6.3 Federico Moreno Torroba: Sonatina in A, Allegro, mm. 49–51, with metric accents.

It's harder to accent the middle finger (*m*) in this context, which is one of the reasons why exercises employing different rhythms and accents are so important.

In his 1885 *Principles of Expression in Pianoforte Playing*, Adolph Christiani writes that an accent "should not surpass the unaccented notes by more than one degree of strength."[27] He gives a few examples, such as a *pianissimo* passage in which an accent shouldn't exceed *piano*. Things like this are difficult to describe and quantify, but accents in the above example should help define the meter and not obscure it.

Below are applications of some of the rhythmic variants presented earlier to the first two measures of Mauro Giuliani's etude Op. 48, No. 5. The first two exercises allow one to work on the problem presented above with the Moreno Torroba example, although in the event the Giuliani should be performed as two groups of three.

Dynamics and Voicing

Many have written about the necessity of varying exercises and passages from pieces by applying different dynamics to them. Several pianists make this clear through notated examples. Malwine Brée gives an example of various dynamic treatments for a two-octave C-major scale. Cortot gives the same example but for a one-octave scale.[28]

Below is Brée's example, which she says should first be practiced *forte* then *pianissimo*. When those have been mastered, then *crescendo* and *diminuendo* as notated in example 6.4. She adds, "In these also, to begin with, play slowly."[29]

Cortot adds in his example that one is "to pass through all the degrees of intensity of tone from pp to ff."[30]

Variety in repetition to gain dynamic control was also used in the study of chords. In his discussion of Chopin's Prelude Op. 28, No. 20, Cortot recommends the practice of repeating the same chord with "progressive-gradation in intensity of attack."[31] Cortot uses a c-minor chord—the tonic chord of the piece. Francisco Tárrega made a transcription of this prelude for guitar and

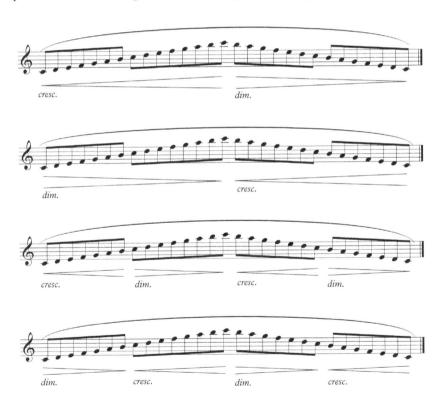

EXAMPLE 6.4 Dynamic variants for scale practice from Malwine Brée, *The Groundwork of the Leschetizky Method* (1902).

EXAMPLE 6.5   Alfred Cortot's practice example in preparation for dynamic shading in Chopin Op. 28, No. 20.

transposed it to c-sharp minor, and example 6.5 uses the tonic chord of the guitar transcription. It can serve as an introduction for guitarists to the practices Cortot suggests as well as help one connect those practices to musical ends.

The first four-bar phrase of the piece is marked **ff**. Cortot suggests that each chord of the first four bars be repeated four times following the dynamic gradations above, *piano* to *fortissimo*, as I've given below in example 6.6 for the chords of the first measure:

EXAMPLE 6.6   Alfred Cortot's practice suggestion to develop dynamic gradations.

Cortot writes, "the most delicate piece of shading" is in the second phrase (m. 5), which is marked *piano*. To express the grandeur of the opening phrase while at *piano*, Cortot brings out the outer voices, as shown in example 6.7:

EXAMPLE 6.7   Chopin Prelude, Op. 28, No. 20, m. 5.

To achieve this effect, Cortot recommends that one practice thusly:

EXAMPLE 6.8 Cortot's exercise for voicing.

The right-hand fingers—in this case, *i* and *m*—should return to their strings to damp them as shown by the eighth rests. The technique of projecting a voice or voices above others in a chord is beyond the scope of this book, but if you have trouble, reduce the problem further and practice on open strings, as Frank Thistleton recommended to violinists so they could master bowing difficulties before adding the left hand:

EXAMPLE 6.9 Open string template of m. 5.

In the last phrase (m. 9), marked **pp** in Cortot's edition, the voicing is reversed, and it's the middle voice that needs projection. Cortot suggests the following practice technique to bring out the inner voice:

EXAMPLE 6.10 Chopin Prelude, Op. 28, No. 20, m. 9.

Tárrega's transcription of this prelude allows one to follow what Frank Merrick calls, "the thread of musical discourse," with the exception of the penultimate measure. Tárrega has inexplicably moved the melody from the top voice to an inner voice, which buries it. I've re-notated this measure to reveal the line (Tárrega's notation can be seen in example 6.13):

EXAMPLE 6.11 Chopin Prelude, Op. 28, No. 20, m. 12.

Guitarists can benefit by applying Cortot's practice suggestions for other parts of the piece to this measure:

EXAMPLE 6.12 Practice exercise for voicing.

Avoid projecting notes through arpeggiation. Rather, play all chord notes simultaneously and let the stroke of a right-hand finger draw out the sound of the desired note at the level you want, which practice of the above exercises will help develop. Note that the above exercises are to gain control of individual voices. In performance, one would not damp the notes.

Voicing is an oft-neglected facet of guitar study and technique, although, according to Hilda Gervers, pianists didn't always have this skill. She writes that Liszt was a master at bringing out melodic lines wherever they might appear:

> Liszt was able to differentiate each contrapuntal line with clarity, through variety of touch and nuance. In the early nineteenth century, it had not been considered possible to separate the voices except on the organ or in the string quartet, through their variety of timbres.[32]

Her source is Lina Ramann's *Franz Liszt als Künstler und Mensch*, published in 1894. Ramann was Liszt's disciple and first biographer. It seems unbelievable that early nineteenth-century pianists didn't voice contrapuntal lines, which was made possible by the invention of the fortepiano in the early eighteenth century. Centuries earlier, lutists had been bringing out the lines in their fantasias and intabulations (arrangements) of vocal music (chansons, frottole, motets, masses, and popular tunes), and melodic voicing is made explicit by the frequency with which melodic notes were played on the *chanterelle* (the single-string first course of the lute). Voicing is mentioned in guitar methods, most notably by Dionisio Aguado in his 1843 *Nuevo Método para Guitarra*: "[C]are must be taken to ensure that the melody stands out as the main part, while the accompaniment is soft, and the bass is clearly audible."[33]

Example 6.13 is a modified version of Tárrega's transcription. I've kept his notes, except for one correction in measure three that Cortot says Chopin made on a student's copy (Jane Stirling), but have left the piece un-fingered. I've added back Chopin's phrasing marks—missing in Tárrega's transcription—modified by Cortot. Cortot also says that the *ritenuto* given in most editions (measure eleven) doesn't fit the fateful rhythm of the prelude.

Cortot's practice suggestions for this Chopin prelude can serve as examples of how to work intelligently and artistically and to avoid the pitfalls of massed repetition.

Prelude

Frederic Chopin

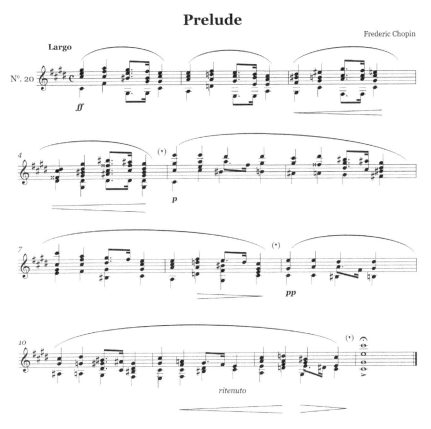

EXAMPLE 6.13 Modified version of Francisco Tárrega's transcription of Chopin's Op. 28, No. 20.

Cortot makes a direct connection between the practice of exercises incorporating variety and the development of interpretive freedom. In chapter 1 of *Rational Principles of Pianoforte Technique*, he writes,

> Legato or staccato playing, portando or brilliant and distinct execution, evenness of finger touch or variety of tone created by diversity of attack, such are the many modes of expression *which here come into being*, and whose immediate application is to be found in the interpretation of the works of the principal composers mentioned above.[34]

(The composers to whom he's referring are Mendelssohn and Chopin.) The phrase "*which here come into being*" refers to the exercises that follow in his book.

As one introduces variety to the practice of one's repertoire, one introduces variety to one's ears. Variety in repetition helps one hear interpretive nuances more clearly, but more importantly, the practice of variety helps one imagine levels of artistic nuances that would otherwise lie dormant.

Notes

1. Galamian, *Principles of Violin: Playing & Teaching*, 97.
2. Ignace J. Paderewski, "Practical Hints on Piano Study," *Modern Music and Musicians* (1918): 152.
3. Lhévinne, *Basic Principles in Pianoforte Playing*, 44.
4. Leon Conus, *Fundamentals of Piano Technique: Advanced Technique* (Chicago: Clayton F. Summy Co., 1953), 2.
5. Földes, *Keys to the Keyboard*, 53.
6. Berg, *Mastering Guitar Technique*, 8.
7. Darrin Fox, "Liona Boyd," *Guitar Player*, January 2011, 54.
8. Ibid., 57.
9. Ibid.
10. Ibid.
11. Gillian Porter and Lara Taggart, "The Neurological Hand," in *Fundamentals of Hand Therapy: Clinical Reasoning and Treatment Guidelines for Common Diagnoses of the Upper Extremity*, ed. Cynthia Cooper, 2nd ed. (St. Louis: Mosby, 2013), 554.
12. Schonbrun, *The Performance Cortex*, 53.
13. I have received dozens of inquiries from guitarists suffering from focal dystonia. On the day I accessed the Wikipedia entry for "Focal Dystonia" (May 1, 2017), eight of the seventeen musicians listed as notable cases were guitarists or bassists. Most of these eight were classical guitarists.
14. Coyle, *The Talent Code*, 18.
15. Brown, *Make It Stick*, 79.
16. Coyle, *The Talent Code*, 18.
17. Quoted in ibid.
18. Austin, "A Computational Theory," 47.
19. Ibid., 49.
20. Ibid., 50.
21. Alberto Jonás, *Master School of Piano Playing and Virtuosity* (New York: Carl Fischer, Inc., 1922), 23.
22. Bryan Wallick, "Piano Practice: Practice Routines and Techniques for Concert Pianists" (DMus Thesis, Pretoria, South Africa: University of Pretoria, 2013), 96–98.

23. Frederic Chopin, *24 Preludes, Students'*, ed. *Alfred Cortot*, trans. Davis Ponsonby (Paris: Editions Salabert, 1926), 14.
24. Ibid., 48.
25. Ibid.
26. Berg, *Mastering Guitar Technique*, 130–131.
27. Adolph Christiani, *The Principles of Expression in Pianoforte Playing* (New York: Harper, 1885), 25.
28. Chopin, *24 Preludes*, 42.
29. Brée and Baker, *The Groundwork of the Leschetizky Method*, 19.
30. Chopin, *24 Preludes*, 42.
31. Ibid., 65.
32. Gervers, "Franz Liszt as Pedagogue," 389.
33. Aguado, *New Guitar Method*, 144.
34. Cortot and Le Roy, *Rational Principles of Pianoforte Technique*, 9. [Italics added].

Sources

Aguado, Dionisio. *New Guitar Method*. Edited by Brian Jeffry. Translated by Louise Bigwood. London: Tecla Editions, 1981.

Austin, Howard. "A Computational Theory of Physical Skill." PhD diss., Massachusetts Institute of Technology, 1976.

Berg, Christopher. *Mastering Guitar Technique: Process & Essence*. Pacific, MO: Mel Bay Publications, 1997.

Brée, Malwine, and Theodor Baker. *The Groundwork of the Leschetizky Method*. New York: G. Schirmer, 1902.

Brown, Peter C., Henry L. Roediger III, and Mark A. McDaniel. *Make it Stick: The Science of Successful Learning*. Cambridge, MA: Belknap Press, 2014.

Chopin, Frederic. *24 Preludes, Students' Edition by Alfred Cortot*. Translated by Davis Ponsonby. Paris: Editions Salabert, 1926.

Christiani, Adolph F. *The Principles of Expression in Pianoforte Playing*. New York: Harper, 1885.

Conus, Leon. *Fundamentals of Piano Technique: Advanced Technique*. Chicago: Clayton F. Summy Co., 1953.

Cortot, Alfred, and Métaxas Le Roy. *Rational Principles of Pianoforte Technique*. Paris: M. Senart: Boston: Oliver Ditson Company, 1930.

Coyle, Daniel. *The Talent Code: Greatness Isn't Born: It's Grown: Here's How*. New York: Bantam, 2009.

Földes, Andor. *Keys to the Keyboard, a Book for Pianists: With Explanatory Music*. New York: E.P. Dutton, 1948.

Fox, Darrin. "Liona Boyd." *Guitar Player* (January 2011): 54–59.

Galamian, Ivan. *Principles of Violin: Playing & Teaching*. Englewood Cliffs, NJ: Prentice-Hall, 1962.

Gervers, Hilda. "Franz Liszt as Pedagogue." *Journal of Research in Music Education* Vol. 18, No. 4 (1970): 385–391.

Giuliani, Mauro. *The Complete Works in Facsimiles of the Original Editions*. Vol. 6. Edited by Brian Jeffery. London: Tecla, 1984.

Jonás, Alberto. *Master School of Piano Playing and Virtuosity*. New York: Carl Fischer, Inc., 1922.

Lhévinne, Josef. *Basic Principles in Pianoforte Playing*. Philadelphia: Theo. Presser Company, 1924.

Moreno Torroba, Federico. *Sonatina*. Edited by Andrés Segovia. Washington, DC: Columbia Music Co, 1966.

Paderewski, Ignace, J. "Practical Hints on Piano Study." *Modern Music and Musicians* (1918): 153–155.

Porter, Gillian, and Lara Taggart. "The Neurological Hand." In *Fundamentals of Hand Therapy: Clinical Reasoning and Treatment Guidelines for Common Diagnoses of the Upper Extremity*, edited by Cynthia Cooper. St. Louis: Mosby, 2013.

Schonbrun, Zach. *The Performance Cortex: How Neuroscience Is Redefining Athletic Genius*. New York: Dutton, 2018.

Villa-Lobos, Heitor. *Douze Études Pour Guitare*. Paris: M. Eschig, 1953.

Wallick, Bryan. "Piano Practice: Practice Routines and Techniques for Concert Pianists." D.Mus. diss., Pretoria, South Africa: University of Pretoria, 2013.

7

CONTINUITY

Continuity in music performance may seem so obvious that it doesn't bear discussion. A performance of a piece of music exists in time, and time is the container of the continuous. But everything we've explored previously—foundation work, chunking, mental work, slow practice, variety in repetition—has been in service of achieving unbroken continuity in performance and imbuing that continuity with artistic meaning. Frank Merrick writes that "there are few, if any, factors that do so much to ensure that the audience will be carried away by the music."[1] Continuity is not more important than the areas of study mentioned above; *it is made possible by them.*

Performing Time

We've seen that Ivan Galamian called time devoted to foundation work "building time," and in the next chapter we'll encounter what he called "interpreting time." He had a third division of practice hours that he called "performing time." During performing time, the entire composition is played through. Galamian has recognized that a passage that has been mastered by itself sometimes falls apart when the piece is played in its entirety. This lapse isn't the fault of having approached the passage from a technical point of view, which is indispensable, but that distinct factors are present when the passage is integrated into a larger whole. Galamian says that the passage must be practiced

> in the context of a larger section and with the expression that is its due. Only then has one a right to expect that the isolated section can be successfully integrated again into the piece and made to grow together with the rest of the work without showing a seam or a scar.[2]

A Fluttering of Chaff

Mark Hambourg also writes about the practice of continuity as a goal of practice:

> A vital point is the bridging over of one passage to another, the securing of continuity in the performance of a work. Without this bridging over we have neither breadth nor cohesiveness; it is a fluttering of chaff in the wind; there is neither the mastery of intellectuality nor the value of artistic finish.[3]

George Kochevitsky narrows down the reason why continuity work is so important. He suggests that when one can play a passage at tempo but is unable to play the sections in continuity, it is a problem of the mind; one is unable to think fast enough to "anticipate and prepare one's playing apparatus for each situation without the slightest delay."[4] Anticipating and preparing for what's coming up means, in part, transcending latency involved with the initiation of a difficult movement.

Continuity practice is designed to move the joining of passages from an explicit skill to an implicit skill. As this is primarily a mental skill, continuity practice speaks to the importance of mental work.

An Unbroken Mood-Line

Frank Merrick writes of a conversation he had with a journalist when he competed in the 1910 Rubinstein Competition in St. Petersburg, Russia. When a competitor displayed a particularly noteworthy "unified presentation," the journalist referred to it as an "unbroken mood-line."[5] This mood-line incorporates all aspects of a polished performance in the context of continuity. Merrick sets about to offer suggestions to help achieve an unbroken mood-line.

The most obvious is to play the piece straight through, although Merrick points out that a preoccupation with one aspect of the piece—accuracy of notes, legato of inner voices—reduces the benefits of continuity practice, although it may accustom one's ear to it. Merrick's goal in continuity work is to integrate all aspects of artistic performance, but one can benefit from continuity practice well before all the artistic aspects of an unbroken mood-line are in place. Some artistic ideas may not reveal themselves until one's ear gains a grasp of the whole.

As an intermediate step, it can be helpful to play a piece, or sections thereof, while focusing on one interpretive element, such as voicing, rubato, accents, etc. (This presupposes one has already mastered the technical exigencies of the piece.) Then, perhaps, one will be able to engage in the artistic practice of continuity and bring these elements together in service of Merrick's unbroken mood-line.

Merrick has some other suggestions, one of which we've already seen. Merrick suggests that "thinking the pieces right through without any playing at all

(either with or without the music) is another good idea."[6] Here Merrick anticipates Kochevitsky's recognition of the importance of mental work in achieving
continuity.

Merrick also suggests one play nothing but the main melodic line, which
he sees as "the thread of musical discourse."[7] Another suggestion of Merrick's
is to play a piece through softly and on the slow side,[8] a practice of Tausig's
that Heinrich Neuhaus describes in chapter 5. We know that this improves
proprioception.

The Floating Fermata

Merrick recognizes the relationship between mastering individual chunks and
continuity. He acknowledges that it may seem out of place to discuss working
on isolated phrases in a discussion about playing the piece in its entirety, but
mastery of separate phrases, he says, is the "foundation upon which larger and
ever larger units can gradually be reared." As we've seen, Merrick uses the
technique of stopping-practice to join the chunks into larger units, eventually
reaching a continuous, unbroken mood-line.

Merrick's approach is much like Tilly Fleischmann's, although Merrick suggests mentally or actually singing each phrase *before* playing, in addition to
pausing afterward to evaluate. The pauses should be at least as long as the
phrases, especially "if the thinking is a really expressive mental rehearsal of
what is to come."[9]

The Forest *and* the Trees

Continuity practice is a good way to develop and maintain mental focus of a
piece. Heinrich Neuhaus tells the story of Busoni combining slow practice and
continuity work on the day of a recital:

> Zadora, a well-known pupil of Busoni, told me that on the day of a recital
> Busoni frequently played his whole programme from beginning to end
> slowly and without 'expression' which is what Tausig used to do after a
> recital (but as a matter of fact he probably did it before the recital too).[10]

What this achieves, in addition to perceiving the piece as one large chunk,
is that one's ability to concentrate lengthens and acquires continuity. One's
focus can narrow and widen as needed. Because one need not rely on muscle
memory, one can focus on the forest, the trees, or both at will.

Continuity in Performance

Musicians, scholars, and critics write a lot about performance, but they write
about the result of a performance or a performer's style, which is, of course,

what matters to the listener. We learn from the August 2001 issue of *Early Music*, for example, that Chopin

> placed a premium on the beauty of sound, the art of touch, simplicity, subtlety, suppleness and colouristic variety. He continually advocated intensive listening coupled with imaginative fingering to produce a legato *cantabile*, a sense of phrase and a natural breathing rivalling the *bel canto* singers he so admired, whose style he translated into his unique pianistic idiom.[11]

All of this is good and useful information, but for those wishing to learn how to develop the *act* or *skill* of performance, there is a vacuum at the heart of these writings. How would a young Chopin have taken his first steps in developing the freedom to perfect his art of touch in an actual performance situation? Jane O'Dea writes:

> It takes courage, for example, to go out on a stage and perform in front of people. As every performer knows . . . musical performance is a tricky, risky business. It entails more often than not minute, subtle, physical and mental readjustments, all of which have to be made in a split second and can spell the difference between success and failure. It takes courage to engage publicly in such an endeavor. It takes bravery to tap your creative resources, to open yourself, and relying on your own sense of what is fitting, worthy and right, to tackle on stage a complex and often technically difficult piece of music. There are any number of ways in which you may fail in the attempt and give a less than successful performance.[12]

In chapter 4, the authors of *Practicing Perfection: Memory and Piano Performance* expressed surprise that there was no pedagogical tradition of memorization in music schools. Similarly, there exists no specific and dedicated pedagogy for concert performance, although some teachers are better able than others to help their charges navigate the terrain of mastering each necessary physical, mental, and artistic skill and then help them combine them successfully in a performance environment. The assumption seems to be that playing a piece well in practice leads inexorably to skill in performance. The usual approach is akin to that outlined by Australian concert pianist and artist-teacher Ernest Hutchinson (1871–1951) in 1915:

> I have had a large studio, seating 150 or 200, and generally have had a musicale once a week, the pupils inviting their parents and friends. There is nothing which will take the place of the routine of playing before others. The only way to learn to play in public is to play. Pupils who play their pieces correctly and well for me, will make shocking mistakes and go all to pieces through sheer nervousness, if playing for the first time in

a musicale. They soon get used to it however. Even three or four performances during the season will be of great benefit.[13]

Advice like Hutchinson's borders on the tautological, and there is no reason
for the ritual humiliation. Beyond learning their repertoire, students need a
framework for the work of developing performance skills to save them from
making "shocking mistakes" and "going all to pieces" when they present their
first public offerings. Both of these can give rise to fractured concentration,
which interferes with continuity. Although music performance is an act that
requires mastery of a variety of skills, it is itself a skill that can be developed.
Hutchinson's students would have been better served had their teacher been
able to design learning goals for performance.

Before one can begin to develop performance skills, one must understand
that fluency with the material in the practice room does not guarantee mastery of the material in performance. Performance creates a vulnerability to the
wrong sort of expectations and a heightened awareness of areas orbiting our
sense of self and self-worth. Chief among these are our thoughts about and
reactions to:

- Perfection. Our attitude toward perfection can derail us, and it is a form
  of arrogance to think we're capable of it. Its usefulness may lie more in its
  ability to keep us humble. There is a paradox here: the more we can let go
  of our preoccupation with perfection, the closer we can come to whatever
  we think perfection is. We'll have a deeper look at attitudes about perfection when we discuss feedback and self-criticism.
- Expecting a specific result. The expectation of a specific result locks us into
  one version of the future. When reality doesn't meet our expectation, we
  can become disappointed or distracted and lose our sense of being present.
  Performance is a living art, and many results are possible to the prepared. It
  is best to remain open to the unfolding of the experience. Lauren Tashman
  pointed out in chapter 2 that novices don't have the experience to formulate realistic expectations for situations. Consequently, they often develop
  expectations that are unanchored to the way they've been working.
- Failure. Although there is such a thing as failure, as you practice performing, all you're doing is collecting information. There is no failure, only a
  chance to learn what's working, what isn't, and how to adjust your practice
  accordingly. This means having a learning goal about performance. The
  only failure is the failure to learn from these experiences, which will better
  prepare you for when the stage is no longer virtual.
- Environment. A performance space is different from a practice space, even
  if they are physically the same. Students are sometimes thrown by the sudden shock of facing a performance environment, which often doesn't happen until they're walking on stage before an audience for the first time.

There's nervousness and one's senses seem distorted and function not at all like they did in practice.
- Variability. Our inability to handle things when they don't go as they did in practice can unnerve us. Neurologist Frank R. Wilson, writing about juggling, says:

> Intuitively one might suppose that practice pays off by making movements more and more precise: you learn to toss the balls to exactly the same height all the time. That, however, turns out to be a terrible mistake, because this kind of practicing inevitably leads to serious limitations in a juggler's development. An inflexible routine built on the expectation of a long sequence of perfect tosses would be extremely vulnerable to deviations in the behavior of the object being juggled.[14]

Wilson's comment does not consider the behavior of the juggler, which is also subject to variability. Music critic Anne Midgette reminds us that "human variability is supposed to be one of the exciting things about live music, making it like a high-wire act"[15] and points out

> a tacit and incorrect assumption: that live performance can be equated with a book or a film [or a recording], and that a constantly changing art is comparable to something that is fixed and will be encountered in the same form by everyone who apprehends it.[16]

There is variability everywhere in live performance, but solid mental preparation will help you respond well to it, as will having added variety to your practice. In performance, you are both the juggler and the object being juggled.

The next step is to try to simulate playing in a performance situation. This is based on good preparation and the use of imagination.

Once you can visualize and play a piece, have smoothed out technical difficulties, and have an idea of your phrasing and interpretive nuances, it is time to practice performing it. Below are some steps to help heighten your perceptions to simulate the nervousness that accompanies live performance. Eventually, nervousness will be stripped of its devitalizing effects. The more imaginatively you can conjure up the details, the better. These are to be done by yourself, as preparation for playing for others:

1. Set up to play in an environment that's different from where you normally practice: Go to a different room, face a different direction, anything that's different will suffice.
2. Walk to the chair, music stand, empty stage, or piano bench and bow to imaginary applause. This helps signal the start of the performance and that there's no going back. If you're nervous, great. You're doing a good job of

simulation. As you invite nervousness into this process, it will lose its grip over you and will no longer be a surprise in the event.

3. Tune quietly, if needed. Compose yourself and mentally hear the start of the piece. This will help settle you and give you a chance to set your tempo.

4. Begin playing and keep going no matter what. Do not go back to fix errors. Learn to trust your previous mental work with the piece. Try to cultivate an attitude of exploration. Whatever is happening is giving you a reflection of where you are with the piece. Do not evaluate the performance as it happens; that will only serve to distract you and take you out of the flow of time. There will be time set aside for this later. If you do have to stop and can't continue, cancel the performance and evaluate what happened so you can resolve the problem in practice.

5. When the piece is finished, stand up and bow. This signals the end of the performance. The bowing on either side of the performance acts as a frame or container for the time in which you create art. And when you are creating art, you should not be thinking of the effect of your creation.

Once you've left the virtual concert platform, it is time to evaluate the performance. Whatever happened is simply information about how your studies have been going. Try to see the results in a dispassionate way. Take this information and use it to inform your next practice sessions. You now know more about what works and what doesn't and can make adjustments to your practice. After several practice sessions, repeat and evaluate again. As your performance skills develop, you will move closer to achieving freedom and spontaneity in your work.

Don't attribute something not working well to an external force—you have no control over those—which renders one helpless. Assume that something not working is something you do have control over and exercise that control in your next practice session. (We'll look at this in more detail in the discussion of psychologist Carol Dweck's work on "mindsets" in chapter 9.) You may need more technical work in some passages, you may need more mental work, or you may need to set aside more time for these practice performances.

A final step is to use imagery as presented by sports psychologists. The difference between imagery and visualization is that the former seeks to recreate the event in the larger context of the venue; visualization focuses primarily on the relationship between your mind, the music, and the instrument. To effectively use imagery for your preparation, *imagine* yourself performing the steps above: Walk on stage, see the venue if you're familiar with it, bow, perform the piece while visualizing, and then bow and walk off stage. This will prepare you for the actual performance. With enough practice, the concert stage can become a familiar and enjoyable place, and nervousness and anxiety can be transformed into artistic energy.

Notes

1. Merrick, *Practising the Piano*, 31.
2. Galamian, *Principles of Violin: Playing & Teaching*, 101.
3. Hambourg, "The Making of an Artist," 259.
4. Kochevitsky, *The Art of Piano Playing*, 45.
5. Merrick, *Practising the Piano*, 31.
6. Ibid., 32.
7. Ibid.
8. Ibid.
9. Ibid., 2.
10. Neuhaus, *The Art of Piano Playing*, 214. Neuhaus is referring to Michal Zadora (1882–1946), who was also known as Michael von Zadora.
11. John Rink, "Chopin as Early Music," *Early Music* Vol. 29, No. 3 (August 2001): 339.
12. Jane O'Dea, *Virtue or Virtuosity? Explorations in the Ethics of Musical Performance* (Westport, CT: Greenwood Press, 2000), 27.
13. Brower, *Piano Mastery* (1915), 101–104.
14. Frank R. Wilson, *The Hand* (New York: Pantheon Books, 1998), 109. Quoted in Berg, "Re-Imagination of Guitar Pedagogy," 51.
15. Anne Midgette, "Go to That Opera Again; Singers Are Only Human," *The New York Times*, December 20, 2006.
16. Ibid.

Sources

Berg, Christopher. "The Re-Imagination of Guitar Pedagogy." *The Soundboard* Vol. 24, No. 3/4 (2000): 43–52.

Brower, Harriette Moore. *Piano Mastery: Talks with Master Pianists and Teachers, and an Account of a Von Bülow Class, Hints on Interpretation.* New York: Frederick A. Stokes Company, 1915.

Galamian, Ivan. *Principles of Violin: Playing & Teaching.* Englewood Cliffs, NJ: Prentice-Hall, 1962.

Kochevitsky, George. *The Art of Piano Playing: A Scientific Approach.* Princeton, NJ: Summy-Birchard, 1967.

"The Making of an Artist." *The Musical Standard* (October 25 1902): 259–260.

Merrick, Frank. *Practising the Piano.* London: Barrie and Rockliff, 1958.

Midgette, Anne. "Go to That Opera Again; Singers Are Only Human." *The New York Times*, December 20, 2006.

Neuhaus, Heinrich. *The Art of Piano Playing.* New York: Praeger, 1973.

O'Dea, Jane. *Virtue Or Virtuosity?: Explorations in the Ethics of Musical Performance.* Westport, CT: Greenwood Press, 2000.

Rink, John. "Chopin as Early Music." *Early Music* Vol. 29, No. 3 (2001): 339–340.

Wilson, Frank R. *The Hand: How Its Use Shapes the Brain, Language, and Human Culture.* New York: Vintage, 1999.

8

PHRASE-STORMING

Practice is preparation for those moments when you can create art through your interpretation of a piece of music. The artist sculpts sound as time moves forward, just as the potter shapes clay on the turning wheel.

But what shape? How does one decide? Unless you want your interpretations to have the spontaneity of a metronome or "run the gamut of emotions from A to B," to use Dorothy Parker's famous phrase, the answer lies neither in imitation nor well-rehearsed mannerisms. It inheres in a never-ending cascade of decisions made possible by all the freedom you have acquired to date.

Pianist Paul Ulanowsky (1908–1968), Lotte Lehmann's favorite accompanist and member of the renowned Bach Aria Group, warned the graduating class at Cincinnati College-Conservatory in June of 1962 against imitation and the adoption of another artist's mannerisms:

> If some musicians have successfully developed certain characteristics or mannerisms into hallmarks of their style, it doesn't mean that you will attain equal success by copying them. First of all, it isn't quite as easy to make that imitation sound genuine, secondly, the graft will always show at the seams, and thirdly, it is an odd thing that people who are quick to compare any newcomers of consequence to the outstanding representatives in their field, really don't want a second Rubinstein or Heifetz or Lehmann, even if this were imaginable for a moment.[1]

Galamian thought mimicking recordings was deplorable and saw that the student would become "unable to think of the composition except in terms of the recording artist."[2] The long-term effect of this practice would stunt a student's growth and prevent one's imagination from developing.[3]

John Dewey thought that imitation throws no light upon what's behind an act and that it is comparable to repeating a "fact as an explanation of itself."[4] Emerson thought that in imitation one would lose oneself, and he didn't mean the egoless surrender of self to creative inspiration. He bluntly wrote that "imitation is suicide."[5]

The situation is worse today as the first thing many students do is to seek a performance of a newly assigned piece they can stream or watch on YouTube. As Galamian noted, it's difficult to separate the listening "to see how it goes" from the listening that stealthily embeds another's interpretation into one's conception of the piece. Beyond this, though, *one isn't learning how to make artistic decisions.*

Imitation needs no decision-making, and it may seem to be an easy way to approach a new piece, *but decision-making itself requires practice.* If one is only trying to solve a problem, then the results may be constrained by the definition of the problem. The interpreter, much like an artist facing a blank canvas, must *create, articulate,* or *find* the problem to solve. Artistic problems are more discovered than given.

Through the act of phrase-storming, one can explore the minutest nuance of a phrase. Try out an idea. Let the sound roll around in your ear, discard the idea, and create another, and another, and perhaps two of the others will combine to form an interpretive idea that would never have been conceived of otherwise. Many musicians, of course, have written about the nuances of interpretation without accounting for how one learns to conceive of them, but some artists connect the capacity to explore nuance in interpretation with having explored rhythmic and dynamic variety in their technical practice.

The Kernel of the Profession

Pianist Harold Bauer (1873–1951) was no friend of mechanical scale practice and thought scale practice should be full of "variety and life" and that interpretation "should be full of tonal and rhythmic modifications. Briefly, it may be said that expression may be exemplified in four ways: loud, soft, fast, and slow. But within these crude divisions what infinite shades and gradations may be made! Then the personal equation also comes in. Variety and differentiation are of supreme importance—they are life!"[6]

In *Technique and Interpretation in Violin-Playing* from 1920, Rowsby Woof elaborates on these tonal and rhythmic modifications:

> To interpret music adequately many diverse qualities are required. Much variety of tone, judicious changes of tempo, suitable rubato, many shades of vibrato, musicianly phrasing, a sense of climax, and an appreciation of the different styles in music—all are complementary parts of a complete whole.[7]

Andor Földes thought the well-designed practice of exercises beneficial for accustoming the student to the technical requirements of nuance. The real value of exercises, he writes,

> lies in using [them] in different keys, rhythms, and dynamics. If we practice Hanon every day the same old way, our time will be wasted after a while because the practicing will get stale, mechanical, and dull. If we succeed in making our practice exciting by changing the keys, using interesting and difficult rhythms and varied dynamics, then we will profit by it.[8]

Mark Hambourg, who thought that in interpretation the artist must find "the kernel of his whole profession,"[9] thought it necessary to use "all possible technical means" to that end, which is done

> by means of accents, variations of tone-values (*crescendo* and *diminuendo*), variations of rhythm (*accelerando* and *ritardando*), variety of touch, and manipulation of the pedals. Accents enable the pianist to bring into prominence certain notes, or groups of notes, which might be comparable to cries, exclamations, interjections in the elocutionary art, or to sudden bursts of colour in painting.[10]

Hambourg clearly posits a relationship between interpretation and many of the practice variations explored in chapter 6. "The well-trained hand," Hambourg writes, is "the pliant tool of his imagination."[11] Note the direction of this equation: Being well-trained leads to the ability to bring life to one's vision.

Try Practicing for Beauty

Josef Lhévinne gives a too-brief description of what I call "phrase-storming":

> [I]t would be a very good plan to take a book of standard studies or pieces *very much below your grade of accomplishment* and by means of careful, thoughtful, devout study, in which your 'ears' play an equal role with your fingers, take phrase after phrase and play them over and over again.[12]

Note that Lhévinne wants to ensure that there are no technical barriers so that one's ears can do their work. He writes, "Try practicing for beauty as well as practicing for technic."[13] Lhévinne thought that "centuries of practice" are wasted because the search for beauty is ignored:

> Thousands of pianoforte recitals are given in the great music centers of the world by aspiring students every year. They look forward to great careers. They play their Liszt Rhapsodies, their Concertos and their Sonatas, often with most commendable accuracy, but with very little of

the one great quality which the world wants and for which it holds its highest rewards—Beauty.[14]

We saw in chapter 2 that Ivan Galamian called practice devoted to technical study "building time," and in chapter 7 we looked at "performing time." He also had students set aside a part of their practice for "interpreting time":

> During the interpreting time the emphasis should be placed on musical expressiveness, the shaping of a phrase, of a larger section, of a whole movement, and finally of several movements, as a convincing unit. Whereas during building time one should never permit a mistake to go uncorrected, during practice for interpretation (and still more so during performing time) it is advisable not to interrupt the execution every time a note is missed or some other small accident occurs.[15]

Note that Galamian recommends that one's interpretation grow by chunks: a phrase, a larger section, a movement.

In 1930, Sydney Robjohns writes about the joy of experimenting during practice, although he makes clear that this can only happen when "all musical and technical details have been studied and mastered, and when teaching has done its utmost."[16]

Studying and mastering these details is usually when students think their work is finished, but Robjohns says there remains a final effort, and by this effort "there comes into that individual's playing the life and charm that he alone, from the light of his poetic imagination, can give it."[17] Rachmaninoff thought this work was a "vital spark that seems to make each interpretation of a masterpiece—a living thing."[18] He added:

> Fine playing requires much deep thought away from the keyboard. The student should not feel that when the notes have been played his task is done. It is, in fact, only begun. He must make the piece a part of himself. Every note must awaken in him a kind of musical consciousness of his real artistic mission.[19]

By way of illustration, Robjohns relays a story about the great Belgian violinist, Eugène Ysaÿe. A pupil of Ysaÿe, Thomas Fussell, who told the story to Robjohns, called at Ysaÿe's home to get some music. Ysaÿe was practicing and not to be disturbed, so someone else in the house searched for the music, which took forty minutes. Fussell had one of the finest lessons of his life:

> He listened from another room, and for forty minutes he heard nothing but one short phrase. This was repeated over and over again—not to overcome technical difficulty: there was none;—not to memorize it, for any one could have memorized those few notes in fewer minutes;—but just

in the effort to find the ideal expression he knew that phrase could give. As the pupil left the house, the same few notes were still being repeated![20]

Anthony Tommasini, writing in *The New York Times* in 2016, gives an account of modern-day phrase-storming that is similar to Robjohn's description. Tommasini observed Russian pianist Daniil Trifonov practicing Schumann's *Kreisleriana* two days before Trifonov's Carnegie Hall recital: "Mr. Trifonov would repeat a rhapsodic flight—not to nail it technically, it seemed clear, but rather to highlight inner voices or bring out a milky coloring as harmonies mingled, what he described as paying 'attention to resolutions,' 'the way sounds connect.'"[21]

Violinist Achille Rivarde thought that not enough musicians did the type of work that Fussell (or Tommasini) overheard: "It would be interesting to know how many instrumentalists there are, even among artists of repute, who spend as much time in developing their musical ideas as they do in developing their muscles and making their fingers go."[22]

One pianist who did was Liszt. Hilda Gervers notes that Liszt would make students repeat musical fragments many times until it came close to his conception. Liszt's own interpretations did not rely on caprice or the muse of the moment. Gervers writes that "he worked them out searchingly beforehand then relied on his genius to breathe life into them in performance."[23]

Vision and a Passion for Variants

In *After the Golden Age: Romantic Pianism and Modern Performance*, Kenneth Hamilton gives an account of a lesson Franz Liszt gave in 1828 to Wilhelm von Lenz (1809–1883), taken from von Lenz's book, *The Great Piano Virtuosos of Our Time* from 1872.

Lenz played Weber's *Invitation to the Dance*. "Liszt," writes Lenz, "could hardly tear himself away from the piece. He played through the different parts over and over again. He tried various reinforcements. He played the second part of the minor movement in octaves, and was inexhaustible in his praise of Weber."[24] About the A-flat sonata, Lenz writes, "He played the first part over and over again in various ways. . . . He experimented in every direction." Lenz concludes, "So I had the experience of observing how one genius looks upon the work of another, and turns it to his own account."[25]

Hamilton quotes from an 1863 letter of Liszt's: "The fact is that the passion for variants, and for what seems to me to be ameliorations of style, has got a particular grip on me and gets stronger with age."[26]

In *Fire in the Crucible*, John Briggs writes about *themata*, or "nuance-laden themes,"[27] and how they evolve over time in creators of genius and dominate their work. Liszt's passion for variants helped form his creative vision. Briggs writes, "Great creators are different in the sense that they feel compelled to show the world that their themata in fact point to a hidden reality that people pursuing the consensual themata of the moment have failed to notice."[28]

But what happens when there is no vision?

The Thousand Cuts of Competence

Flannery O'Connor (1925–1964) gave many lectures during her short life. In an undated speech for an unknown audience, she said,

> Any idiot with a nickel's worth of talent can emerge from a writing class able to write a competent story. In fact, so many people can now write competent stories that the short story as a medium is in danger of dying of competence. We want competence, but competence by itself is deadly. What is needed is the vision to go with it.[29]

Leopold Auer thought many violinists were content to play the notes as written. He thought the result was a "dead level of monotony," which he attributed to a lack of phrasing.[30] The antidote to this monotony? Phrase-storming, although by another name:

> Play a phrase or a succession of passages in various ways, with varying inflections, with changing emphasis, now softly, now loudly, until you have found the natural interpretation, until those factors which, collectively, make up what we know as nuance have merged in a harmonious entirety of expression.[31]

Carl Flesch thought the harm done by a few ill-determined phrases insignificant compared to the aesthetic damage caused "when a specific phrasing is not attempted at all, but one follows only the composer's dynamic indications, and even observes the measure-beat as traditionally prescribed."[32] Flesch regarded the composer's indications, bars, and meter, as the "centers of gravity" of the phrases and points of support for

> *crescendo* and *diminuendo*, but also for the *stringendo* and *ritardando*; that is to say, for the dynamic as well as for the agogic shadings, the two principal factors of expressive performance. On the other hand, when we read and accentuate measure by measure, we have no motive to depart in any way from a rigid monotony of movement.[33]

What happens when there is no "center of gravity," to use Flesch's phrase? If the centers of gravity are the composer's interpretive indications—as well as an understanding of meter and metric hierarchies—and are to support *crescendo, diminuendo, stringendo, ritardando*, in short, *dynamic as well as agogic shadings*, how does one interact with the score when there are no indications to stimulate one's imagination?

In 2009, I argued in The Guitar Foundation of America's *Soundboard* that phrase markings are almost entirely absent in guitar music, even when the subject of a transcription had them (we saw this with Tárrega's transcription of

Chopin's prelude, Op. 28, No. 20 in chapter 6), and dynamic indications are scarce: "Guitarists don't have an original phrasing model in their Urtext editions, and they don't have a model of a later artist's interpretive edition. *There aren't even interpretive editions containing ideas with which we can disagree.*"[34] The lack of interpretive indications in many guitar scores shields from students the idea that nuance even exists. There may be many who can play a piece but who don't know how to search for beauty.

Example 8.1 shows the main theme and A section of Agustín Barrios Mangoré's Vals, Op. 8, No. 4, which, after an eight-bar introduction (not shown) and a four-bar wind-up, goes from measure thirteen to measure twenty-eight. These sixteen bars are made up of two eight-bar phrases, but the phrases do not fall into a predictable four-plus-four pattern. The first phrase proceeds by two-by-three-by-three, and the second phrase contrasts that by proceeding two-by-six, as I've marked below with accompanying dynamic indications:

EXAMPLE 8.1 Agustín Barrios Mangoré: Vals, Op. 8, No. 4, mm. 9–33.

This waltz was published in 1928 by Casa Romero Fernandez in Argentina and later in a posthumous collection of twenty-three pieces produced around 1952 by the luthier Romeo DiGiorgio. I've not seen the Casa Romero edition, but the DiGiorgio edition has one *crescendo* mark in measure fifteen, which sometimes shows up in later editions, but there are no dynamic indications, such as *f* or *pp*, sprinkled throughout the score to guide the performer. Other than the one *crescendo* mark, there are no interpretive indications. Guitarists who play the piece accenting measure by measure fall victim to Flesch's "monotony of movement." Without knowing the phrases, one cannot understand their "center of gravity" and will have little basis for understanding how to apply artistic nuance to give the phrases shape.

Busoni compares the search for artistic phrasing to the hours and hours great actors spend "seeking for the best method of expressing the author's meaning. No pianist of ability would think of giving less careful attention to phrasing."[35] For Busoni, fine phrasing is not a detail to be tacked on at the end of the study of a repertoire piece. It is the act of creating an artistic design over a work's underlying structure, although he acknowledges that "rules" need to change as one advances, as we saw in chapter 1:

> In instructing very young pupils it may be necessary to lead them to believe that the time must be marked in a definite manner by such accents, but as the pupil advances he must understand that the measure divisions are inserted principally for the purpose of enabling him to read easily. He should learn to look upon each piece of music as a beautiful tapestry in which the main consideration is the principal design of the work as a whole and not the invisible marking threads which the manufacturer is obliged to put in the loom in order to have a structure upon which the tapestry may be woven.[36]

The Wet Sponge

In 1948, Arnold Schoenberg wrote an essay called "Today's Manner of Performing Classical Music" in which he castigated artists for suppressing "all emotional qualities and all unnotated changes of tempo and expression."[37] Although he acknowledged that many artists at the turn of the twentieth century overdid things, Schoenberg connected the lack of tempo changes, *ritardando*, or *Luftpause* to express musical feelings with the influence of American popular dance music, where "no old culture regulated presentation."[38] Schoenberg writes that "a change of character, a strong contrast, will often require *a modification of tempo*" and that "over-accentuation of strong beats shows poor musicianship."[39]

Richard Wagner (1813–1883) wrote about tempo modification in 1869: "We may consider it established that in classical music written in the later style *modification* of tempo is a *sine qua non*."[40] Richard Hudson, in *Stolen Time: The History of Tempo Rubato*, gives an overview of Wagner's ideas:

> The central idea is that each theme, even within a single movement, has its own personality and hence requires its own proper tempo. This involves not only changing the tempo to suit each melody, but also making a transition from one tempo to another, with the appropriate ritards and accelerations occurring in the proper places. In addition, fast movements are taken faster and slow movements much slower than formerly. These concepts are applied, then, to the various themes in the sonata forms.[41]

Schoenberg's essay ends with a description of a performance that seemed "as if the conductor had taken a wet sponge, erasing all traces of problems by playing whole movements in one stiff, inflexible tempo."[42] Schoenberg thought that great artists of the past "could venture far-reaching changes of every kind without ever being wrong, without ever losing balance, without ever violating good taste."[43]

It takes a technique well-practiced in applying all manner of variety to incorporate the artistic nuances required to shape and contrast the phrases within a piece. Without this expressive shaping, one's performances may sound as lifeless as the performance Schoenberg heard that was wiped clean of any artistic shading.

Preconceived Notions

Rivarde complains about the enormous number of recitalists before the public who were:

> more or less efficiently equipped instrumentally, but with no claim whatsoever to any interpretative power. The regrettable result is that the general standard of interpretation remains at a very low level in this country. Great interpreters are exceedingly rare. There are many good artists and an overwhelming number of excellent players; but the great artists can generally be numbered on the fingers of one hand at any epoch, taking all the different branches of music into consideration.[44]

Could Rivarde have tapped into what historian and film critic Neal Gabler later identified as the difference between *entertainment values and art values*? "Art," writes Gabler, "is thought of as *in*ventional and entertainment as *con*ventional or formulaic."[45] Gabler quotes art critic Clement Greenberg, who compared Picasso to Repin, a representational painter of kitsch: "Where Picasso paints *cause*, Repin paints *effect*."[46] Isn't this the error John Dewy pointed out in chapter 1 and what pianist Email Sauer complained about in chapter 2: musicians who perform masterworks and try to reach the "lovers of sensation" through the use of "nauseating perfume"?

How does Rivarde account for this? These artists approach a piece of music with preconceived notions that prevent their intuitions from interacting with the work in the spirit of exploration, experimentation, and play, after which they'd be open to receive varying impressions from the work. Rivarde says they are more focused on their ability to *transmit* impressions than to *receive* them.[47] Having too rigid a preconceived idea about a piece shuts down the possibility of interesting problems emerging from creative work, which is what psychologists Mihaly Csikszentmihalyi and J. W. Getzels discovered in their research.

Exploration, Experimentation, and Playfulness

Guy Claxton relates an experiment carried out by University of Chicago faculty members Mihaly Csikszentmihalyi, the author of *Flow: The Psychology of Optimal Experience,* and J. W. Getzels, a professor in the Department of Education and Behavioral Sciences. The experiment was designed to see if they could find a correlation between the working methods of art students and the finished product, in this case, a still life.[48]

The students were presented with a wide choice of objects to use in their still life. Unlike a clearly defined problem with a well-defined method of solution, the students were free to decide what to paint and how to paint it.

The students *did* work in different ways. Claxton writes:

> From the large selection of objects available, from which to compose their still life, some students selected and handled as few as two, while others played with many more before settling on their selection. And some of them did "play": they did not just pick the objects up; they stroked them, threw them in the air, smelled them, bit into them, moved their parts, held them up to the light and so on. The students also varied in the actual objects they selected. Some chose from the "pool" those that were conventional, even clichéd, still-life subjects—a leather-bound book, a bunch of grapes. Others went for objects that were more surprising, or less hackneyed.[49]

Most surprising, though, were the differences in *how* the students worked once they started their pictures:

> Some continued to change the composition of the objects, or even the objects themselves, for quite a long time, so that the finished structure of the picture did not emerge until rather late in the creative process. Others, once they had made their composition, stuck to it religiously, and their pictures took on recognisable form rather early.[50]

What Getzels and Csikszentmihalyi learned was clear:

> The pictures produced by the students who had considered more objects, and more unusual ones, who played with them more, and who delayed foreclosing on the final form of the picture for as long as possible, changing their minds as they went along, were judged of greater originality and "aesthetic value" than the others. What is more, when the students were followed up seven years later, of those who were still practising artists, the most successful were those who had adopted the more playful and patient modus operandi.[51]

A too-precise definition of the problem to be solved in interpretation carries a double constraint. It limits one's artistry to the boundaries of the problem as defined, and it prevents one's artistic intuition from discovering or formulating other interesting problems, which is what Rivarde means by receiving an impression from the piece. Either of these can cause artistic paralysis as one may feel restricted and unable to act upon something interesting outside the defined problem. One then becomes unable, as Emerson advises, to "learn to detect and watch that gleam of light which flashes across his mind from within."[52]

Variety in repetition is the musical equivalent of interacting with a phrase and can be a musician's version of stroking an object, throwing it in the air, smelling it, biting it, manipulating its parts, and holding it up to the light.

Phrase-storming embraces exploration, experimentation, and, most importantly, playfulness. This open attitude can release a spark of creative intuition which in turn can connect with a body of knowledge, experience, and skill. The richer these are, the richer the possibility of high-level creative and artistic expression

Notes

1. This address is unpublished and was probably given when the school awarded Ulanowsky an honorary doctorate. My friend and the pianist's son, Philip Ulanowsky, has kindly provided me with a copy of his father's address.
2. Galamian, *Principles of Violin: Playing & Teaching*, 8.
3. Ibid.
4. Dewey, *Democracy, and Education*, 41.
5. Emerson, *Essay on Self-Reliance*, 10.
6. Brower, *Piano Mastery* (1915), 101.
7. Woof, *Technique and Interpretation*, 67.
8. Földes, *Keys to the Keyboard*, 90.
9. Hambourg, *How to Play the Piano*, 76.
10. Ibid., 79.
11. Ibid.
12. Lhévinne, *Basic Principles in Pianoforte Playing*, 39. [Italics added].
13. Ibid.
14. Ibid.
15. Galamian, *Principles of Violin: Playing & Teaching*, 100.

16. Robjohns, *Violin Technique*, 45.
17. Ibid.
18. Cooke, *Great Pianists on Piano Playing*, 217.
19. Ibid., 219.
20. Robjohns, *Violin Technique*, 45
21. Tommasini, "Fleet Fingers and Red-Eye Flights: A Pianist Is a Study in Stamina," *The New York Times*, C1.
22. Rivarde, *The Violin and Its Technique*, 46.
23. Gervers, "Franz Liszt as Pedagogue," 388.
24. Quoted in Kenneth Hamilton, *After the Golden Age: Romantic Pianism and Modern Performance* (New York: Oxford University Press, 2008), 201. (Wilhelm von Lenz, *The Great Piano Virtuosos of Our Time* (1872; London: Kahn and Averill, 1983), 19.)
25. Quoted in Ibid. (Von Lenz, *The Great Piano Virtuosos of Our Time*, 20–21).
26. Hamilton, *After the Golden Age*, 229.
27. Briggs, *Fire in the Crucible*, 155.
28. Ibid., 32.
29. Flannery O'Connor, *Mystery and Manners: Occasional Prose* (New York: Farrar, Straus and Giroux, 1970), 86.
30. Auer, *Violin Playing as I Teach It*, 162.
31. Ibid., 159.
32. Flesch, *The Art of Violin Playing, Book Two*, 58.
33. Ibid.
34. Berg, "The Re-Imagination of Performance," 8.
35. Cooke, *Great Pianists on Piano Playing*, 104.
36. Ibid., 104–105.
37. Arnold Schoenberg, "Today's Manner of Performing Classical Music," *Style and Idea*, ed. Leonard Stein (London: Faber and Faber, 1975), 320.
38. Ibid.
39. Ibid., 321. [Italics added].
40. Richard Wagner, *On Conducting: A Treatise on Style in the Execution of Classical Music*, trans. Edward Dannreuther (London: W. Reeves, 1897), 43.
41. Richard Hudson, *Stolen Time: The History of Tempo Rubato* (Oxford: Clarendon Press, 1997), 312.
42. Schoenberg, "Today's Manner of Performing Classical Music," 322.
43. Ibid., 321.
44. Rivarde, *The Violin and Its Technique*, 53.
45. Neal Gabler, *Life: The Movie, How Entertainment Conquered Reality* (New York: Vintage Books, 2000), 19.
46. Ibid.
47. Rivarde, *The Violin and Its Technique*, 53.
48. Details of the experiment can be found in J. W. Getzels and M. Csikszentmihalyi, *The Creative Vision: A Longitudinal Study of Problem Finding in Art* (New York: Wiley, 1976).
49. Claxton, *Hare Brain, Tortoise Mind*, 83.
50. Ibid.
51. Ibid., 83–84.
52. Emerson, *Essay on Self-Reliance*, 10.

Sources

Auer, Leopold. *Violin Playing as I Teach It*. New York: Frederick A. Stokes Company, 1921.
Berg, Christopher. "The Re-Imagination of Performance, Part One: Portamento." *The Soundboard* Vol. 35, No. 1 (2009): 6–18.

Briggs, John. *Fire in the Crucible: The Alchemy of Creative Genius*. New York: St. Martin's Press, 1988.

Brower, Harriette Moore. *Piano Mastery: Talks with Master Pianists and Teachers, and an Account of a Von Bülow Class, Hints on Interpretation*. New York: Frederick A. Stokes Company, 1915.

Claxton, Guy. *Hare Brain, Tortoise Mind: How Intelligence Increases When You Think Less*. New York: Harper Perennial, 1998.

Cooke, James Francis. *Great Pianists on Piano Playing*. Philadelphia: Theodore Presser Co., 1913.

Dewey, John. *Democracy and Education: An Introduction to the Philosophy of Education*. New York: The Macmillan Company, 1916.

Emerson, Ralph Waldo. *The Essay on Self-Reliance*. East Aurora, NY: The Roycrofters, 1908.

Galamian, Ivan. *Principles of Violin: Playing & Teaching*. Englewood Cliffs, NJ: Prentice-Hall, 1962.

Flesch, Carl. *The Art of Violin Playing, Book Two*. New York: Carl Fischer, Inc., 1930.

Földes, Andor. *Keys to the Keyboard, a Book for Pianists: With Explanatory Music*. New York: E.P. Dutton, 1948.

Gabler, Neal. *Life: The Movie: How Entertainment Conquered Reality*. New York: Vintage, 2000.

Gervers, Hilda. "Franz Liszt as Pedagogue." *Journal of Research in Music Education* Vol. 18, No. 4 (1970): 385–391.

Getzels, J. W., and M. Csikszentmihalyi. *The Creative Vision: A Longitudinal Study of Problem Finding in Art*. New York: Wiley, 1976.

Hambourg, Mark. *How to Play the Piano*. New York: George H. Doran Company, 1922.

Hamilton, Kenneth. *After the Golden Age: Romantic Pianism and Modern Performance*. New York: Oxford University Press, 2008.

Hudson, Richard. *Stolen Time: The History of Tempo Rubato*. Oxford: Clarendon Press, 1997.

Lhévinne, Josef. *Basic Principles in Pianoforte Playing*. Philadelphia: Theo. Presser Company, 1924.

O'Connor, Flannery. *Mystery and Manners: Occasional Prose*. New York: Farrar, Straus and Giroux, 1970.

Rivarde, A. *The Violin and Its Technique as a Means to the Interpretation of Music*. London: Macmillan, 1921.

Robjohns, Sydney. *Violin Technique: Some Difficulties and Their Solution*. London: Oxford University Press and H. Milford, 1930.

Schöenberg, Arnold. "Today's Manner of Performing Classical Music." In *Style and Idea*, edited by Leonard Stein, 320–322. London: Faber and Faber, 1975.

Tommasini, Anthony. "Fleet Fingers and Red-Eye Flights: A Pianist Is a Study in Stamina." *The New York Times*, December 10, 2016, C1.

Ulanowsky, Paul. *Unpublished Commencement Address Given at Cincinnati College-Conservatory of Music*, June, 1962.

Wagner, Richard. *On Conducting: A Treatise on Style in the Execution of Classical Music*. Translated by Edward Dannreuther. London: W. Reeves, 1897.

Woof, Rowsby. *Technique and Interpretation in Violin-Playing*. New York: London: Longmans, Green and E. Arnold, 1920.

9
FEEDBACK AND SELF-CRITICISM

I ended the last chapter with words from Emerson's essay *Self-Reliance*, but I didn't give you the end of quotation: "In every work of genius we recognise our own rejected thoughts; they come back to us with a certain alienated majesty."[1] Here we explore ways of looking at our thoughts with discernment so that we can recognize whether they are majestic or still need polishing.

It's unfortunate that the word "criticism" has an antagonistic and hostile character. It wasn't always so. One of the two definitions given in the 1913 Webster's Revised Unabridged Dictionary defines criticism as, "The rules and principles which regulate the practice of the critic; the art of judging with knowledge and propriety of the beauties and faults of a literary performance, or of a production in the fine arts; as, dramatic criticism." The definition given in Webster's 1828 dictionary is virtually identical. The first definition presented in today's Merriam-Webster's dictionary focuses on condemnation and rebuke: "The act of expressing disapproval and of noting the problems or faults of a person or thing: the act of criticizing someone or something." The second definition also implies negative judgment. It is only in the third definition that we learn about "careful judgments about . . . good and bad qualities".

Who wouldn't want to be able to make careful judgments about their work?

Contaminated Perceptions and Points of View

Self-criticism doesn't come easily to people, though, because it's so easily contaminated. As an adage puts it, "We do not see things as they are; we see things as we are."[2] In his *System of Subjective Public Laws* from 1892, Austrian lawyer Georg Jellinek (1851–1911) looked at what he called the "normative power of the factual."[3] One's sense of normality doesn't exist outside the facts of one's environment, even when one's environment becomes terribly distorted.

Rolf Dobelli, in *The Art of Thinking*, calls the *confirmation bias* "the father of all fallacies."[4] Those under its influence look for confirmation of their approach and simply cannot see information that would contradict this. Nassim Nicholas Taleb points out that chess grand masters are an exception because they "focus on where a speculative move might be weak."[5] Chess masters look for instances that would falsify a move and show it to be flawed, whereas novices look for information that confirms their choice.

Imaginary States and Other Illusions

Perfection has long been viewed as a laudable goal by musicians past and present. It is a goal against which one measures oneself, but it is a goal absent both definition and the means to reach it. It is a benighted synonym for John Dewey's "endless ends." The problem with perfection is that its definition keeps changing; even if you think you have defined it today, and reach it tomorrow, defining it and reaching it have expanded your vision, and "perfect" must be redefined. As with the horizon, wherever you are, there's *always* a distant horizon. At best, the term is used as shorthand for the minimal standard of getting the correct notes and rhythms; at its worst, it encourages measuring oneself against a master without understanding what went into how that master developed, like Dewey's mention of taking a "fact as an explanation of itself." As a measure of performance, it's meaningless, unless perfection is understood as one of the definitions given in the OED: "Fully accomplished; thoroughly versed or trained in," but this is not the way the word is commonly used. George Leonard, in his book *Mastery*, includes perfectionism in a chapter called "Pitfalls Along the Path."[6] Contaminated points of view can sometimes beget perfectionism.

Many artists have written about the paralyzing effects of perfectionism, whether one is facing a blank page, a blank canvas, or an uninterpreted score. Writer Anne Lamott calls perfectionism "the voice of the oppressor" and that it will "ruin your writing, blocking inventiveness and playfulness and life force."[7] Perfectionism compromises one's ability to size up what one has done and accurately settle upon the next steps. Christopher Hitchens equates perfectionists with zealots: they "can break but not bend; in my experience they are subject to burnout from diminishing returns or else, to borrow Santayana's definition of the fanatic, they redouble their efforts just when they have lost sight of their ends."[8] In his *Devil's Dictionary* from 1911, Ambrose Bierce defined perfection as: "An imaginary state of quality distinguished from the actual by an element known as excellence."

The "iceberg illusion," a term used by Anders Ericsson, sheds light on why concepts of perfection based upon another's experience are pointless. Syed describes this as "witnessing the end product of a process measured in years."[9] We see the result, but we don't see all the submerged, decades-long work. One may even become misled by the effortless quality honed by years of work and believe it's easy to obtain. Nassim Nicholas Taleb has a passage about the opacity of history in *The Black Swan*, which can easily be adapted to illustrate the opaqueness of performance:

> Performance is opaque. You see what comes out, not the practice that produces the work, the generator and developer of ability and talent. There is a fundamental incompleteness in your grasp of such work, since you do not see what's inside the box, how the mechanisms work. What I call the generator and developer of ability and talent is different from ability and talent themselves, much as the minds of the gods cannot be read just by witnessing their deeds. You are very likely to be fooled about their intentions.[10]

Mark Hambourg says: "To the properly equipped pianist nothing is difficult, nor are there certain passages that some have described as a hurdle which is sometimes made at a leap and sometimes missed."[11] But it's hard work to make a thing easy, and as we saw with the curse-of-knowledge effect in chapters 3 and 4, those who have done it are not always masterful when it comes to guiding others.

David Dunning and Justin Kruger, who described the Dunning-Kruger Effect, suggest that incompetent people seldom receive honest feedback about their skills.[12] Peter Brown explains that some people overestimate their competence and can't distinguish between their performance and the standard in their field. If one can't distinguish between incompetence and competence, how can one improve?[13]

A few great musicians and teachers have been aware of the deleterious effects of falling prey to a contaminated point of view. Ivan Galamian writes about the difficulty students have listening to themselves: "The things they actually hear are strongly distorted by what they want and hope to hear. When they have an opportunity to make a recording they are shocked to find things they would never believe they had actually done."[14] We've seen Paul Ulanowsky inveigh against trying to imitate great artists, which is a version of mistaking the goal for the means, as are perfectionism and the iceberg illusion.

The quest for perfection should be rationed out in small, manageable doses, like rich food, so that one's self-criticism does not result in bingeing on a self-directed *ad hominem* attack. Peter Brown unequivocally states that "we are poor judges of when we are learning well and when we're not."[15] There needs to be an apprenticeship period when, according to John Briggs, one learns creative working routines, develops focus, gains an understanding of a discipline's structures, learns to explore material from different directions, and, most importantly, learns to "recognize the nuances of other works in the creative field as having both relevance and irrelevance to the personal creative purpose."[16] Unfortunately, if one's teacher is giving feedback that compares one's performance to a distant goal but has not explored how to reach it, feedback won't be very healthy or useful.

Motivation and Reward

How do we receive feedback in a way that is focused and helps us solve what needs to be solved, or fix what needs to be fixed, without affecting our creativity? This question is worthwhile and sets the stage for the usefulness of self-criticism. The answer lies in whether one's motivations are extrinsic or intrinsic and whether there's an external reward.

Mihaly Csikszentmihalyi's groundbreaking research on flow explores a state of maximum performance characterized by concentration so strong that it results in immunity to irrelevant thoughts, the disappearance of self-consciousness, and a distorted sense of time.[17] Csikszentmihalyi found that an "activity that produces such experiences is so gratifying that people are willing to do it for its own sake, with little concern for what they will get out of it, even when it is difficult or dangerous."[18] High-level performers are experts in their ability to produce flow experiences, which is another way of describing what should happen in good practice: One works to *create the conditions* for flow to occur in performance. John Briggs presents a one-line description of a prerequisite for flow: "Flow occurs when there is a proper alignment of skill and challenge."[19] The alignment of skills and challenges should be the object of all good students and teachers and describes the most beneficial relationship between means and ends. One's awareness of artistic nuance can increase challenges, even in a simple piece. As a corollary, students who are bored with their practice should first question the awareness of artistic nuance they bring to their work.

Csikszentmihalyi presents a diagram in his book that shows boredom results when skills are high and challenges are low, and anxiety results when challenges are high and skills are low.[20] These descriptions are useful, but gauging when skills and challenges are aligned requires one to have accurate perceptions, and we know perceptions can become contaminated.

Csikszentmihalyi discusses traits that are obstacles to flow. Although a self-conscious self and a self-centered self are different, Csikszentmihalyi suggests that they are alike in that they both "are condemned to permanent exclusion from enjoyment."[21] The former because of a preoccupation with the perceptions of others; the latter because nothing has value except in its relationship to the desires of the self-centered self.

John Briggs, in *Fire in the Crucible*, looks at the nature of absorption, which he sees as a condition for creativity: "[T]he ability to be absorbed in the creative activity is the mirror if not the essence of talent."[22] Briggs suggests that absorption is a condition of flow and is also intrinsically rewarding.[23] Matthew Syed notes that when one's motivation is *internal*, practice is enjoyable. He quotes tennis legend Monica Seles: "I just love to practice and drill and all that stuff."[24] Serena Williams said, "It felt like a blessing to practice because we had so much fun."[25] Absorption in practice is its own reward.

Teresa Amabile, a psychology professor at Brandeis University, writes, "The more complex the activity, the more it's hurt by extrinsic reward."[26] She has shown that *creativity may depend on it being its own reward.*[27] Amabile's research reveals that when her subjects "thought they were working for an external remuneration, they became less creative."[28] Geoffrey Colvin cites studies showing "that virtually any external attempt to constrain or control the work results in less creativity. Just being watched is detrimental. Even being offered a reward for doing the work results in less creative output than being offered nothing."[29]

The danger this can pose to giving oneself useful and reliable self-criticism is that one may evaluate oneself in terms of whether one has received a reward, or by the amount of the reward, rather than by the quality of the activity itself. When this happens, self-criticism can become contaminated.

This doesn't mean that artists shouldn't receive rewards for their work, but it does mean that seasoned artists have learned to place a preoccupation with rewards in the background *during the act of creation*. Flannery O'Connor describes why this is important: "[I]n art the self becomes self-forgetful in order to meet the demands of the thing seen and the thing being made."[30] In "On Being a Writer," an essay that appeared in *The New York Review of Books* in 1987, V. S Naipaul quotes Marcel Proust (1871–1922): "A book is the product of a different *self* from the self we manifest in our habits, in our social life, in our vices."[31] Briggs summarizes this nicely: "The self that is ambitious for success and takes credit for a great work is not, in fact, the same self that created it."[32]

When it comes to self-criticism, which self is making the criticism, and what are its values?

Corrective Feedback

Anders Ericsson sees quality feedback vital to the success of one's practice. Without good feedback, even when students have plenty of motivation, "efficient learning is impossible and improvement only minimal."[33] If a student is engaged in well-designed practice, feedback must correlate with these well-designed steps.

The process of making corrections based on sound feedback amounts to working with desirable difficulties, which enhances learning. When students make mistakes but are given good feedback and fix the mistakes, the errors are not learned.[34] The work required to fix the errors helps to increase mastery.

Howard Austin found that those who acquire fluency easily are open to feedback and are able to give themselves good advice. Those who have difficulty learning are not as open to what Austin calls "advice techniques."[35] He found it surprising that intellectual analysis and the consequent advice should play such a large role throughout one's development, as opposed to only the early stages of study, but we've seen that it's the ability to change direction (that is, re-design one's work) that accounts for the continued growth of a musician. Whether Alexander's process of inhibition or Jorge Bolet's ability to solve technical and musical problems away from the keyboard, this work is based on trustworthy feedback. The key word here is "trustworthy." Austin acknowledges that "some experts give bad advice while others are definitely worth listening to."[36] The ideas in this book may provide musicians with an enhanced ability to assess whether the feedback they receive or the self-criticism they've learned is trustworthy and reliable.

Sometimes students can't act upon feedback, no matter how good it might be. Psychologist Carol Dweck was curious why some people are helpless in the face of a new problem, and others are undaunted and set about trying new strategies. Dweck came to see that the former had adopted what she calls a "fixed mindset," whereas the latter had adopted a "growth mindset." Those with a fixed mindset see failure as a lack of innate abilities that are beyond their control; those with a growth mindset view failure as caused by a lack of effort or the wrong kind of effort. The amount and type of effort are things a person can change and control.[37] Being labeled "talented" or "untalented"—it doesn't matter which—can increase the chances of one developing a fixed mindset.

Errorless Learning?

In the 1950s and 1960s, psychologist B. F. Skinner promoted the idea of "errorless learning." The problem with this approach, says Syed, is that it assumes errors to be the result of faulty instruction and to be counterproductive.[38] Syed concludes that this results in a fear of failure and can "poison learning by creating aversions to the kinds of experimentation and risk taking that characterize striving, or by diminishing performance under pressure, as in a test setting."[39]

Shortly after I stopped studying with Aaron Shearer (1919–2008), my teacher at the Peabody Conservatory, he implemented a procedure he termed "developmental performance." These performances were slow, memorized run-throughs of a piece before an audience of other students in a class devoted to this purpose. The object was to achieve a flawless rendition of a piece to develop confidence and security in performance. I don't know whether Shearer knew about Skinner's idea of "errorless learning" or came up with this idea on his own, but those who have had these "performances" as a regular part of their training can end up afraid of failure and overly cautious. Whether the promise of perfection was part of Shearer's original idea, or something tacked on by those who taught it in his name, is impossible to know, but it's easy to see how students might equate the object of these performances with achieving perfection. Perfection admits no degree, so the slightest flaw means a performance is imperfect. If these imperfections are viewed as failures, they can inculcate in students an aversion to risk, but a willingness to take risks is necessary, as Horowitz said, "to make the music really live." Another danger—as Carl Flesch noted in chapter 3—is that one's ear can become dull.

The ability to effect an errorless performance is not the first step to greatness.

The First Step to Greatness

Why the long wind-up before getting to how musicians regarded self-criticism? One must come to understand the bias or point of view a teacher has when offering feedback because this will inform the way one evaluates one's work. Students must know their own biases in case these compromise their ability to provide themselves with healthy and useful self-criticism. Samuel Johnson gives a clue to the first step: "The first Step to Greatness is to be honest."[40]

Self-Criticism as Self-Cultivation

Most of the famous artists and teachers from whom we've heard often mention self-criticism as a crucial ingredient to success. Malwine Brée writes,

> There is still another stage in correct piano-playing: self-criticism. Whoever has got so far as to criticize himself as sharply as his neighbor, is far advanced; for even the recognition of one's faults means much, although there is yet a long step to their amendment.[41]

To the modern ear, phrases like "criticize sharply" have a harsh, judgmental tone. It has been a "tradition" in high-level music instruction for some teachers to wield harsh condemnations unanchored to insights about what a student can do to fix the object of the criticism. Amy Fay wrote of Carl Tausig in a letter from 1870, "Tausig is so hasty and impatient that to be in his classes must be a fearful ordeal. He will not bear the slightest fault. The last time I went into his class to hear him teach he was dreadful."[42] Six months later, she was accepted to his class and noted, "It is his principle to rough you and snub you as much as he can, even when there is no occasion for it, and you can think yourself fortunate if he does not hold you up to the ridicule of the whole class."[43] Tausig hovered over her as she played a Chopin scherzo commenting, "Terrible! Shocking! Dreadful!"[44] Fay ran from the room in tears when she finished. Later, Tausig asked her why she was crying, oblivious to the reason.

Contrast this with a description of a Liszt master class in 1877:

> Liszt was standing by the piano, surrounded by about fifteen pupils. . . . He
> sometimes interrupted his pupils, sat down and played himself, making
> various comments, generally full of humor, witty and good-natured . . .
> He did not scold or get angry, the pupils did not feel affronted . . . In all
> his comments he was . . . gentle and delicate and sparing of his pupils'
> vanity.[45]

It's easy for students to internalize a Tausig-like invective, which compromises their ability to see accurately their weaknesses as well as their strengths. The feedback given by teachers should be possessed of the honesty Dr. Johnson requires and the sensitivity and insight an interpretive art requires. Teachers need to practice self-criticism regarding their teaching.

Fernando Sor wrote about self-criticism and correction in his work but insisted upon the same level of reflection from those who disagreed with him:

> I made mistakes, and have been indebted to them for a multitude of reflections which I never should have made perhaps without the necessity of self-correction: so true it is that, when we reason, we can derive advantage from the involuntary errors we may have committed. I request the reader to examine well my reasons, and not to sanction them without judging of their validity. I may deceive myself, being no more exempt from error than another person; but I am for plain dealing, and, because I endeavour to prove what I advance, I can never admit a contrary opinion but by virtue of sufficient reasons. A smart saying, raillery, quoting an authority, will not amount to proof, and I have a right to require a just reciprocity.[46]

The language of criticism can be made more palatable by thinking of it the way one thinks of critical thinking in the best sense of those words: continuously striving to uncover the value and meaning of something.

Stop and Think

Marie von Unschuld ends her book with advice that it is better to think than play. She acknowledges that playing before others is a great help in becoming sure of the piece but that "self-criticism must not rest even then," and that praise from others shouldn't lull one to sleep.[47] She includes a curious injunction from pianist Anton Rubinstein (1829–1894) *not* to play for family members but for strangers, "and observe closely the impression which the playing makes. Ask yourself then what is to be blamed for the greater or less pleasure, and learn from that."[48] (The assumption is, I suppose, that family members would have less-objective responses.) It is "listening to one's self, proving [another archaic use of the word 'prove'] and criticizing one's self which alone leads to progress, to an ever higher grade of perfection in artistic ability."[49]

Leopold Auer ties self-criticism to close self-observation: "When [my pupils] practise without observing and criticizing themselves they merely develop and perfect their faults. They are worse than wasting their time."[50] The real source of progress, according to Auer, lies in the mental labor needed to control and direct one's efforts.

Pianist Frank Merrick connects self-criticism with mental work. He writes, "When time is also taken for self-criticism, all sorts of practical questions like 'Did the fingering, pedalling, etc., all conduce to give me a recognisable copy of that mental rehearsal?' can be seriously faced."[51] Merrick is connecting the technique of stopping-practice to self-criticism.

Spaced Repetition Helps Self-Criticism

Pianist and composer John McEwen (1868–1948), writing in 1919, finds spaced practice to be of help. He stresses that one's full attention needs to be concentrated on one's practice but admits that mental effort can't continue indefinitely:

> After a certain amount of concentrated attention the brain becomes numb and the work in general suffers from a want of *self-criticism*. To avoid this, I have found it very useful to divide one's practice time into periods of fifteen to thirty minutes each, with a general average of twenty minutes per period, followed by a period of rest of from two to five minutes.[52]

For McEwen, self-criticism underlay all practice.

The Difference Between Theory and Practice

Violinist Theodore Spierling, also writing in 1919, saw self-criticism as the means of discovering whether "theory and practice conform with one another."[53] Earlier we discussed how Robert Bjork's desirable difficulties present students with a focused struggle to overcome or a problem to solve. Self-criticism is the way this comes about, and Spierling's description lines up with distinct actions given by Coyle:

1. Pick a target.
2. Reach for it.
3. Evaluate the gap between the target and the reach.
4. Return to step one.[54]

Spierling's "theory" is Coyle's "target"; reaching for it is Spierling's "practice"; self-criticism is step three: evaluating the gap between the two.

Pianist Ruth Deyo, like Spierling, connects self-criticism to discerning the gap between one's inner hearing of a work and what she calls "exteriorizing." Exteriorizing is

> the ability to give to the audience the exact impression of the music you desire to present to them, thereby making the composition clear and intelligible and not muddled, which it is bound to be if you only hear it in the inner ear and do not put the necessary technical work on it to express all your inner thoughts to the listener.[55]

Deyo takes us back to technique work if we present the composition in a way that is muddled.

Deyo requires one to analyze the musical components of a composition with care and then to apply equal care to the technique required to avoid what she calls "this natural and insidious fault," that is, an unintelligible and muddled reading of the piece. She advises:

> Try to listen to yourself from the outside. You will find this one of the most difficult things to do and one of the most fatal things to neglect. Self-criticism is the artist's safeguard and the moment he becomes influenced by the audience's good opinion of him, in that moment is he bound to deteriorate unless he constantly keeps strict standards before him of what is artistically right.[56]

Pianist Wilhelm Bachaus implies that through a continuous process of self-criticism, evaluating the gap between the effects he wants and what comes out, he added to his interpretive palette: "I produce them by listening, criticizing, judging—working over the point, until I get it as I want it. Then I can reproduce it at will, if I want to make just the same effect."[57]

Learning to Listen

It's hard to hear oneself accurately, but it is something one can learn to do. In 1913, pianist Max Pauer spoke about how surprised he was upon hearing himself on a recording for the first time: "I heard things which seemed unbelievable to me. Was I, after years of public playing, actually making mistakes that I would be the first to condemn in any one of my own pupils? I could hardly believe my ears."[58] Pauer heard "dislocation" (pianists' word for playing one hand slightly after the other) and many small errors he didn't know he had made. He also heard some good things: "I had unconsciously brought out certain nuances, emphasized different voices and employed special accents without the consciousness of having done so."[59]

Busoni thought that every sound produced during practice "should be heard with ears open to give that sound the intelligent analysis which it deserves."[60] Busoni extends this type of listening to performance and self-improvement:

> At my own recitals no one in the audience listens more attentively than I do. I strive to hear every note and while I am playing my attention is so concentrated upon the one purpose of delivering the work in the most artistic manner dictated by the composer's demands and my conception of the piece, that I am little conscious of anything else. I have also learned that I must continually have my mind alert to opportunities for improvement. I am always in quest of new beauties and even while playing in public it is possible to conceive of new details that come like revelations.[61]

Decades later, violinist Yehudi Menuhin (1916–1999) praised recording technology as a boon to more accurate performance: "[I]t is only with the gramophone that self-criticism has reached its present high standard."[62]

Self-Criticism as a Learned Skill

Teresa Carreño was taught how to criticize herself:

> Part of my training consisted in being shown how to criticize myself. I learned to listen, to be critical, to judge my own work; for if it was not up to the mark I must see what was the matter and correct it myself. The earlier this can be learned the better. I attribute much of my subsequent success to this ability. I still carry out this plan, for there on the piano you will find all the notes [the scores] for my coming recitals, which I work over and take with me everywhere. This method of study I always try to instill into my pupils.[63]

The Teacher's Deputy

Carl Courvoisier makes explicit the relationship between feedback from one's teacher and self-criticism:

> Let him try to be as critical with himself as he finds his teacher to be, and he will see the reason why he should not be permitted to do any guesswork, or to rush to difficult tasks. Thus he will avoid both negligence and impatience.[64]

Galamian makes the same connection and regards practice as the continuation of the lesson, which is why teachers need to teach their students how to practice well. When I discussed the trial-and-error fallacy in chapter 1, I acknowledged that one practices, evaluates the results, and moves on from there, *but one needs to learn how to do this*, as Teresa Carreño did. Practice as the continuation of the lesson means practice is "a process of self-instruction in which, in the absence of the teacher, the student has to act as the teacher's deputy, assigning himself definite tasks and supervising his own work."[65]

Notes

1. Emerson, *Essay on Self-Reliance*, 10.
2. It's been impossible to track down the origin of this saying. It has been attributed to the Talmud, Anaïs Nin, Immanuel Kant, Steven Covey, and numerous minor writers.
3. Discussed in Christopher Clark, *The Sleepwalkers, How Europe Went to War in 1914* (New York: Harper, 2013), 361.
4. Rolf Dobelli, *The Art of Thinking Clearly* (Reprint, New York: Harper Paperbacks, 2014), 22.
5. Nassim Nicholas Taleb, *The Black Swan: Second Edition: The Impact of the Highly Improbable: With a New Section: "On Robustness and Fragility"* (New York: Random House Trade Paperbacks, 2010), 59.
6. Leonard, *Mastery*, 140.
7. Anne Lamott, *Bird by Bird: Some Instructions on Writing and Life* (New York: Pantheon Books, 1994), 28.
8. Christopher Hitchens, *Letters to a Young Contrarian* (New York: Basic Books, 2001), 33.
9. Syed, *Bounce*, 22.
10. See the original quote in: Taleb, *The Black Swan*, 8.
11. Hambourg, "The Making of an Artist," 259.
12. Brown, *Make It Stick*, 122.
13. Ibid., 121.
14. Galamian, *Principles of Violin: Playing & Teaching*, 101–102.
15. Brown, *Make It Stick*, 3.
16. Briggs, *Fire in the Crucible*, 264.
17. Mihaly Csikszentmihalyi, *Flow: The Psychology of Optimal Experience* (New York: HarperPerennial, 1991), 71.
18. Ibid.
19. Briggs, *Fire in the Crucible*, 150.
20. Csikszentmihalyi, *Flow*, 74.
21. Ibid., 84.
22. Briggs, *Fire in the Crucible*, 200.
23. Ibid., 210.
24. Syed, *Bounce*, 63.
25. Ibid., 63–64.
26. Briggs, *Fire in the Crucible*, 111.
27. Ibid., 210.
28. Ibid.
29. Colvin, *Talent Is Overrated*, 191.
30. O'Connor, *Mystery and Manners*, 82.
31. V. S. Naipaul, "On Being a Writer," *The New York Review of Books* Vol. 34, No. 7 (April 23, 1987): 7. The quote is from Proust's *Against Sainte-Beuve*, which Naipaul called, "—a strange and original and beautiful form, part autobiography, part literary criticism, part fiction."

32. Briggs, *Fire in the Crucible*, 78.
33. Ericsson, "The Role of Deliberate Practice," 367.
34. Syed, *Bounce*, 90.
35. Austin, "A Computational Theory," 212.
36. Ibid., 329.
37. Brown, *Make It Stick*, 179–180. Carol Dweck devotes an entire book to this: *Mindset: The Psychology of Success* (New York: Ballantine Books, 2007).
38. Ibid.
39. Ibid., 91.
40. Freya Johnston, *Samuel Johnson and the Art of Sinking 1709–1791* (New York: Oxford University Press, 2005), 99.
41. Brée and Baker, *The Groundwork of the Leschetizky Method*, 77.
42. Fay, *Music-Study in Germany*, 40.
43. Ibid., 82.
44. Ibid., 83.
45. Gervers, "Franz Liszt as Pedagogue," 390.
46. Sor, *Method for the Spanish Guitar*, 47.
47. Unschuld, *The Pianist's Hand*, 64.
48. Ibid.
49. Ibid.
50. Auer, *Violin Playing as I Teach It*, 42.
51. Merrick, *Practising the Piano*, 2.
52. John B. McEwen, *The Foundations of Musical Aesthetics: Or the Elements of Music* (London: K. Paul, Trench, Trubner & Co., 1917), 5. [Italics added].
53. Martens, *Violin Mastery*, 249.
54. Coyle, *The Talent Code*, 92.
55. Brower, *Piano Mastery: Second Series* (1917), 140–141.
56. Ibid.
57. Ibid., 168.
58. Cooke, *Great Pianists on Piano Playing*, 201–202.
59. Ibid.
60. Ibid., 98.
61. Ibid., 99.
62. Yehudi Menuhin, *Theme and Variations* (New York: Stein and Day, 1972), 49.
63. Brower, *Piano Mastery* (1915), 162. Carreño, like Hans von Bülow, Percy Grainger, and Amy Fay, uses "the notes" to mean "the scores."
64. Courvoisier, *The Technics of Violin Playing*, 7.
65. Galamian, *Principles of Violin: Playing & Teaching*, 93.

Sources

Auer, Leopold. *Violin Playing as I Teach It*. New York: Frederick A. Stokes Company, 1921.

Austin, Howard. "A Computational Theory of Physical Skill." PhD diss., Massachusetts Institute of Technology, 1976.

Brée, Malwine, and Theodor Baker. *The Groundwork of the Leschetizky Method*. New York: G. Schirmer, 1902.

Briggs, John. *Fire in the Crucible: The Alchemy of Creative Genius*. New York: St. Martin's Press, 1988.

Brower, Harriette Moore. *Piano Mastery: Second Series; Talks with Master Pianists and Teachers*. New York: Frederick A. Stokes Company, 1917.

Brower, Harriette Moore. *Piano Mastery: Talks with Master Pianists and Teachers, and an Account of a Von Bülow Class, Hints on Interpretation.* New York: Frederick A. Stokes Company, 1915.

Brown, Peter C., Henry L. Roediger III, and Mark A. McDaniel. *Make It Stick: The Science of Successful Learning.* Cambridge, MA: Belknap Press, 2014.

Clark, Christopher. *The Sleepwalkers: How Europe Went to War in 1914.* New York: Harper, 2013.

Colvin, Geoffrey. *Talent Is Overrated: What Really Separates World-Class Performers from Everybody Else.* New York: Portfolio Trade, 2010.

Cooke, James Francis. *Great Pianists on Piano Playing.* Philadelphia: Theodore Presser Co., 1913.

Courvoisier, Karl. *The Technics of Violin Playing.* London: The Strad, 1894.

Coyle, Daniel. *The Talent Code: Greatness Isn't Born: It's Grown: Here's How.* New York: Bantam, 2009.

Csikszentmihalyi, Mihaly. *Flow: The Psychology of Optimal Experience.* New York: Harper Perennial, 1991.

Dobelli, Rolf. *The Art of Thinking Clearly.* New York: Harper Paperbacks, 2014.

Emerson, Ralph Waldo. *The Essay on Self-Reliance.* East Aurora, NY: The Roycrofters, 1908.

Ericsson, K. A., R. T. Krampe, and C. Tesch-Römer. "The Role of Deliberate Practice in the Acquisition of Expert Performance." *Psychological Review* (1993): 363–406.

Fay, Amy, and Fay Peirce. *Music-Study in Germany, from the Home Correspondence of Amy Fay.* Chicago: A. C. McClurg, 1886.

Galamian, Ivan. *Principles of Violin: Playing & Teaching.* Englewood Cliffs, NJ: Prentice-Hall, 1962.

Gervers, Hilda. "Franz Liszt as Pedagogue." *Journal of Research in Music Education* Vol. 18, No. 4 (1970): 385–391.

Hitchens, Christopher. *Letters to a Young Contrarian.* New York: Basic Books, 2001.

Johnston, Freya. *Samuel Johnson and the Art of Sinking 1709–1791.* Oxford: Oxford University Press, 2005.

Lamott, Anne. *Bird by Bird: Some Instructions on Writing and Life.* New York: Pantheon Books, 1994.

Leonard, George. *Mastery: The Keys to Success and Long-Term Fulfillment.* New York: Plume, 1992.

Martens, Frederick Herman. *Violin Mastery: Talks with Master Violinists and Teachers, Comprising Interviews with Ysaÿe, Kreisler, Elman, Auer, Thibaud, Heifetz, Hartmann, Maud Powell and Others.* New York: Frederick A. Stokes company, 1919.

McEwen, John B. *The Foundations of Musical Aesthetics: Or the Elements of Music.* London: K. Paul, Trench, Trubner & Co., 1917.

Menuhin, Yehudi. *Theme and Variations.* New York: Stein and Day, 1972.

Merrick, Frank. *Practising the Piano.* London: Barrie and Rockliff, 1958.

Naipaul, V. S. "On Being a Writer." *The New York Review of Books* Vol. 34, No. 7, (April 23, 1987): 7.

O'Connor, Flannery. *Mystery and Manners: Occasional Prose.* New York: Farrar, Straus and Giroux, 1970.

Sor, Fernando. *Method for the Spanish Guitar.* Translated by A. Merrick. London: R. Cocks & Co., n.d. Reprint, New York: Da Capo Press, 1971.

Syed, Matthew. *Bounce: Mozart, Federer, Picasso, Beckham, and the Science of Success.* Harper Perennial, 2011.

Taleb, Nassim Nicholas. *The Black Swan: Second Edition: The Impact of the Highly Improbable: With a New Section: "On Robustness and Fragility".* New York: Random House Trade Paperbacks, 2010.

Unschuld, Marie von. *The Pianist's Hand.* Translated by Henry Morgan Dare. Leipzig: Breitkopf & Härtel, 1903.

10

CODETTA

When practice advice is vague—as was Theodor Kullak's to Amy Fay—students become susceptible to wasting time as they cast about for direction. When advice is overly regimented—as it is in books that have listings of specific exercises and times to be spent on each—one is just as likely to waste time. Advice that is regimented and tightly ordered allows no redesign, yet one's practice should be under almost sacred observation and vary as one develops. The question is always: "Upon what basis does one modify one's work?"

Witnessing a concert performance—the audible and visible result of practice—does not contain information about all the behind-the-scenes work. Even when Thomas Fussell eavesdropped on Eugène Ysaÿe, as valuable as that was, what he heard was only a fleeting moment among the thousands and thousands of hours Ysaÿe had spent practicing. What had Ysaÿe done previously to get to the point where he could exercise his musical imagination unfettered by technical concerns? The *practice* practices of renowned artists will always surprise amateurs and students.

We saw in chapter 7 that Busoni played through his program slowly and without expression the day of a concert. Who could have inferred that from his performances? Tilly Fleischmann tells of how her friend, Edward Martyn (1859–1923), managed to discover the time of day that Liszt practiced and listened outside the window. What did Martyn hear? Nothing but scales for as long as he stayed.[1] When Liszt was younger, he practiced technique up to twelve hours a day; when he was older and giving his master classes in Weimer in the 1870s and 1880s, he was bored by technique and refused to teach it.[2] But here was the aged Liszt practicing scales.

Sometimes artists say one thing about practice but practice something else. Oscar Beringer (1844–1922), Piano Professor at the Royal Academy of Music in London, wrote in 1907 that Carl Tausig so disliked people hearing him practice that he had extra felt put on the hammers of his piano to deaden the sound.[3] Beringer, who studied with Tausig for three years, wrote in 1914 that in those three years Tausig never showed him a single technical exercise. Yet, after Tausig's death in 1871, a huge amount of technical material Tausig had made for his personal use was found among his papers.[4]

Autocratic teachers, or those who teach a system rather than a student, can know *what* a student doesn't understand, but they don't usually know *how* a student doesn't understand. There is a multiplicity of ways students can misunderstand something, and instruction can be futile if it isn't designed to create understanding. Overly prescriptive written instructions are like autocratic teachers, but authors of written instructions don't know what their readers don't understand. Music practice involves more than learning how to navigate the exigencies of one's instrument. Understanding material from disciplines outside of music that explore the development of exceptional skill can help students understand the reasons behind the decisions they need to make once they are alone in the practice room.

I mentioned in the preface that *Practicing Music by Design* is more of a "why-do" book than a "how-to" book. The best practice advice is that which helps students identify real problems rather than be misled by symptoms of problems. Then teachers can work toward developing a student's ability to design practice that works on these problems. Understanding why some practice techniques work and others don't, knowing how skill best develops, and seeing examples of how great artists and teachers applied this knowledge in the service of artistic development can help students identify their needs with precision.

After learning what legendary artists and teachers have written and said about how they work and why, it's impossible not to note the consistencies among their approaches. It's impossible not to be stunned by how their practices presaged later discoveries by neurologists, physiologists, and psychologists. If the consistency of the ways in which great masters spoke about practice and its relationship to art doesn't inspire you, then perhaps modern research on learning will inspire you, and the experiences of the musicians in this book can serve as models for how to apply ideas from this book to your work. Practice is too important to be reduced to a bunch of tired bromides. But today, it seems the future of the pedagogy of practice lies in writings like these:

- 8 Things Top Practicers Do Differently
- 5 Steps to Mastering Sight-Reading
- 5 Laws of Confident Performance
- 4 Templates for Classical Guitar Practice Sessions[5]

Even if there's good advice in these blog posts, how can you know? What stands behind the advice? The subjective experiences of the author? Dogma?

Intuition? Extensive research? Misconceptions consecrated by tradition? Can one reduce how best to design practice to a series of bullet points?

As you gain a deeper understanding of the tenets of good practice explored in this book, you will be able to design intelligent practice sessions for yourself regardless of your level. You will regain and strengthen agency over your work; if you get off track, you will be able to figure out why and adjust accordingly. Rather than be in the grip of some incomprehensible mystery about why things aren't going smoothly, you'll be able to see clearly the relationship between cause and effect. You'll become an expert at spotting specious reasoning about practice. As your technique, artistry, intellect, and experience move forward, you will be able to redesign your practice to progress evermore toward higher levels of creativity in performance.

Notes

1. Fleischmann, *Tradition, and Craft in Piano-Playing*, 8.
2. Walker, *Franz Liszt: The Virtuoso Years*, 302.
3. Oscar Beringer, *Fifty Years' Experience of Pianoforte Playing and Teaching* (London: Bosworth & Co., 1907), 31.
4. Within a decade of Tausig's death, these exercises were published by his friend, Heinrich Ehrlich.
5. These are titles of actual blog posts.

Sources

Beringer, Oscar. *Fifty Years' Experience of Pianoforte Teaching and Playing*. London: Bosworth & Co., 1907.
Fleischmann, Tilly. *Tradition and Craft in Piano-Playing*. Dublin: Carysfort Press, 2014.
Walker, Alan. *Franz Liszt: The Virtuoso Years, 1811–1847*. Vol. 1. Ithaca, NY: Cornell University Press, 1988.

BIBLIOGRAPHY

Aguado, Dionisio. *New Guitar Method*. Edited by Brian Jeffry. Translated by Louise Bigwood. London: Tecla Editions, 1981.

Alexander, F. Matthias. *Constructive Conscious Control of the Individual*. New York: E.P. Dutton & Company, 1923.

Alexander, F. Matthias. *Constructive Conscious Control of the Individual*. Kent: Integral Press, 1986.

Alexander, F. Matthias. *Man's Supreme Inheritance; Conscious Guidance and Control in Relation to Human Evolution in Civilization*. New York: E.P. Dutton & Company, 1918.

Alexanian, Diran, and Frederick Fairbanks. *Traité Théorique et Pratique du Violoncelle: Theoretical and Practical Treatise of the Violoncello*. Paris: A. Z. Mathot, 1922.

Arnold, Matthew. *Culture and Anarchy*. New York: Macmillan and Co., 1882.

Artzt, Alice. *The Art of Practising*. Dorset: Musical New Services, LTD., 1978.

Arx, Victoria A. von. *Piano Lessons with Claudio Arrau: A Guide to His Philosophy and Techniques*. New York: Oxford University Press, 2014.

Auer, Leopold. *Violin Playing as I Teach It*. New York: Frederick A. Stokes Company, 1921.

Augustine, Jack H. "Combining Physical and Mental Practice with Muscle Memory Training to Improve a Motor Skill." Ed.D. diss., Fayetteville, AR: The University of Arkansas, 1990.

Austin, Howard. "A Computational Theory of Physical Skill." PhD diss., Cambridge, MA: Massachusetts Institute of Technology, 1976.

Berg, Christopher. *Mastering Guitar Technique: Process & Essence*. Pacific, MO: Mel Bay Publications, 1997.

Berg, Christopher. "The Re-Imagination of Guitar Pedagogy." *The Soundboard* Vol. 26, No. 3/4 (2000): 43–52.

Berg, Christopher. "The Re-Imagination of Performance, Part One: Portamento." *The Soundboard* Vol. 35, No. 1 (2009): 6–18.

Beringer, Oscar. *Fifty Years' Experience of Pianoforte Teaching and Playing.* London: Bosworth & Co., 1907.

Berman, Boris. *Notes from the Pianist's Bench.* New Haven, CT: Yale University Press, 2002.

Bilson, Malcolm. "The Future of Schubert Interpretation: What Is Really Needed?" *Early Music* Vol. 25, No. 4 (1997): 715–722.

Blumenberg, Marc A., ed. "Achille Rivarde." *The Musical Courier* Vol. 31, No. 12 (1895): 8.

Bone, Philip J. *The Guitar and Mandolin: Biographies of Celebrated Players and Composers.* 2nd ed. London and New York: Schott, 1954.

Bonpensiere, Luigi. *New Pathways to Piano Technique: A Study of the Relations between Mind and Body with Special Reference to Piano Playing.* New York: Philosophical Library, 1953.

Boorstin, Daniel J. *The Discoverers, a History of Man's Search to Know His World and Himself.* New York: Random House, 1985.

Brée, Malwine, and Theodor Baker. *The Groundwork of the Leschetizky Method.* New York: G. Schirmer, 1902.

Breithaupf, R. M. *Natural Piano Technique.* Leipzig: C. F. Kahnt Nachfolger, 1909.

Briggs, John. *Fire in the Crucible: The Alchemy of Creative Genius.* New York: St. Martin's Press, 1988.

Brower, Harriette Moore. *Piano Mastery: Second Series: Talks with Master Pianists and Teachers.* New York: Frederick A. Stokes Company, 1917.

Brower, Harriette Moore. *Piano Mastery: Talks with Master Pianists and Teachers, and an Account of a Von Bülow Class, Hints on Interpretation.* New York: Frederick A. Stokes Company, 1915.

Brown, Peter C., Henry L. Roediger III, and Mark A. McDaniel. Cambridge, MA: *Make it Stick: The Science of Successful Learning.* Belknap Press, 2014.

Buechner, Sara Davis. "Jeepney Ride: A Tribute to Reynaldo Reyes on the Occasion of His Retirement from 50 Years of Teaching at Towson University." Talk given at the Reynaldo Reyes Retirement Celebration, Towson University, Towson, MD, April 11, 2015.

Caland, Elizabeth. *Artistic Piano Playing as Taught by Ludwig Deppe.* Translated by Evelyn Sutherland Stevenson. Nashville, TN: The Olympian Publishing Co., 1903.

Chaffin, Roger, Gabriela Imreh, and Mary Crawford. *Practicing Perfection: Memory and Piano Performance* (Expertise: Research and Applications Series). New York: Psychology Press, 2012.

Chopin, Frederic. *24 Preludes, Students' Edition by Alfred Cortot.* Translated by Davis Ponsonby. Paris: Editions Salabert, 1926.

Christiani, Adolph F. *The Principles of Expression in Pianoforte Playing.* New York: Harper, 1885.

Clark, Christopher. *The Sleepwalkers: How Europe Went to War in 1914.* New York: Harper, 2013.

Clary, Christopher. "Olympians Use Imagery as Mental Training." *The New York Times,* February 23, 2014.

Claxton, Guy. *Hare Brain, Tortoise Mind: How Intelligence Increases When You Think Less.* New York: Harper Perennial, 1998.

Colvin, Geoffrey. *Talent Is Overrated: What Really Separates World-Class Performers from Everybody Else.* New York: Portfolio Trade, 2010.

Conus, Leon. *Fundamentals of Piano Technique: Advanced Technique.* Chicago: Clayton F. Summy Co., 1953.

Cooke, James Francis. *Great Pianists on Piano Playing*. Philadelphia: Theodore Presser Co., 1913.

Cortot, Alfred, and Métaxas Le Roy. *Rational Principles of Pianoforte Technique*. Paris: M. Senart and Boston: Oliver Ditson Company, 1930.

Courvoisier, Karl. *The Technics of Violin Playing*. London: The Strad, 1894.

Coyle, Daniel. *The Talent Code: Greatness Isn't Born: It's Grown: Here's How*. New York: Bantam, 2009.

Csikszentmihalyi, Mihaly. *Flow: The Psychology of Optimal Experience*. New York: Harper Perennial, 1991.

Culkin, John M. "A Schoolman's Guide to Marshall McLuhan." *Saturday Review* Vol. 50, No. 11 (1967): 51–53, 70–72.

Currier, T. P. "Some Characteristics of Paderewski the Pianist." *Modern Music and Musicians. Vol. 1: The Pianist's Guide*, 24–25. New York: The University Society, 1918.

Cutter, Benjamin. *How to Study Kreutzer: A Handbook for the Daily Use of Violin Teachers and Violin Students, Containing Explanations of the Left Hand Difficulties and of Their Solution, and Directions as to the Systematic Acquirement of the Various Bowings, Both Firm and Bounding*. Boston: O. Ditson Co., 1903.

Day, Timothy. *A Century of Recorded Music: Listening to Musical History*. New Haven, CT: Yale University Press, 2000.

Dewey, John. *Democracy and Education: An Introduction to the Philosophy of Education*. New York: The MacMillan Company, 1916.

Dewey, John. *Experience and Education*. New York: Free Press, 1997.

Dewey, John. *Human Nature and Conduct: An Introduction to Social Psychology*. New York: Holt, 1922.

Dobelli, Rolf. *The Art of Thinking Clearly*. New York: Harper Paperbacks, 2014.

Dowland, Robert. *Varietie of Lute Lessons: A Lithographic Facsimile of the Original Edition of 1610*. London: Schott, 1958.

Dubal, David. *The World of the Concert Pianist*. London: Victor Gollancz, 1985.

Duncan, Charles. *The Art of Classical Guitar Playing*. Princeton, NJ: Summy-Birchard Music, 1980.

Dunning, David, Kerry Johnson, Joyce Ehrlinger, and Justin Kruger. "Why People Fail to Recognize Their Own Incompetence." *Current Directions in Psychological Science* Vol. 12, No. 3 (2003): 83–87.

Emerson, Ralph Waldo. *The Essay on Self-Reliance*. East Aurora, NY: The Roycrofters, 1908.

Ericsson, K. Anders, R. T. Krampe, and C. Tesch-Römer. "The Role of Deliberate Practice in the Acquisition of Expert Performance." *Psychological Review* (1993): 363–406.

Ericsson, K. Anders, Michael J. Prietula, and Edward T. Cokely. "The Making of an Expert." *Harvard Business Review* Vol. 85, No. 7/8 (2007): 114–121.

Ericsson, K. Anders, and Paul Ward. "Capturing the Naturally Occurring Superior Performance of Experts in the Laboratory: Toward a Science of Expert and Exceptional Performance." *Current Directions in Psychological Science* Vol. 16 (2007): 346–350.

Fay, Amy and Fay Peirce. *Music-Study in Germany, from the Home Correspondence of Amy Fay*. Chicago: A. C. McClurg, 1886.

Feldenkrais, Moshé. *Awareness through Movement: Health Exercises for Personal Growth*. New York: Harper & Row, 1972.

Fleischmann, Tilly. *Tradition and Craft in Piano-Playing*. Dublin: Carysfort Press, 2014.

Flesch, Carl. *The Art of Violin Playing, Book One*. New York: Carl Fischer, Inc., 1924.

Flesch, Carl. *The Art of Violin Playing, Book Two*. New York: Carl Fischer, Inc., 1930.

Flesch, Carl. *Carl Flesch Scale System a Supplement to Book 1 of the Art of Violin Playing*. Edited by Max Rostal. New York: Carl Fischer Music, 1987.

Földes, Andor. *Keys to the Keyboard, a Book for Pianists: With Explanatory Music*. New York: E.P. Dutton, 1948.

Gabler, Neal. *Life: The Movie: How Entertainment Conquered Reality*. New York: Vintage, 2000.

Galamian, Ivan. *Principles of Violin: Playing & Teaching*. Englewood Cliffs, NJ: Prentice-Hall, 1962.

Galamian, Ivan, and Frederick Neumann. *Contemporary Violin Technique*. Vol. 1. Boston, MA: Galaxy Music Corporation, 1966.

Gallot, Jacques. *Pièces De Luth: Composées Sur Différents Modes*. Edited by François Lesure. Genève: Minkoff Reprint, 1978.

Garfield, Charles A., and Hal Zina. *Peak Performance Mental Training Technique of the World's Greatest Athletes*. New York: Warner Books, 1984.

Gaultier, Denis, and Ennemond Gaultier. *Pièces De Luth and Livres De Tablature Des Pièces De Luth*. Genève: Minkoff Reprint, 1975.

Gervers, Hilda. "Franz Liszt as Pedagogue." *Journal of Research in Music Education* Vol. 18, No. 4 (1970): 385–391.

Getzels, J. W., and M. Csikszentmihalyi. *The Creative Vision: A Longitudinal Study of Problem Finding in Art*. New York: Wiley, 1976.

Giuliani, Mauro. *The Complete Works in Facsimiles of the Original Editions*. Vol. 6. Edited by Brian Jeffery. London: Tecla, 1984.

Goodchild, Neil L. "Liszt's Technical Studies: A Methodology for the Attainment of Technical Virtuosity." Unpublished.

Grant, Heidi, and Carol S. Dweck. "Clarifying Achievement Goals and Their Impact." *Journal of Personality and Social Psychology* Vol. 85, No. 3 (2003): 541–553.

Green, Barry, and W. Timothy Gallwey. *The Inner Game of Music*. Garden City, NY: Anchor Press and Doubleday, 1986.

Green, Elizabeth A. H., Judith Galamian, and Josef Gingold. *Miraculous Teacher: Ivan Galamian & the Meadowmount Experience*. Bryn Mawr, PA: Theodore Presser, 1993.

Greene, Graham. *The Power and the Glory*. London: William Heinemann, 1940.

Groot, Adrianus Dingeman de. *Thought and Choice in Chess*. The Hague: Mouton, 1965.

Hambourg, Mark. *How to Play the Piano*. New York: George H. Doran Company, 1922.

Hamilton, Kenneth. *After the Golden Age: Romantic Pianism and Modern Performance*. New York: Oxford University Press, 2008.

Harbach, Chad. *The Art of Fielding*. New York: Little, Brown and Company, 2011.

Hill, Nicole M., and Walter Schneider. "Brain Changes in the Development of Expertise: Neuroanatomical and Neurophysiological Evidence About Skill-Based Adaptations." In *The Cambridge Handbook of Expertise and Expert Performance*, edited by K. A. Ericsson, N. Charness, P. J. Feltovich, and R. R. Hoffman, 653–682. New York: Cambridge, 2006.

Hitchens, Christopher. *Letters to a Young Contrarian*. New York: Basic Books, 2001.

Hofmann, Josef. *Piano Playing: A Little Book of Simple Suggestions*. Philadelphia: Theodore Presser Co., 1920.

Hofmann, Josef, and Harriette Brower. *Piano Playing, With Piano Questions Answered*. Philadelphia: Theodore Presser, 1920.

Hofstadter, Richard. *Anti-Intellectualism in American Life*. New York: Alfred A. Knopf, 1963.

Huang, Chungliang Al. *Embrace Tiger, Return to Mountain: The Essence of Tai Ji*. Moab, Utah: Real People Press, 1973.

Hudson, Richard. *Stolen Time: The History of Tempo Rubato*. Oxford: Clarendon Press, 1997.

Hughes, Edwin. "Rafael Joseffy's Contribution to Piano Technic." *The Musical Quarterly* Vol. 2, No. 3 (1916): 349–364.

Hullah, Annette. *Theodor Leschetizky*. London and New York: J. Lane Company, 1906.

Iznaola, Ricardo. *Kitharologus: The Path to Virtuosity*. Pacific, MO: Mel Bay Publications, Inc., 1997.

Jacoby, L. L., R. A. Bjork, and C. M. Kelley. "Illusions of Comprehension, Competence, and Remembering," In *Learning, Remembering, Believing: Enhancing Human Performance*, edited by D. Druckman and R. A. Bjork, 57–80. Washington, DC: National Academy Press, 1994.

Jain, Aditya, Ramta Bansall, Avnish Kumar, K. D. Singh. "A Comparative Study of Visual and Auditory Reaction Times on the Basis of Gender and Physical Activity Levels of Medical 1st Year Students." *International Journal of Applied and Basic Medical Research* Vol. 5, No. 2 (2015): 124–127.

Johnston, Freya. *Samuel Johnson and the Art of Sinking 1709–1791*. Oxford University Press, 2005.

Jonás, Alberto. *Master School of Piano Playing and Virtuosity*. New York: Carl Fischer, Inc., 1922.

Jones, John Gerald. "Motor Learning without Demonstration of Physical Practice, Under Two Conditions of Physical Practice." *Research Quarterly* Vol. 36 (1965): 270–276.

Kahneman, Daniel. *Thinking, Fast and Slow*. New York: Farrar, Straus and Giroux, 2013.

Kochevitsky, George. *The Art of Piano Playing: A Scientific Approach*. Princeton, NJ: Summy-Birchard, 1967.

Lamott, Anne. *Bird by Bird: Some Instructions on Writing and Life*. New York: Pantheon Books, 1994.

Langer, Ellen J. *The Power of Mindful Learning*. Reading, MA: Addison-Wesley Publishing Company, Inc., 1998.

Lasch, Christopher. *Culture of Narcissism: American Life in an Age of Diminishing Expectations*. New York: W. W. Norton & Company, 1991.

Leimer, Karl, and Walter Gieseking. *Piano Technique Consisting of the Two Complete Books the Shortest Way to Pianistic Perfection and Rhythmics, Dynamics, Pedal and Other Problems of Piano Playing*. New York: Dover Publications, 1972.

Leonard, George. *Mastery: The Keys to Success and Long-Term Fulfillment*. New York: Plume, 1992.

Lhévinne, Josef. *Basic Principles in Pianoforte Playing*. Philadelphia: Theo. Presser Company, 1924.

Liszt, Franz. *Études Techniques Pour Le Piano*. Edited by A. Winterberger. 12 bks. Leipzig: J. Schuberth & Co., 1887.

Liszt, Franz. *Technical Exercises for the Piano*. Edited by Julio Esteban. Van Nuys, CA: Alfred Publishing Co., 1971.

Liszt, Franz, Mara La, and Constance Bache. *Letters of Franz Liszt*. St. Clair Shores, MI: Scholarly Press, 1972.

Mach, Elyse. *Great Pianists Speak for Themselves*. New York: Dodd Mead, 1988.

"The Making of an Artist." *The Musical Standard* (October 25, 1902): 259–260.

Martens, Frederick Herman. *Violin Mastery: Talks with Master Violinists and Teachers, Comprising Interviews with Ysaÿe, Kreisler, Elman, Auer, Thibaud, Heifetz, Hartmann, Maud Powell and Others*. New York: Frederick A. Stokes company, 1919.

Masin, Gwendolyn. "Violin Teaching in the New Millennium: In Search of the Lost Instructions of Great Master: An Examination of Similarities and Differences between Schools of Playing and How These Have Evolved, or Remembering the Future of Violin Performance." PhD diss., Dublin: Trinity College, 2012.

McCarthy, Harold E. "Review of Zen in the Art of Archery by Eugen Herrigel: R. F. C. Hull." *Philosophy East and West* Vol. 5, No. 3 (1955): 263–264.

McEwen, John B. *The Foundations of Musical Aesthetics, or the Elements of Music.* London: K. Paul, Trench, Trubner & Co., 1917.

Menuhin, Yehudi. *Theme and Variations.* New York: Stein and Day, 1972.

Merrick, Frank. *Practising the Piano.* London: Barrie and Rockliff, 1958.

Midgette, Anne. "Go to That Opera Again: Singers Are Only Human." *The New York Times,* December 20, 2006.

Miller, G. A. "The Magical Number Seven, Plus or Minus Two: Some Limits on Our Capacity for Processing Information." *Psychological Review* Vol. 63 (1956): 81–97.

Montagu-Nathan, M. "Ottakar Ševčík." *The Musical Times* Vol. 75, No. 1093 (1934): 217–218.

Moreno Torroba, Federico. *Sonatina.* Edited by Andrés Segovia. Washington, DC: Columbia Music Co, 1966.

Morris, Errol. "The Anosognosic's Dilemma: Something's Wrong But You'll Never Know What It Is (Part Five)." *The New York Times,* June 24, 2003.

Nabokov, Vladimir. *Strong Opinions.* New York: Vintage, 1990.

Naipul, V. S. "On Being a Writer." *The New York Review of Books* (April 23, 1987): 7.

Naylor, J. C., and G. E. Briggs. "Effects of Task Complexity and Task Organization on the Relative Efficiency of Part and Whole Training Methods." *Journal of Experimental Psychology* Vol. 65 (1963): 217–224.

Neuhaus, Heinrich. *The Art of Piano Playing.* New York: Praeger, 1973.

Newell, K. M. "Motor Skill Acquisition." *Annual Review of Psychology* Vol. 42 (1991): 213–237.

New York Times. "A Young Violinist Makes a Successful First Appearance in America." November 18, 1895.

Noad, Frederick M. *Solo Guitar Playing.* 3rd ed. New York and Toronto: Schirmer Books, 1994.

Oakeshott, Michael. *What Is History? And Other Essays.* Exeter, UK and Charlottesville, VA: Imprint Academic, 2004.

O'Connor, Flannery. *Mystery and Manners: Occasional Prose.* New York: Farrar, Straus and Giroux, 1970.

O'Dea, Jane. *Virtue or Virtuosity?: Explorations in the Ethics of Musical Performance.* Westport, CT: Greenwood Press, 2000.

Paderewski, Ignace, J. "Practical Hints on Piano Study." *Modern Music and Musicians* (1918): 153–155.

Parkening, Christopher, Jack Marshall, and David Brandon. *The Christopher Parkening Guitar Method.* Milwaukee, WI: Hal Leonard, 1997.

Pascual-Leone, Alvaro. "The Brain That Plays Music Is Changed by It." *Annals of the New York Academy of Sciences* Vol. 930 (2001): 451–456.

Porter, Gillian, and Lara Taggart. "The Neurological Hand." In *Fundamentals of Hand Therapy: Clinical Reasoning and Treatment Guidelines for Common Diagnoses of the Upper Extremity,* edited by Cynthia Cooper. St. Louis: Mosby, 2013.

Rachmaninoff, Sergei. "New Lights on Piano Playing." *The Etude* Vol. 41 (1923): 223–224.

Rafal, Robert D., Albrecht W. Inhoff, Joseph H. Friedman, Emily Bernstein. "Programming and Execution of Sequential Movements in Parkinson's Disease." *Journal of Neurology, Neurosurgery, and Psychiatry* Vol. 50 (1987): 1267–1273.

Reder, Lynne M., Xiaonan L. Liu, Alexander Keinath, and Vencislav Popov. "Building Knowledge Requires Bricks, Not Sand: The Critical Role of Familiar Constituents in Learning." *Psychonomic Bulletin & Review* (2015): 1–7.

Rink, John. "Chopin as Early Music." *Early Music* Vol. 29, No. 3 (2001): 339–340.

Rivarde, A. *The Violin and Its Technique as a Means to the Interpretation of Music*. London: MacMillan, 1921.

Robjohns, Sydney. *Violin Technique: Some Difficulties and Their Solution*. London: Oxford University Press and H. Milford, 1930.

Rosenthal, Eleanor. "The Alexander Technique: What It Is and How It Works." *Medical Problems of Performing Artists* (June 1987): 53–57.

Rywerant, Yochanan. *The Feldenkrais Method: Teaching By Handling: A Technique for Individuals*. 1st ed. San Francisco: Harper & Row, 1983.

Safonoff, Wassili. *New Formula for the Piano Teacher and Piano Student, Chester Edition*. London: J. & W. Chester, 1916.

Sand, Barbara Lourie. *Teaching Genius Dorothy Delay and the Making of a Musician*. Portland, OR: Amadeus Press, 2000.

Savary, Michel. *Encyclopedia of Guitar Virtuosity: 210 Difficult Passages*. Heidelberg: Chanterelle Verlag, 1987.

Schmidt, Richard. "A Schema Theory of Discrete Motor Skill Learning." *Psychological Review* Vol. 82, No. 2 (1975): 225–260.

Schöenberg, Arnold. "Today's Manner of Performing Classical Music." *Style and Idea*, edited by Leonard Stein, 320–322. London: Faber and Faber, 1975.

Schonbrun, Zach. *The Performance Cortex: How Neuroscience Is Redefining Athletic Genius*. New York: Dutton, 2018.

Segovia, Andrés. *Diatonic Major and Minor Scales*. Washington, DC: Columbia Music Co, 1953.

Segovia, Andrés, Napoléon Coste, Fernando Sor, and Mauro Giuliani. "The Guitar and I: My Early Years in Granada and Córdoba." (1970): 2 s. 12 in. 33 1/3 rpm. microgroove. stereophonic.

Shearer, Aaron. *Learning the Classic Guitar*. Pacific, MO: Mel Bay, 1990.

Shinn, Frederick G. "The Memorizing of Piano Music for Performance." *Proceedings of the Musical Association* (1898): 1–25.

Shōji, Yamada. "The Myth of Zen in the Art of Archery." *Japanese Journal of Religious Studies* Vol. 28, No. 1/2 (2001): 1–30.

Smith, Joseph. *Voice and Song*. New York: G. Schirmer, 1907.

Sor, Fernando. *Method for the Spanish Guitar*. Translated by A. Merrick. London: R. Cocks & Co., n.d. Reprint, New York: Da Capo Press, 1971.

Start, K. B. "Relationship between Intelligence and the Effect of Mental Practice on the Performance of a Motor Skill." *Research Quarterly* Vol. 31, No. 4 (1960): 644–649.

Stembridge-Montavont, Michael. "Variations on a Theme of Chopin." *Piano* (September/October 2004): 34–45.

Stuart, Douglas G. "Integration of Posture and Movement: Contributions of Sherrington, Hess, and Bernstein." *Human Movement Science* Vol. 24 (2005): 621–643.

Sunstein, Cass R., and Adrian Vermeule. "Conspiracy Theories: Causes and Cures." *Journal of Political Philosophy* Vol. 17, No. 2 (2009): 202–227.

Syed, Matthew. *Bounce: Mozart, Federer, Picasso, Beckham, and the Science of Success*. New York: Harper Perennial, 2011.

Taleb, Nassim Nicholas. *The Black Swan: Second Edition: The Impact of the Highly Improbable: With a New Section: "On Robustness and Fragility"*. New York: Random House Trade Paperbacks, 2010.

Tashman, L. S. "The Development of Expertise in Performance: The Role of Memory, Knowledge, Learning, and Practice." *Journal of Multidisciplinary Research* Vol. 5, No. 3 (2013): 33–48.

Teague, Ross C., Stuart S. Gittleman, and Okchoon Park. "A Review of the Literature on Part-Task and Whole-Task Training and Context Dependency." *United States Army Research Institute for the Behavioral Sciences*, Technical Report 1010 (October 1994): 1–33.

Thistleton, Frank. *The Art of Violin Playing for Players and Teachers*. London: The Strad, 1924.

Thistleton, Frank. *Modern Violin Technique, How to Acquire It, How to Teach It*. London: Longmans Green & Co., 1913.

Tocqueville, Alexis de. *Democracy in America*. New York: Knopf, 1951.

Tocqueville, Alexis de. *Democracy in America: Historical-Critical Edition of De La Démocratie en Amérique*. Vol. 4. Edited by Eduardo Nolla. Translated from the French by James T. Schleifer. Indianapolis: Liberty Fund, 2010.

Tommasini, Anthony. "Fleet Fingers and Red-Eye Flights: A Pianist Is a Study in Stamina." *The New York Times*, December 10, 2016, C1.

Unschuld, Marie von. *The Pianist's Hand*. Translated by Henry Morgan Dare. Leipzig: Breitkopf & Härtel, 1903.

Vandell, Roland A., Robert A. Davis, and Herbert A. Clugston. "The Function of Mental Practice in the Acquisition of Motor Skills." *The Journal of General Psychology* Vol. 29 (1943): 243–250.

Villa-Lobos, Heitor. *Douze Études Pour Guitare*. Paris: M. Eschig, 1953.

Wade, Graham. *Maestro Segovia*. London: Robson Books, 1986.

Wagner, Richard. *On Conducting: A Treatise on Style in the Execution of Classical Music*. Translated by Edward Dannreuther. London: W. Reeves, 1897.

Walker, Alan. *Franz Liszt: The Virtuoso Years, 1811–1847*. Vol. 1. Ithaca, NY: Cornell University Press, 1988.

Wallace, David Foster. "How Tracy Austin Broke My Heart." In *Consider the Lobster and Other Essays*. New York: Little, Brown, 2005.

Wallick, Bryan. "Piano Practice: Practice Routines and Techniques for Concert Pianists." D.Mus. diss., Pretoria, South Africa: University of Pretoria, 2013.

Whone, Herbert. *The Simplicity of Playing the Violin*. London: Victor Gollancz LTD, 1989.

William, James, "The Social Value of the College-Bred." In *Memories and Studies*, edited by Henry James, Jr., 307–325. New York: Longmans, Green, 1912.

Wilson, Frank R. *The Hand: How Its Use Shapes the Brain, Language, and Human Culture*. New York: Vintage, 1999.

Wolff, Konrad. *Schnabel's Interpretation of Piano Music*. New York: W. W. Norton & Company, 1979.

Woof, Rowsby. *Technique and Interpretation in Violin-Playing*. New York: London: Longmans, Green and E. Arnold, 1920.

Wullner, Ludwig. "Solo Building Is Structure Building." *The Musical Standard* (September 13, 1902): 162.

ABOUT THE AUTHOR

Guitarist Christopher Berg received his training at the Peabody Conservatory of Music, in master classes with Andrés Segovia at the University of Southern California, and at the Schola Cantorum Basilensis in Switzerland. He has performed recitals in Carnegie Recital Hall and Merkin Hall in New York in addition to hundreds of recital and concerto appearances throughout the United States including the *Dame Myra Hess Memorial Concert Series* in Chicago.

He is a *Carolina Distinguished Professor* at the University of South Carolina where he directs the classical guitar program. His students have won top prizes in regional and national competitions. During 1999–2000, he was honored by the University of South Carolina as a recipient of a *Michael J. Mungo Award for Excellence in Undergraduate Teaching*; in 2003, he was awarded the *Cantey Outstanding Faculty Award* by the School of Music for performance, research, and teaching. In 2003, his former students created the *Christopher Berg Guitar Endowment Fund* at USC in his honor, which supports *The Christopher Berg Guitar Award* presented annually to an outstanding undergraduate guitar student in the School of Music at the University of South Carolina.

He has been honored by the National Endowment for the Arts as a recipient of a *Solo Recitalist Fellowship* and by the South Carolina Arts Commission as a recipient of two *Solo Artist Fellowships*. *The Post and Courier* (Charleston, SC) called his playing "a stellar display of guitar virtuosity" and *The State* (Columbia, SC) found his performance of Joaquin Rodrigo's *Concierto de Aranjuez* "electrifying . . . hugely enjoyable and freshly played."

The Pilgrim Forest, his recent recording of original compositions for solo guitar, has been released on Laughing Heart Records. Critics have praised it as "a journey through a new geography . . . nothing less than radiant and compelling," (*The State*) and an "uncharted forest of music that is free-flowing, vibrant, expansive and modern—even postmodern." (*The Free Times*).

He is the author of *Mastering Guitar Technique* and *Giuliani Revisited* (Mel Bay Publications) and *The Classical Guitar Companion* (Oxford University Press).

INDEX

Note: Page numbers in *italics* indicate examples; page numbers in **bold** indicate tables.